WITHOUT
RESERVATIONS

RANDOM HOUSE

NEW YORK

WITHOUT
RESERVATIONS

The Travels of an Independent Woman

ALICE STEINBACH

Grateful acknowledgment is made to the following for
permission to reprint previously published material:

Music Sales Corporation: Excerpt from "We'll Meet Again" by Ross Parker and
Hugh Charles. Copyright © 1939 and renewed for all countries by Irwin Dash
Music Co., Ltd. All rights for the western hemisphere controlled by Music Sales Corp. Reprinted
by permission.

Warner Bros. Music Publishing and Williamson Music: Lyric excerpt from "My Funny Valentine" by
Richard Rodgers and Lorenz Hart. Copyright © 1937 (renewed) by Chappell & Co. Rights for the
extended renewal term in the United States controlled by the Estate of Lorenz Hart (administered
by W.B. Music Corp) and the Family Trust u/w Richard Rodgers and the Family Trust u/w
Dorothy F. Rodgers (administered by Williamson Music). All rights outside of the United States
controlled by Chappell & Co. All rights reserved. Reprinted by permission of Warner Bros.
Publications U.S. Inc., Miami, FL 33014 and Williamson Music.

The author encountered many people during the course of her travels.
Their names and in some cases identifying details have been changed
in order to protect the privacy of those individuals.

Library of Congress Cataloging-in-Publication Data
Steinbach, Alice.
Without reservations : the travels of an independent woman / Alice Steinbach.
p.   cm.
ISBN 0-375-50188-6
1. Steinbach, Alice—Journeys—Europe.   2. Europe—Description and
travel.   3. Women journalists—Biography.   4. Women travelers—
Biography.   5. Women—Travel—Europe.   I. Title.
PN4874.S682A3   2000
818'.5403—dc21
[B]   99-32959

Random House website address: www.atrandom.com

Printed in the United States of America on acid-free paper

2 4 6 8 9 7 5 3

First Edition

Book design by Caroline Cunningham

*This book is for Shelby
and Patricia Carter*

There are years that ask questions

and years that answer.

—ZORA NEALE HURSTON

Acknowledgments

For making this book possible, the author wishes to thank Gail Ross, who, from the first, stood behind its publication every step of the way. I am also deeply grateful to Kate Medina for her elegant eye and insightful editing. For their invaluable contributions, I thank Jean-Isabel McNutt, Robin Pinnel, and Meaghan Rady.

I am also indebted to the *Baltimore Sun*, where, over the years, many of my writing thoughts took shape.

Contents

INTRODUCTION

I write this sitting in my cozy kitchen on a wintry morning, my old cat dozing beside me on the warm, hissing radiator. An ice storm passed through Baltimore last night, and I can hear the evergreen trees outside my window creaking under the weight of their glazed branches. Six years ago, on a winter's day not unlike this one, I sat at the same table and made a decision that, for me, was quite daring: I decided to take a chance and temporarily jump ship, so to speak, from the life I'd fashioned for myself.

This morning I got out a box containing some reminders of where that decision took me. Although I've been searching for a particular item, it's fun seeing whatever turns up.

Here, for instance, is the bill for the ten-dollar cappuccino I drank one morning in Venice at the caffè Florian. And here's a program from a student production in Oxford of *Much Ado About Nothing*. Next comes a ticket to the Museum of Garden History in London, and the receipt for a pair of black silk pumps with four-inch heels, bought in Milan and worn once. The menu from a dinner enjoyed in the Umbrian town of Perugia follows, reminding me of how delicious the Veal Escalope with Red Chicory was that night.

Finally, in a smaller box labeled PARIS, I find what I'm looking for: a postcard with a view of the city's loveliest bridge, Pont Alexandre III. Dated 9 May 1993, and sent from me to me, the postcard signals the beginning of an adventure:

Dear Alice,

   It is my first morning in Paris and I have walked from my hotel on the Left Bank to the Seine. The river is silver; above it, an early morning sun the color of dull nickel burns through a gray sky, its light glancing off the ancient buildings that line the quai Voltaire. It is the Paris I have come to know from the photographs of Atget and Cartier-Bresson: a city of subtle tonalities, of platinum and silver and gray; a city of incomparable beauty. Now, from this perfect place, I begin a journey.

The postcard is signed: *Love, Alice.*

It is the first of many such postcards that I would write and send home to myself as I traveled over the next several months. Or, as I affectionately came to call that interlude in my life, The Year of Living Dangerously.

Most of us, I suppose, have had at one time or another the impulse to leave behind our daily routines and responsibilities and seek out, temporarily, a new life. Certainly, it was a fantasy that more than once had taken hold of me. At such times I daydreamed about having the freedom to travel wherever chance or fancy took me, unencumbered by schedules and obligations and too many pre-planned destinations.

But the daydream always retreated in the face of reality. I was, after all, a working, single mother and my life was shaped in large measure by responsibilities toward my two sons and my work as a newspaper reporter at the *Baltimore Sun.*

By 1993, however, I was entering a new phase of my life, one that caused me to rethink its direction. My sons had graduated from college and were entering new adult lives of their own; one as a translator in Japan, the other as a graduate physics student in Colorado. I was happy for them, and proud too. After all, watching a child march successfully into the larger world is one of the greatest satisfactions parenthood has to offer. Still, letting go of my sons left me feeling vulnerable in a way I didn't understand. The powerful bonds between us remained; but physically the boys I had raised were gone.

If I close my eyes, I can see them still, on a long-ago summer's night. Two boys, so different: one lying in bed listening to an Orioles game and bouncing a ball off the wall; the other outside in the backyard, setting up his telescope under a starry indigo sky. *Holy moments*, I think now of such times. Without such moments, the house felt quiet and empty.

At work my life went on as before. I continued to interview interesting people as well as write a column. It was a challenging, sometimes next-to-impossible job and I was completely invested in it. My work was not only what I did but who I was.

Occasionally, though, I found myself wondering: was I *too* invested in it? At times I felt my identity was narrowing down to one thing—being a reporter. What had happened, I wondered, to the woman who loved art and jazz and the feeling that an adventure always lurked just ahead, around some corner? I hadn't seen her in quite a while. Had she disappeared? Or had I just been too busy writing about other people's lives to pay attention to her?

There was nothing wrong with my life. I liked its order and familiarity and the idea of having a secure place in the world. Still, the image of that woman who had gone missing kept popping up. One day, after reading about a photography course offered in Tuscany, I thought, *She would find a way to do that.* I had the same reaction when I read an article offering room and board on a Scottish sheep farm that trained Border collies: *I'll bet she'd be on the phone trying to work something out.* I found myself wondering if there was some way to reconnect with this missing woman. I sort of admired her.

The answer, one that arrived in bits and pieces over the next few months, surprised me.

What you need to do, a voice inside me said, *is to step out and experience the world without recording it first in a reporter's notebook. After fifteen years of writing stories about other people, you need to get back into the narrative of your own life.*

It made sense to me. But how to go about doing that? I thought of taking a leave of absence from my job, of traveling to an unfamiliar place where all the old labels that define me—both to myself and others—would be absent. Maybe then, somewhere along the way, I would bump into that other woman. Or, if she no longer existed, maybe such a trip could help me find out who took her place. Although the idea appealed to me, I pushed it aside as impractical, both personally and professionally.

Yet I couldn't let go of the fantasy; it sprang out at odd times. In the middle of the night, I would get up and start figuring out what such a plan might cost and how to finance it. I spent hours in the bookstore's travel section poring over possible destinations. At dinner, talking and laughing with friends, I would wonder about my capacity to be a woman in a strange city, without an identity, without friends.

Then I ran through all the reasons why I shouldn't do it. What would I do with my house? Who would take care of my cat? What if some emergency arose at home? Would my editors give me a leave? And if they did, what about the column I wrote twice a week? Would it be assigned to someone else? Suppose I got sick in some strange place? Suppose I disappeared, never to be seen again?

But something was working deep inside me and, like a tropical storm, it gathered momentum before hitting me full force with its message: *you are a woman in search of an adventure,* said the voice inside. *Take the risk. Say "Yes" to life instead of "No."*

Still I hesitated. It was time, I thought, to get some feedback from friends. When I ran the idea by those closest to me, the response was unanimous: *Go. Your children are grown and, except for your cat, you're an independent woman.*

They were partly right. In many ways, I *was* an independent woman. For years I'd made my own choices, paid my own bills, shoveled my own snow, and had the kind of relationships—with the exception of sons and cats—that allowed for a lot of freedom on both sides.

But lately I'd come to see that no matter how much I was in charge of my finances and my time, I was quite dependent in another way. Over the years I had fallen into the habit—a quite natural one, I believe—of defining myself in terms of who I was to other people and what they expected of me as mother, as daughter, as wife, as ex-wife, as reporter, as friend. For a while, at least, I wanted to stand back from these roles and see who emerged.

I arrived at the decision to take a leave of absence in January of 1993. With great anxiety I approached my editor and told him what I'd like to do. Within days I had his approval; we agreed I would leave in April and return the following January. I was elated. Then it hit me: I had no real plan for all the free time now available to me. Except for the first stop. In some unspoken way I'd known all along that I would begin my new life in Paris.

"Why Paris?" friends asked. "Why not?" I would reply breezily, reluctant to reveal the truth. The truth was that I was pursuing a fantasy—the fantasy of living in a small hotel on the Left Bank just as my journalistic idol, Janet Flanner, had done. From 1925 to 1975, Flanner's famous "Letter from Paris" appeared in *The New Yorker.* The pieces, now collected in book form, still stand as small master-pieces of intelligence and style; like many writers, I studied them as a painter does Cézanne. For years I had wanted to walk, book in hand, through the streets and into the cafés Flanner described so vividly. Now I was about to do it.

But after Paris, what? I wanted to keep my plans flexible, but not so loose that I was just wandering aimlessly about. After think-ing it over, I came up with two ground rules. One: I did not want to flit from place to place; I wanted to stay a while in the places I chose to visit. And two: my agenda would not include exotic locales. This allowed me to immediately rule out such places as Las Vegas and Katmandu. I reasoned that while part of my goal was to see if I still had the skills—and the nerve—to make it in a new setting, some kind of cultural connection was necessary.

For the next several weeks I pieced together a list of possibilities from clippings, articles, and guidebooks I'd collected. Several places in England and Scotland were on the list. So was almost every region in Italy, from the Veneto to Campania. At one point I considered spending all my time, after leaving Paris, in Italy. But when I came across an article in my travel file on a course given at Oxford on the history of the English village and another on traveling by train through the Scottish Highlands, I abandoned the all-Italy plan. I also moved two of my initial "Possibilities"—Ireland and Provence—into a lesser category headed: "Possible Possibilities."

In the end I left Baltimore with a hotel booked in Paris, an apart-ment almost secured in London, a place reserved in the Oxford course, and a room of my own on a Scottish sheep farm. The rest, I figured, would be negotiated as opportunities presented themselves.

But even the slightest of plans can go awry. Life intruded while I was away, more than once. On my way to Scotland, word came of the sudden death of a beloved sister-in-law, and I returned to Baltimore for her funeral. Later, another urgent family matter caused a change in my plans. Life's like that, I told myself on a sad plane trip back to Italy: with awesome impersonality it ambushes us, changing our lives and the lives of those we love in an instant.

Of course, on the day I arrived in Paris to begin my leave, I knew nothing of what lay ahead, good or bad. All I knew was a feeling of utter astonishment at finding myself in a small hotel on the Left Bank of the world's most beautiful city.

It was from this hotel, at the end of my first week, that I wrote the simple truth of what I had been seeking:

Last night on the way home from a concert at Sainte-Chapelle, I stopped on the Pont Royal to watch the moon struggle through a cloudy night sky. From the bridge my eyes followed the lights of a tourist boat as it moved like a glowworm across the water. Here in Paris, I have no agenda; here I can fall into step with whatever rhythm presents itself. I had forgotten how wonderful it is to stand on a bridge and catch the scent of rain in the air. I had forgotten how much I need to be a part of water, wind, sky.

Reading this postcard I see myself, carefree and exhilarated, standing in the middle of the bridge, halfway between the Louvre on the Right Bank and the quai Voltaire on the Left. What I see is a woman who is not thinking about observing life but experiencing it. The observations would come later, in postcards sent home.

From Milan and Siena, from tiny villages along the Amalfi Coast and small towns in the Cotswolds, from London and Oxford, the postcards were waiting for me when I returned, each one recounting like a spontaneous child the impressions of a day spent exploring the world. As I read them, I relived the days spent at Brasenose College in Oxford; the momentous meeting in Paris with Naohiro, a Japanese man who read my soul; the sunny Italian days in Sorrento; the days of self-discovery in Asolo, a village at the foot of the Dolomites.

It was not a new habit, writing postcards to myself. It had begun about fifteen years ago, while traveling alone to Bornholm, a remote island in the Baltic Sea. It was homesickness that prompted me to write that first time; the postcard served as a companion, someone with whom I could share my feelings.

Over the years, the postcards took on another role: they became a form of travel memoir, preserving and recapturing the feelings of certain moments during a trip. When I see such a postcard, the handwriting oddly familiar, it startles me and, like Proust's madeleine, has the power to plunge me back into the past.

Until recently I was convinced—quite smugly so—that I'd invented this form of travel writing. But about four months ago, while going through a box of papers collected from my mother's apartment after her death, I came across a postcard she'd written to herself from Dublin. The picture is a charming view of O'Connell Street and the Gresham Hotel. She writes:

> We stayed here for eight days. A lovely, comfortable hotel, with Irish poetry readings in the evenings. The food was very good. And Dublin has the loveliest zoo in all of Europe.

Tears sprang to my eyes as I read these simple words in a handwriting as familiar as my own. It is the handwriting that signed my grade-school report cards; the handwriting that scribbled out the lists I carried to the corner grocery store; the handwriting that, over the years, in countless letters, supported and encouraged me in good times and bad.

Holding the postcard in my hands, I thought of my sons and of the future. Would they someday read my postcards, I wondered, and think of me, as I do now of my mother?

If so, I hope they see me soaring like a bright kite into a big blue sky; happy and adventurous, going wherever the wind takes me.

—Baltimore,
January 1999

Paris

PARIS

1

THE NOVICE

Dear Alice,

    Each morning I am awakened by the sound of a tinkling bell. A cheerful sound, it reminds me of the bells that shopkeepers attach to their doors at Christmastime. In this case, the bell marks the opening of the hotel door. From my room, which is just *off the winding staircase, I can hear it clearly. It reminds me of the bell that calls to worship the novice embarking on a new life. In a way I too am a novice, leaving, temporarily, one life for another.*

Love, Alice

For weeks I had imagined my first day in Paris: I could see myself sipping a *citron pressé* at the Flore, a famous Saint-Germain café that was once the haunt of Picasso, Sartre, de Beauvoir, and Camus; then darting in and out of the shops on the rue du Bac or browsing the bookstores in the historic rue Jacob. Always in this fantasy I saw myself responding with curiosity and excitement to the pulsing street life of Paris.

I had night dreams, too, along with the daydreams. In one particularly appealing dream, I bumped into Scott and Zelda Fitzgerald, who once lived on the Left Bank in a hotel just blocks from where I would be staying. I accepted their invitation to Sunday breakfast at their favorite café, the Deux Magots. Waking from this dream, I scribbled a note to myself: *Must have Sunday brunch at Deux Magots.*

In another dream I entered an unnamed passageway on the Left Bank and, after a short walk, emerged on the Right Bank in the Marais district. Both during the dream and after, I felt quite pleased with myself at having made this historic discovery, one that eliminated the need to cross the Seine by bridge.

I liked these dreams, both the day and night versions. They seemed to signal a willingness on my part to go where the moment took me and to trust it would take me to an interesting place. They also reminded me of how it felt to approach every day as I once had, guided less by expectations than by curiosity.

On the day I left for Paris, I drank champagne with a friend in the Air France lounge at Dulles airport. "Here's to a successful trip," said my friend, raising her glass. I raised mine in reply, saying, "And to an interesting one."

What I didn't say was that "success" was not something I was seeking from this venture. In fact, I was determined *not* to judge this trip, or its outcome, in terms of success or failure. Too much of life—my life, anyway—seemed to be aimed at achieving success and avoiding failure. I was determined not to carry that baggage with me on this trip.

"You must be excited," my friend said. "I know I would be."

I laughed. "That's an understatement. I'm probably the most excited person in this airport," It was true. I felt the way I did at twenty when, on the spur of the moment, I threw some clothes into a suitcase, bought a ticket at the airport, and left for Turkey.

But later, while waiting to board the plane, another feeling crept in, one I couldn't quite identify. Was it apprehension? Or just too much champagne? Such thoughts were swept aside, however, once I felt the plane lift off the runway, headed for Paris. *This is it,* I thought, tightening my seat belt, *the beginning of the next part of my life.*

To my dismay, I arrived in Paris not an excited woman but an anxious one. Without warning, halfway through the flight, my sense of excitement deserted me and a new, less welcome companion arrived: a complete failure of nerve. *What am I doing on this plane?* I asked myself. Panic was lurking beneath the question. What had seemed a wonderful idea—*une grande aventure,* as my friends put it—began to feel like an ill-conceived fantasy that should have provided fifteen minutes of amusement before being discarded.

By the time my plane landed in Paris I had considered every bad outcome—from loss of livelihood to loss of life—that was likely to result from my incredible mistake in judgment. It was a little before eight in the morning and the air terminal was chilly and deserted. A tiring wait to get through customs was followed by a longer and more tiring vigil at the luggage carousel. By the time I had retrieved my bags and made the long trek to the public transportation area, my mood was dangerously low. I decided to cheer myself up by taking a taxi to my hotel instead of the bus that dropped passengers off at some central location.

"Rue de l'Université," I told the driver, directing him to my hotel. He'd never heard of it. "On the Left Bank," I said. "Rue de l'Université. Off the quai Voltaire." He shook his head and sighed wearily, as if to say, *It's no use trying to understand these Americans.* Then suddenly he lurched into gear and abruptly hurled his taxi into the traffic headed for Paris.

It is a long drive from the airport into the city, one that offers little in the way of scenic diversion. The truth is, there is no difference between the morning rush-hour traffic in Paris and that of any big American city: bumper-to-bumper cars and lots of ugly industrial parks separated by the occasional cluster of sterile high-rise buildings. The hour-long trip did nothing to bolster my morale.

Just as I was wondering whether it was madness or stupidity that had landed me in the back of this taxi, something happened: we entered the city of Paris and the Seine came into view. Silvery and serpentine, it moved like mercury through the center of the city, a mesmerizing force. From the taxi window I could see the tree-lined quais along the river. A few more minutes and we were on the quai Voltaire, driving past ancient buildings, their stone façades tinted a rosy pink by the morning sun.

Here it was that Voltaire had lived and died, I thought, looking at the silent buildings, each one with a story to tell. As I allowed myself to be drawn into the net of beauty and history that hangs like a bridal veil over Paris, my excitement grew.

We drove along the Seine, turning finally into the heart of the Left Bank, into the narrow, picturesque streets lined with book-shops and galleries and cafés. Ernest Hemingway once lived in this neighborhood, and so did Edna St. Vincent Millay. The thought buoyed my mood even more.

By this time the sun had burned through the early mist, leaving the air fresh and damp, as fragrant as the ocean. I felt elated; it was the same feeling I'd had as a child when, headed for the beach with my parents, the first whiff of sea and salt air would blow through the open windows of our trusty green Plymouth.

The taxi made another turn and then stopped in front of a small old building that from the outside bore little resemblance to a hotel. I was more or less dumped out into the middle of the narrow street, and with the traffic piling up behind us, horns blaring, I counted out seventy dollars' worth of francs. The driver pocketed the money, unloaded my belongings, and immediately drove off, leaving me and my suitcase—a large black number about the size of a baby hippopotamus—at the curb in front of the hotel.

I peered through the glass door, looking for someone to assist me. The place appeared deserted. Draping my raincoat around my neck, I slung my tote-sized handbag over one shoulder, a small duf-fel bag over the other, propped open the door with my left foot, and proceeded into the lobby, dragging my suitcase behind me.

It was my first look at the small hotel, once a private residence dating back to the seventeenth century. I'd decided to stay there on the advice of friends who knew and liked it. Immediately upon entering, something about the small reception area put me at ease. The furniture, under the original vaulted ceilings, was old and beautiful; the winding wooden staircase was polished and gleaming; and in one corner a young woman was arranging long-stemmed, fresh-cut flowers in large Chinese porcelain vases. There was a sense of history here. And, just as important to me, a sense of order.

It was also, I might add, the hotel's first look at me; at the rumpled, tired, luggage-intensive figure slouching toward the small reception desk. But those who work in hotels are not unused to seeing people at their worst. After all, the word "travel" comes from the Latin "trepalium." Which, loosely translated, means "instrument of torture." So whatever judgmental thoughts may have passed through the mind of the receptionist, she tactfully kept them from appearing on her face.

It was still early, a little before nine, and my room, she informed me, would not be ready until 12:30. She suggested I take a walk.

Outside, the shopkeepers were washing down the narrow sidewalks. In the air I could smell bread baking. I headed for a café I'd seen on the rue Bonaparte. I stopped on the way to buy a *Herald-Tribune* at a newsstand where a large gray cat sat grooming himself on a stack of *Le Monde* newspapers. Timidly, I touched the cat's head. "His name is Jacques," said the elderly proprietor proudly, "and he is very friendly." I scratched Jacques under the chin; he immediately began drooling. After that, my first stop every morning was to see Jacques and, as I came to call his owner, "Monsieur Jacques."

By 10:30 I was seated in a neighborhood café near the rue Saint-Benoît, reading the paper, sipping café-au-lait and wondering, *Is this really happening? Am I really in Paris? Do I really not have to go to the office or write a column or go to the supermarket?*

As if to answer my questions, a tall man wearing a tuxedo and a beret walked by, pushing before him a perambulator. In it I could see an accordion, and behind that a puppy and a cat. I turned to my waiter who answered my question before I asked it. "Madame, he is on his way to the place Saint-Germain-des-Prés to perform for the tourists."

Yes, I thought, *I really am in Paris.*

I left the café and walked along the rue Bonaparte, scanning the numbers above the doors. When I came to Number 36, I stopped. The sign outside said: HÔTEL SAINT-GERMAIN-DES-PRÉS. It was the small hotel where Janet Flanner lived in her early days in Paris, and I had come to pay my respects to her. Of course, she was no longer around—she died in 1978—but it's my belief that you can remain as close in feeling to the dead as you can to the living. Sometimes even closer.

I entered the lobby, an elegant, refined space that in all probability bore no resemblance to the modest surroundings in which Flanner lived in the 1920s. At that time it was a hotel where young American expatriates with talent but little money rented rooms. Still, it was from this hotel that Flanner began filing her fortnightly articles, signed with her *nom de correspondance,* Genêt.

"May I help you, madame?" asked the receptionist.

"No, I am here to meet a friend," I said, walking the few steps to the breakfast room at the rear of the lobby. Breakfast was over and the room was empty. It seemed as good a place as any to deliver my respects to Madame Flanner:

Well, I finally made it here to thank you, my thinking voice said. *So thanks for sharing with me your fifty years in Paris. I couldn't have asked for a better guide.*

After leaving the hotel I walked along the tiny rue Jacob, a charming street that seems to surface suddenly at a little garden near the rue de Seine and then, several blocks later, disappear into the rue de l'Université. *Now this is more like it,* I thought happily, as I popped in and out of the bookshops and antiques galleries along the street. It was at this point that, high on a combination of strong coffee, excitement, and jet lag, I found myself actually skipping.

Later, of course, when the first exhilaration lost its edge, another question would present itself: how does one structure a life that has no responsibilities or set routines? Such an existence, I came to see, had the potential to deteriorate into idle wandering.

But on this particular day I was open to wandering, to idleness, to losing myself in the glorious ether of Paris. I wandered through the narrow streets, my mind spinning, going over all the things I wanted from this trip.

A list began forming itself in my head: I wanted to take chances. To have adventures. To learn the art of talking less and listening more. To see if I could still hack it on my own, away from the security of work, friends, and an established identity.

Of course, I also wanted to lose ten pounds, find the perfect haircut, pick up an Armani suit at 70 percent off, and meet Yves Montand's twin, who would fall deeply, madly, in love with me.

My first chance to get my self-improvement plan rolling presented itself in the form of a cosmetics shop I passed on the rue de Beaune. I stepped inside. It was an elegant shop, staffed by beautiful young Parisiennes with perfect skin, perfect hair, and perfect bodies. Dressed like doctors in crisp white jackets with name tags, they moved like models through the aisles of glass shelves piled high with eye balm, corrective facial masques, and salmon mousse hair balm. I was approached by Françoise, who, in addition to her lab coat, wore a Hermès scarf and Chanel earrings.

Françoise asked if I would like an analysis of my skin. It struck me as a wonderful idea. "What are your problem areas, madame?" Françoise asked, her concerned voice suggesting there might be many of them.

Within minutes I was like an analysand on the couch, blurting out my long list of problems to Françoise. She listened, jotting down notes on a white pad with a Mont Blanc pen. Undaunted by the challenge I presented, she proceeded to fill a white wicker basket with items from various parts of the shop. She then explained the purpose of each product and the miracles that would result from using it. Always, she ended with "I myself use this product, madame."

That was good enough for me. In less than twenty minutes I blew almost half a week's food budget on creams, balms, and restoratives. What better way to celebrate the New Me than by sprucing up the façade of the Old Me? Besides, I told myself, I'd make up for it by eating in cheaper places. Still, I worried a bit. Between the taxi from the airport and my foray into the world of French cosmetics, I'd already spent a lot more than I'd planned.

But what the heck, I thought, heading for the hotel and my first look at the room where I would spend at least the next month. I was excited, but also a little nervous about seeing it. Although I knew many travelers think of a hotel as "just a place to sleep," it was important to me to feel at home in this room.

A young chambermaid proceeded me up the winding staircase, stopping in the middle of it. Pulling out a key, she opened a door I hadn't noticed, one situated between the reception area and the second floor. It was the door to my room. I stepped inside. What I saw disappointed me.

After passing through a narrow entry hall, I entered a long narrow room. It seemed to tilt to one side, the side occupied by a huge, dark armoire. At the far end of the room was the bed; or, to be precise, two twin beds that had been pushed together. In the middle of the room was a round table covered with a fresh linen cloth and flanked by two straight-backed chairs; it served as both desk and dining space. Opposite the bed, near the small entry hall, was a slightly worn loveseat, its wine-velvet arms and back rising and falling in classic Art Deco fashion. All in all, it was not what I had hoped for.

But the room had two big, beautiful French windows that opened out over a small green courtyard. There was one in the large, well-appointed bathroom too, situated in such a way that it could be left open without any lack of privacy. Brushing my teeth in the morning while looking out over the courtyard became one of my real pleasures.

Still, at first glance, I couldn't imagine living in this room for several weeks. Later, when the room became home to me—when I had learned to appreciate how comfortable the bed was and how elegant the linens that covered it, how spotlessly clean the room was kept and how well it actually functioned—I realized that first impressions about hotel rooms are like first loves: neither is based on the concept of how, over time, one can come to appreciate the pleasures of durability over infatuation.

At a little before five in the afternoon I left the hotel and headed for the Café de Flore. It was early, but I was quite hungry and, in fact, almost ready to retire. The Flore, which was only a short distance from my hotel, was a great place to sit and take in Paris while eating the perfect omelette.

It was a mild evening, so I chose a seat on the terrace and ordered wine. This was the best time to come to the Flore, I thought, looking around. Lunchtime here always seemed hectic, a time when people came to see and be seen, to make deals and use their cellular phones. Late afternoon at the Flore, on the other hand, had a relaxed ambience; people laughed a lot and gossiped and seemed not to be in a hurry to go somewhere else.

It was a lesson I hoped to learn in the months ahead: how to stop rushing from place to place, always looking ahead to the next thing while the moment in front of me slipped away unnoticed.

I knew it once, of course—the feeling of connection that comes from seizing the actual world. When I was a child, very little that happened in the real world escaped my attention. Not the brightly colored ice in small paper boats we bought at Mr. Dawson's snowball stand; or the orange-and-white pattern that formed a map of Africa on my cat's back; or the way Mother sat at her dressing table, powdering her beautiful face to a pale ivory color. It used to surprise me, the intensity with which I still remembered these distant memories. But when I entered my fifties—the Age of Enlightenment, as I came to call it—I understood their enduring clarity. By then I'd knocked around enough to know that, in the end, what adds up to a life is nothing more than the accumulation of small daily moments.

A waiter appeared with my omelette and salad. *"Bon appétit,"* he said, placing my meal on the small round table. He reminded me of someone. Belmondo? No. Louis Jourdan? No. I studied his face, a very Gallic one; a little gaunt but handsome in a bony way. It crossed my mind to flirt with him. This was Paris, after all, where women of a certain age were thought quite desirable. But before I could act on my thoughts, the waiter moved to the next table.

After polishing off the salad, omelette, and a bowl of vanilla ice cream, I ordered a *café noir.* Then I settled into one of the great pleasures of café-sitting: surveying the scene. At the next table, a young, shy-looking couple spoke softly in Japanese, trying not to call attention to themselves. Across the way, a darkly handsome man dressed in black sat sketching in a large notebook.

Outside on the terrace, catching the last bit of sun, were the deeply tanned Italians: beautiful women wearing gold jewelry, and sculpted, model-perfect men in Armani suits. And then, of course, there were the Americans—either overdressed or underdressed but always friendly—and the French, who ruled the Flore, rightfully so, and were elegant no matter their attire.

I sat sipping my second *café,* imagining the time when Sartre and Simone de Beauvoir practically lived at the Flore: writing, eating, and even seeing people by appointment there. It was not difficult to imagine. I could imagine doing it myself. Of course, at that moment, I could see myself doing just about anything, including ringing up friends to set up appointments: *"Bonjour, mon ami, it's Alice. Look, I'll be at the Flore most of the afternoon and I've decided to have some friends over. Why don't you come by sometime after one? Dress casual. See you then."*

At about eight I noticed a subtle change in the light. As the sun moved lower in the western skies, it washed the ancient Paris buildings with pale-pink patterns. The faces of those gathered at the Flore were tinted rosy by the softening light; everyone looked years younger. By now my eyes were growing heavy from jet lag. It was bedtime for me.

As I strolled back to the hotel, I stopped to watch a young couple near the tiny, romantic place Furstemberg. From a radio they'd set on the ground, the voice of Frank Sinatra rose like smoke, filling the air with words about a small hotel and the longing of lovers to be there together. I watched as they began to dance slowly to the music, arms wrapped around each other. The square was deserted except for the young dancers beneath the fragrant paulownia trees. Of course, even had the square been bursting with tourists, the dancers would not have noticed; they existed only for one another.

I knew that feeling. As I stood in the shadows, it all came back: the feel of Dick Reavey's arms around me at the high school prom, swaying to the last slow dance of the night, the swish of my silk dress, the sharp edge of his white collar against my face. Swaying back and forth to the music, our cheeks touching, inhaling the scent of his aftershave, nothing else existed. Time stopped, and we hung there, dancing, not looking back, not looking forward. After the music ended, we'd walk off the dance floor hand in hand, dazed with longing. Some part of me still felt I would never feel that alive again.

Does anyone ever forget such moments? I wondered, watching the two dancers in the place Furstemberg. What if more of life could be like that? Like the last slow dance, where, to echo T. S. Eliot, a lifetime burns in every moment.

By 8:30 I was back at the hotel. The bed had been turned down and there were fresh flowers in the room, a bouquet sent by a friend liv-

ing in Paris. The food had revived me, so I decided to try one of Françoise's miracle beauty products. But which one? The mask, I thought, the one that Françoise promised would "tighten the skin and circulate the blood."

With the bathroom window open, I stood in front of the mirror and spread the green cream on my face. I watched as the mask stiffened and small fissures appeared on the surface. For some reason, I thought of my thrifty Scottish grandmother. How she would have laughed at the idea of spending money on cosmetics! Her own beauty habits consisted of going into the garden early in the morning to splash her face with drops of dew.

"Aye, it's nature's own free moisturizer," she would tell me on those Saturday-morning forays into the garden. If I closed my eyes now, I could still see it: a stocky, plain-looking woman in her sixties and a curious, plain-looking child of eight, both dressed in bathrobes and slippers, kneeling in the misty light of dawn and with cupped hands splashing dewdrops onto their faces. Afterward, I would fall back into the warmth of my bed, to doze and dream of the scones I smelled baking in the kitchen.

So strong was the image of that woman and child—one dead now for over thirty years, the other grown—that when I peeled off the stiff green mask, I half expected to see my grandmother's face emerge.

Perhaps tonight I will dream of my grandmother, dream we are back in that garden, together again, I thought, climbing into bed.

But I didn't. Instead I fell into a deep sleep. When I awakened the next morning, the Paris sun had entered my room, falling in slanted golden rays across the floor. I walked to the window and inhaled the golden air. The breeze carried with it the sound of children's voices from a nearby playground; happy, laughing voices that called to one another in high, excited shrieks of irrepressible energy. The language of pleasure, I thought, is the same everywhere.

The sounds floated into my room, swirling around the dark armoire and the red velvet loveseat before drifting out the window into the skies of Saint-Germain-des-Prés. As I listened to the high, childish voices, I imagined them moving like laughing birds along the narrow street outside; I imagined them turning right at the rue de Beaune, a tiny street that ended at the Seine; I imagined them landing on the water, wings tucked back, playfully joining the river's glorious rush through all of Paris, sending small cries of contagious joy throughout the city.

A gentle tapping on the door reminded me I had left a request for breakfast in my room. *"Bonjour, madame,"* said a cheerful young woman carrying a large tray with white china plates and silver pots. She placed it on the table, just between the two open windows. *"Bon appétit."*

I sat down and studied the tray's contents. Carefully laid out on a white linen cloth were fresh orange juice, croissants and brioche, strawberry jam, cheese, and a tall silver pot of coffee, accompanied by a smaller server filled with hot milk. I thought of my usual breakfast at home—coffee and a slice of whole-wheat toast dabbed with peanut butter, served from the top of my television set. Usually I ate this repast while making phone calls and watching Katie Couric on the *Today* show. In my former life, the one that existed until yesterday, it was my habit always to do at least two things at once; three, if possible.

But there would be no hurried phone calls or Katie Couric-watching this morning. Leisurely, I draped the linen napkin on my lap and took a sip of orange juice. Into my large china coffee cup I poured a combination of the strong black coffee and hot milk. I added two small cubes of brown sugar from the sugar bowl and stirred the mixture with a small silver spoon.

This is heaven, I thought, sipping the coffee.

I picked up a croissant, broke it open, and covered it in a painterly way with strokes of red jam. Then, just before taking the first bite, I raised the croissant and, in a celebratory mood, issued a toast to myself: *Welcome to Paris, madame S. And* bon appétit!

2

WOMAN IN THE HAT

Dear Alice,

    At breakfast today in a café near the rue du Bac, I saw Colette. She was drinking coffee and smoking a cigarette, her wild, curly hair and knowing eyes enveloped in smoke. I almost said hello, but then remembered Colette is dead. Still, I decided to visit her in the flesh, so to speak, at Père-Lachaise Cemetery. When I arrived, she was there waiting for me. It pleased me to *see that someone had placed a dozen red roses on the marble stone that says simply:* ICI REPOSE COLETTE 1873–1954.

Love, Alice

During my first week in Paris I left the hotel each morning with a carefully worked out plan for the day. Knowing the plan was tucked safely in my handbag lessened the slightly chaotic feeling of living in a new kind of time, one that had no demands and no deadlines. I was unfamiliar with such a concept of time and it seemed slightly dangerous.

As I set out each day, I felt like a young child again, one who hadn't yet learned the rules of manmade time: the rules of clocks and calendars, of weekdays and weekends. Except for the primitive markers of day and night, time lay ahead of me in a continuous, undefined mass. I began picturing it as some kind of strange but friendly beast whose appetites and desires were unknown to me. How, I wondered, was I to feed such an unpredictable creature? Having an agenda—I sometimes thought of it as a menu—helped give structure to this new kind of time.

At first I followed the plan precisely, as though I were a reporter on a daily deadline: *Wednesday morning, rue de Buci open-air market and rue du Cherche-Midi; afternoon, Picasso Museum and place des Vosges; evening, organ concert at Sainte-Chapelle.* I guess the idea of stepping out from behind the "camouflage of routine," as someone once described it, still intimated me.

By the end of the week, however, I felt confident enough to exchange the old detailed plan for a new and much looser one. Instead of singling out specific places of interest, I decided to concentrate on the neighborhood that was to be my home. This area consisted, roughly, of the streets that lay between the Seine and the boulevard Saint-Germain, plus the square mile or so surrounding the juncture of the 6th and 7th Arrondissements.

The new plan was simple. I would walk—street by fascinating street.

For several days I did just this, getting to know the bookstores and galleries, the cafés and fruit vendors, the patisseries and flower shops. Each day I ventured farther and farther, extending my map of the familiar, gradually finding the places in my neighborhood that were to become part of my daily life. The bookstore in the rue Jacob devoted to gardening. A café on the rue du Bac that served small elegant sandwiches and pastries so delicious they were famous throughout Paris. The small grocery shop near the rue de Verneuil. The newsstand run by Jacques and Monsieur Jacques. The out-of-the-way tea salon on the rue de Beaune. Presided over by Madame Cedelle, this soon became my favorite place for lunch or a late tea in the afternoon.

It was there that I met Liliane, the most extraordinary looking woman in all of Paris.

I first saw her standing at the entry to the crowded tea shop, a woman with dazzling, almond-shaped eyes and skin the color of cognac. Liliane, a slender figure perched on stiletto heels, wore a short, tight, green velvet skirt paired with a peplumed, deep rose satin blouse. Positioned on top of her long, dark hair was a tilted purple hat made of fluted straw; attached to it, a stiff mousseline veil that just covered her eyes. The total effect was that of some exotic parrot set down among sparrows. So physically striking was Liliane that the sight of her caused a brief silence in the tearoom, as diners paused to take in her presence.

I watched as Liliane's eyes scanned the tea salon looking for an empty table. There was none. To my amazement, she approached me. "Would you mind sharing your table with me?" she asked in English, her clipped accent carrying hints of time spent in England.

"Of course not," I said. "Please. Sit down."

Actually, I was delighted to have company. I pushed aside the postcards I'd been writing to my sons and motioned to a chair. Sharing a meal, I had learned, was one of the best ways to meet people when traveling alone. Sometimes a real friendship grew out of such a chance meeting. More often, though, what developed was a temporary friendship, one rooted in the mutual need of two strangers to find companionship in unfamiliar surroundings.

Suddenly, Liliane's voice interrupted my thoughts. "It's one of my favorite photographs," she said, pointing to a postcard lying on top of my purse.

The card, which I planned to send to a friend in New York, was a reproduction of a famous 1926 picture taken in Paris by the great Hungarian-born photographer André Kertész. A bold-looking, vivacious woman reclines on an Art Nouveau love seat, her arms and legs arranged with abandon against the plush velvet cushions. Her pose gives the effect of a woman dancing horizontally. Kertész, whom I had interviewed once for my newspaper, titled the image *Satiric Dancer*. A print of the photograph hung in my living room at home.

"It's a favorite of mine, too," I said, picking up the postcard. "There's such joy and fearlessness in that face, isn't there? It's like the look you see on a child's face before the age of reason sets in." We both laughed. "But I'm curious. How did you become familiar with the photo?"

"I studied photography in New York for a while and fell in love with Kertész's work," she said. "Brassaï, too. Do you know Brassaï's photos of Paris?"

Liliane had hit on a passion of mine: photography. Within minutes we were discussing Brassaï, also a Hungarian, who had moved
to Paris, where he became famous for his pictures of Paris nightlife
in the 1920s; and Atget, the venerated master photographer of the
city, who, beginning in the 1890s, photographed Paris almost every
day for more than twenty years. After agreeing that Atget was the
architectural historian of Paris and Brassaï the Colette of the camera, we compared notes on cameras we liked and why color prints
could never approach the beauty of black-and-white photographs.

We finished lunch and ordered coffee. Then more coffee. By
this time we had traded our personal histories, or at least as much
as we wished to trade. Liliane, who was born in Rio de Janeiro but
grew up in London, ran an interior design business from her
Chelsea flat. Her two children, both teenagers, were away at boarding school. She made no mention of their father. She did mention,
however, that she was not alone in Paris; an Englishman named
Justin had accompanied her. The purpose of the trip to Paris, Liliane said, was to visit her ailing aunt.

I was surprised by the warmth and openness of Liliane's personality; it contrasted so strikingly with her exotic, unapproachable
appearance. But even her warmth and charm could not completely
dissipate my awareness of her astonishing looks; from time to time
I found myself studying her face as one would a painting.

She seemed interested in my trip and asked question after
question: *Don't you get lonely? What did your sons think of your decision to do
this? Don't you worry about your job? Do you know people in Paris?* By the
time we rose to leave, it was as though I'd had lunch with an old
friend.

Outside we walked along the rue du Bac, stopping to peer into
the shop windows at some amazing display of antiques or ancient
jewelry. As we walked, I noticed how much attention Liliane's

appearance commanded. Especially from men. I felt a twinge of
envy, one I tried to brush aside. Liliane, I noticed, was not unaware
of the stares she drew; she seemed to play to her audience in a flirtatious way, something she hadn't done in the tea shop.

Before we parted, Liliane asked if I liked jazz. "Justin and I are
going to a jazz club near your hotel after we visit my aunt," she said.
"Would you like to join us?"

"Yes, very much." I agreed to meet them at La Villa at 10:30
that night. To my surprise, just before we parted, Liliane reached
out and hugged me.

After leaving Liliane, I decided to walk over to the Musée d'Orsay.
Along the way I saw a half-dozen things that made me think about
pulling out my reporter's notebook. A man sitting outside the museum impersonating the Mona Lisa; a dog roller-skating alongside
his master; two women, identical twins who appeared to be in their
seventies, dressed in matching pink outfits by Chanel; a man in a
tall baker's hat bicycling along the quai d'Orsay, a wedding cake
balanced in the bike's basket.

What great stories there are in Paris, I thought, half-convinced
I should phone an editor and see if I could sell some ideas. The
other half of me, however, stepped in quickly to remind me of why
I came to Paris in the first place: *Remember,* this voice whispered,
you're here to take a break from seeing life as "newspaper stories."

But it was a difficult habit to quit. I loved my work; it was an important part of my identity. In the twenty years I'd been a reporter,
I'd met people and gone through doors that were opened to me
only because of my job. I'd met Princess Diana at the British Em-

bassy on her first trip to the United States in 1986 and interviewed Elie Wiesel in his New York apartment just after he'd won the Nobel Prize. I'd done stories on mothers who murdered their children, and spent four months in a psychiatric ward chronicling the life of a young psychiatrist. I'd profiled artists and actors and scientists and what I liked to think of as "extraordinary" ordinary people. I could think of no job more fascinating.

But the work has its perils: spending large chunks of time immersed in another person's life makes it easier to lose track of one's own place in the world. I was determined not to let that happen on this trip.

Still, when I saw a performance artist climbing a thirty-foot beanstalk constructed of green plastic, it took real self-discipline to talk myself out of doing an on-the-spot interview with "Jacques and His Greenstalk."

On the way back to my hotel I passed a shop near rue Bonaparte that featured in its windows several mannequins dressed in Chinese cheongsam-style dresses. One particularly caught my eye—a beautiful black silk number with a mandarin collar and elegant frog fastenings that ran down the left side of the dress. When I moved closer to the window I saw the silk was subtly patterned: raised silk threads, gossamer as spiderwebs, formed what looked like black-on-black calligraphy. The effect was both elegant and mysterious, a design that revealed itself, like a secret, only to the intimate observer. Impulsively, I walked into the shop.

"Bonjour, madame," a voice sang out from somewhere in the back of the shop. It was a pleasant custom, the way French shopkeepers

greeted each customer personally, and one that ran counter to any notion of the French as rude and unfriendly.

"*Bonjour,*" I sang back. Then to my utter surprise I heard myself say: "I'd like to try on the black dress in the window. Well, I mean, not the one in the window but one like it in my size."

"*Oui, madame,*" she said, eyeballing me from head to toe—the typical French approach, I had learned, in determining size.

That was all right with me. The truth is, I was sure that no size existed in this particular dress that would fit me, so unforgiving was its narrow cut. Still, for some reason, I was willing to give the dress a chance, even if—*quelle horreur!*—it meant humiliating myself in the eyes of the salesclerk.

As I waited for her to bring the dress, I wondered what was behind my sudden need to acquire a glamorous black silk cheongsam. Was it the challenge of meeting Liliane—the exotic, fabulous-looking, man-attracting Liliane—at La Villa? The idea almost made me laugh out loud.

"Here it is, madame," said the saleswoman, interrupting my thoughts. She hung the silk dress in a small room and ushered me in, tactfully leaving me alone to try it on.

Without much optimism I removed my slacks and blouse. I slipped the dress on over my head. To my surprise it kept on going, undeterred even when it encountered my hips. After hooking up the little frog closures and pulling in my stomach muscles, I turned to look in the mirror. Not bad. In fact, better than I would have thought possible. When I moved, I noticed that the slits on either side of the dress flashed just the slightest bit of red silk lining, another elegant secret.

That was it. I had to have the dress. Of course, wearing it meant I would have to be intensely aware of my posture, both upper and lower, for the whole evening. But given my infatuation with the image in the mirror, that seemed a reasonable price to pay.

By 5:30 I was back at the hotel. Thirty minutes later the phone rang. It was a radio producer from Baltimore, calling to confirm I was in my room. At six, Paris time—noon, Baltimore time—I was to be a telephone guest on *The Allan Prell Show*.

For the past seven years I'd been a regular guest on this radio talk show. It was something I enjoyed doing. Allan Prell was both smart and funny and so were the listeners who called in to talk about everything from politics to books. Before leaving on my trip, it was suggested I do a radio interview on the show from Paris. I agreed. And now the familiar voice of Allan Prell was on the other end of the long-distance line.

For forty-five minutes Allan and I talked about Paris. About the price of a glass of orange juice at Deux Magots—seven dollars— and the cost of a cup of coffee at the Flore—five dollars. About the hotels on the Left Bank. About what I was doing. Listeners called in to ask questions. Commercials came and went, bringing into my room on the rue de l'Université the voices of Baltimore Oriole Cal Ripken, Jr., and Morris the Remodeler. I could picture the radio studio, could see Allan in his white turtleneck swiveling back and forth in his chair, could even identify the voices of some callers. It was all so familiar.

And yet, sitting in my Paris hotel, only a few blocks away from the Seine and the hotel where Hemingway lived, it already seemed like somebody else's life.

When the interview was over I sat for a while looking around the room. My gaze stopped at the wine-red love seat. Suddenly I thought: *it looks just like the love seat in the Kertész photo.* I got up and walked to the small sofa. Then, without thinking, I tried to arrange myself on it like the woman—the Satiric Dancer—in the picture. It wasn't easy.

Close enough, I said to the empty room when finally I managed to get both legs onto the back cushion. After all, I was not young, not a dancer, and, although I fancied myself amusing at times, definitely not a satirist.

When I arrived at the jazz club that night, there was no sign of Liliane and her friend. I decided to wait at the bar. La Villa was crowded, filled with affluent-looking men dressed in expensive suits worn with black T-shirts, and model-perfect women wearing creations from the salons of hot young Paris designers. The verdict of success was in the air; it rose up through the smoke and dim light, creating a halo of self-approval. I was glad I'd worn the new black silk dress. Although not up to the level of high fashion present in the room, it had a simplicity that might pass for elegance. At least that was my hope.

Just then I spotted Liliane sitting at a small table with a man who could have stepped out of a Brooks Brothers' ad. She waved me over.

"Hello again," she said as I approached them. Liliane looked spectacular. She was wearing a black silk dress with long sleeves made of crisscrossed green silk ribbons. On her head was a small hat of black tulle; a tiny green bird nested inside the tulle. Her companion stood up and nodded but did not speak; his handsome square-jawed face maintained its Mount Rushmore impassivity.

"This is Justin Moore," Liliane said. "But be warned—he is not in a good mood." She laughed but her eyes darted nervously in Justin's direction. I sat down, slightly put off by the awkward beginning to the evening. Immediately, Justin and Liliane returned to some sort of squabble that obviously had been interrupted by my arrival. Embarrassed, I sat there until Liliane turned to me.

"A lover's quarrel," she explained, laughing. "Sorry. But you know how these things are." She laughed again and turned to pick up Justin's hand. He did not look amused. And he made no attempt to smooth over the situation.

Liliane, meanwhile, tried harder and harder to cajole Justin into a better mood. She grew flirtatious and then flattering, telling me about Justin's accomplishments as a banker. And about his exquisite taste. "I met Justin when he hired me to decorate his flat in London. But his eye is so good he really didn't need a designer."

I asked Justin a few questions about himself. He answered in a bored tone, making it quite clear he felt no need to impress me.

His dismissal did not bother me. I was completely oblivious to the idea of personal slights; my attention was focused on the intriguing dynamics between Liliane and Justin. Particularly fascinating to me was how different she was in his presence. Gone was the easy openness I'd seen at lunch; replacing it was an extreme awareness of how Justin reacted to her. She became manipulative, changing her tactics if they seemed not to please him. It struck me that despite the ease with which she attracted men, she wasn't really comfortable around them. Some impulse seemed to take over in the presence of a man, one that changed Liliane from a freestanding entity into a needy, dependent person.

It was a familiar pattern to me. I'd seen it in my mother, a beautiful woman who even in her seventies elicited the attention of men. By that time, however, she no longer wanted it; in fact, she once confessed to me she had never really been comfortable in the company of a man. "Your father came close," she told me when we were both old enough to talk of such things, "but sometimes even with him I found myself pretending to be someone I wasn't."

Still, she married again less than a year after my father's death. It was a sad marriage, one that depended a good deal on both participants giving up their real personalities. Only when my mother reached her sixties was she able to assert her independence, able to free herself of the fear of being on her own. "I always thought of it as being alone, not on my own," was the way she described the fear that dictated so many of her actions.

I thought I saw that fear of being alone in Liliane, too. I watched as she leaned close to Justin, leaned until the tiny green bird on her hat almost touched his forehead. She began talking. Her face looked anxious, crumpled. I couldn't hear what she was saying and I didn't want to.

After all, I was a stranger who knew none of their mutual history. It was like walking into the middle of a movie: I arrived too late for the beginning and wouldn't be around for the end. Still, I was quite caught up in the drama of whatever was being played out between them. It didn't matter that I no longer existed to Liliane and Justin except, perhaps, as a deterrent to things getting really out of hand. By this time, Liliane was no longer a real person to me. The woman I'd met at lunch had vanished. And while I hated to admit it, I found myself deriving some small satisfaction from the belief that I no longer was susceptible to being compromised in such a way by a man.

"Let's go," I heard Justin say to her. "I didn't want to come to begin with." His face was cold and impassive.

Liliane turned to me. "I'm sorry. But we have to leave. I'm not feeling well." I saw she was close to tears.

I didn't know what to say. It was such an intimate situation, one I shouldn't be witnessing. "Never mind," I said. "I'm not uncomfortable staying here alone. I just hope you're all right."

Liliane and Justin rose to go. He nodded coldly. I nodded back just as coldly. I watched them thread their way between the small tables. My eyes followed the black hat with its tiny green bird caged in tulle until it disappeared.

I stayed on at La Villa until almost midnight, losing myself in the supple gymnastics of great jazz. Just as I was about to leave, a saxophonist started playing "How High the Moon."

The sound started off slow, almost like a love song, then the drummer weighed in with his steel brushes, coming in softly just behind the beat, then moving into a big sound along with the saxophone until the whole place was jiving. In the middle of all this, a figure ran across the years to meet me:

It is my twenty-year-old self and she is back in New York, sitting in Birdland, listening to Charlie Parker. Next to her is Will, an artist and the man she loved. Or thought she loved. How young they both look. And how fearless. I'd forgotten how fearless she was, this young, laughing woman whose head is tilted toward her companion, just as Liliane's had been.

But then my twenty-year-old self leans back and I see something else in her face, something similar to what I'd seen earlier in Liliane's: an anxious look that telegraphs a willingness to be whatever the man sitting next to her wants her to be. Even if it means betraying her own needs.

How easy it was, still, to conjure up those old feelings. Not just for Will, but for all the boyfriends and lovers that I'd reinvented myself for in the name of love. Along the way I'd made some bad choices when it came to men. And a few good ones.

For some reason, I thought of Colette; wise, resilient Colette, who knew about "that lightheartedness which comes to a woman when the peril of men has left her." I never interpreted Colette's observation as meaning she thought women would be better off without men. What I took it to mean was: women would be better off when they no longer needed men more than they needed their own independent identities.

It came to me then, sitting at La Villa, that it had been a long while since I'd thought of love as the center of my life. The peril of men, it seemed, had left me some years back. I no longer believed that romantic love had the power to shape or transform me. My life had a shape, one that suited me just fine.

When I arrived back at the hotel, the night manager handed me, along with my room key, a telephone message from Liliane. I climbed the stairs to my room and sat on the bed reading Liliane's words: "Please forgive Justin's rudeness. He was not feeling well. I'll call before I leave Paris."

I thought again about the look on Liliane's face that night; that anxious look that says no price is too high to pay if it means not being alone. I thought of my own slow conversion to independence, of how long a time it took me after my divorce to understand that being alone is not the same as being lonely.

But I also thought of the twinge of envy I'd felt earlier in the day about Liliane's attractiveness to men. There was pleasure in that, too; in being the focus of a man's attention.

As I soon would be reminded in my unexpected encounter with a man named Naohiro.

BIJOUX ANCIENS - OBJETS ANCIENS

Magnolia

TÉL. 42. 22. 31

78 RUE DU BAC
75007 PARIS

3

At Sainte-Chapelle

Dear Alice,

    There is a certain mysterious quality about Paris that I find in no other city. Paris, it seems, has her hidden, secret places. Walk down any street in the city and you will see the huge wooden gates with peeling green paint that separate the passerby from the lush courtyards and elegant mansions inside. Paris guards her inner beauty from the casual observer. To find it one *must look beyond the façades. It is true of people also, I think: their spirits exist behind their façades, beyond their words.*

Love, Alice

I met Naohiro on the train to Giverny. I'd noticed him earlier at the St.-Lazare station, buying a ticket: a slim, attractive man, elegantly dressed completely in black except for a white sweater thrown across his shoulders. He was Asian; Japanese, I thought, although I wasn't absolutely certain.

For weeks I'd looked forward to visiting Giverny, a small village halfway between Paris and Rouen. It was there that the great French painter Monet had lived for the last forty years of his life, devoting himself to his painting and his gardens. I'd been putting off my visit to Giverny, waiting for the perfect day: one with a breeze, when sun and shadow would play across the surface of Monet's Japanese water garden, just as it had when he painted it.

Such a day arrived at the end of May. *A perfect day for Giverny,* I thought the instant I saw the fast-moving, slightly overcast sky through my window. Wonderful as the streets of Paris were, I longed for the countryside, for the fertile smell of the earth and the feel of grass beneath my feet.

It was from my mother that I had learned the guiding role nature plays in how we map out the geography of self. She was the granddaughter of a landscape gardener who worked on the grounds of a castle in Scotland. For a time, her world was one of towering trees and rose gardens, of heathered hills that stretched to the horizon, of clear water that revealed the salmon, gleaming like silver arrows just beneath the surface.

Later, my mother's interest in the natural world was encouraged by both her parents. From her stern father she learned the botanical names and the science of nature; from her sturdy mother the pleasures of planting and digging in the earth, of being a part of nature's cycle of life and death. But my mother's gift for observation—the mark of a true naturalist—was her own.

A day in the country, I decided, was definitely in order. There was no doubt in my mind that, surrounded by nature's immutable realities, I would find what I needed: a perspective on where I fit into the world.

I had just settled into my seat on the train when Naohiro appeared in the aisle next to me. He tilted his head in a slight bow. "Do you mind if I sit here?" he asked, in almost accentless English. Still, his voice confirmed what I had guessed at the train station: he was Japanese.

"Please do," I said, looking up from the map I was studying. He sat down. Immediately I was aware of a scent about him that seemed familiar. It was crisp; he smelled like pine needles. Quickly it came to me, the reason why it seemed so familiar. It reminded me of Hiroshi, my son's Japanese friend, who had stayed with us during a Christmas holiday. It was the same scent that filled the guest bathroom after Hiroshi had shaved and showered.

But I was aware of something more about Naohiro than his scent. His presence made me feel self-conscious: of my appearance, of the way I was sitting, of my movements and gestures. I was not unfamiliar with such symptoms: it was the behavior of a woman reacting to a man who attracts her.

As the train left the station, Naohiro reached into a small brief-case and pulled out a book. It was the same guidebook to Giverny that I had bought in Paris. I started to say something but stopped, remembering the conversations with my son about the reticence of the Japanese. In his four years as a teacher and translator in Japan, my son had grown to admire the Japanese. And I had grown to re-spect his careful insights into that culture. So I said nothing.

I turned my attention to the view, one that included the Seine winding its way alongside the train. This part of the river bore little resemblance to the glamorous Seine that bisected Paris. Sweet and unsophisticated, this Seine meandered like a country cousin across the pastoral landscape. Through the window I saw young boys fish-ing from its banks, their dogs dozing beside them in the sun.

Naohiro's voice interrupted my thoughts. "Is this your first time to Giverny?" he asked.

"Yes, it is," I said, trying to conceal my surprise that he had ini-tiated a conversation. "What about you?"

"No, I have been before. But this time I go especially to see the Japanese prints."

I had read about Monet's collection of eighteenth- and nineteenth-century Japanese prints, and of their influence on his work. "Are you an artist?" I asked, forgetting my resolve to not ask him personal questions.

He smiled. "No, I am a businessman."

"Do you live in Paris?"

"No, but I come to France two or three times a year."

He seemed not to mind my questions. Still, he asked me nothing about what I did or why I was in France.

As he spoke, I studied his face. It was a handsome face, slightly weathered and somewhat impassive. Except for his eyes. They were the eyes of a man who possessed wit and intelligence and, I thought, a certain sadness. I was drawn to what I saw, or imagined I saw, there.

In the hour or so it took to reach Giverny, Naohiro and I talked mostly about Paris. About our favorite streets—his was the rue de Nevers, a street I did not know, and mine the rue du Bac; about the squares we thought most beautiful—place des Vosges for him, place Furstemberg for me; the open-air markets we liked—one on rue Daguerre, the other on rue de Buci. On one thing we agreed: that the best view of Paris was from any one of the bridges that crossed the Seine. Particularly the Pont Royal or the Pont-Neuf. As we talked I could see that Naohiro knew Paris far better than I did.

In our conversation we exchanged little about the personal details of our lives, but, I realized later, what had been said revealed a good bit about what we each responded to in the larger world.

Finally, I asked: "Is there someplace in Paris that is special to you? That you might suggest I visit?"

"Yes," he said, without hesitating. "Sainte-Chapelle. You must go there to stand in the light."

His answer surprised me. I had been to this medieval chapel on the Île de la Cité to see its famous stained-glass windows, but had never thought of "standing in the light." Although I'd dutifully studied the architecture and used my guidebook to decipher the stories in the windows, I realized I had never actually placed myself there, in the moment, in the light. But I did not tell Naohiro this. Why, I'm not sure. Instead, I said, "I will definitely put Sainte-Chapelle on my list."

We sat in silence for a few minutes. Just when I began to feel awkward about the silence, he asked, "And what place is special to you? That I might visit?"

Unlike him, I felt self-conscious about answering, as though he would somehow judge me by my selection. Nevertheless, I knew what it had to be. "Père-Lachaise Cemetery," I said. After a pause, I added, "You must go there to stand in the past."

I told him about the Sunday I'd spent at Père-Lachaise, walking beneath the trees, picking my way up the crowded hillside through the tilting statues, searching for the graves of Colette and Proust, two writers I admired. I'd found Colette easily but had no such luck in locating Proust. And I told Naohiro of how, just before leaving the area where Proust's grave was marked on the map, I'd come face-to-face with a gravestone engraved ALIX STEINBACH, 1880–1961. Although I had no idea who "Alix Steinbach" was, it pleased me that someone with a name so close to mine was now re-siding in Proust's neighborhood.

"I feel at home in cemeteries," I told Naohiro. "When I was lit-tle, my grandmother would take me on long walks through the cemeteries near our house. We'd read the tombstones and figure out from the dates how old the people buried there were." I laughed. "I think it's how I learned to add and subtract."

Naohiro nodded, but said nothing. I was not surprised. What could he say? I didn't expect him to understand, as most people didn't, my choice of a cemetery as one of my favorite places in Paris.

We sat in silence until the train arrived at Vernon, a village three miles from Giverny. At the taxi stand, Naohiro suggested sharing a ride to Monet's house. I agreed.

When we got to Giverny, the entrance was crowded with buses. Tour groups were heading off in every direction. It was very con-fusing. As I was debating whether to say good-bye to Naohiro and go my own way—whatever way that was—he asked if I would like to look at the Japanese prints with him.

"Yes, very much," I said, following him through the gardens of trellised roses, irises, dahlias, delphiniums, and poppies bordering the paths leading to the house. Inside, Monet's collection of rare Japanese prints lined the walls of nearly every room. Their simplicity and stillness provided a serene contrast to the wild lushness of the gardens outside.

In the dining room, where the walls were painted in two shades of vivid yellow, I stopped to admire a print depicting a mountain-ringed horseshoe of water that ended abruptly at a wide sandy beach. There was no perspective; the flattened-out blue water at the top of the print simply stopped when it met the gray semicircle of sand near the bottom of the paper. It was pure landscape. But its haunting loneliness conveyed something profound, I thought; something having to do with the human condition.

"Do you like that one?" asked Naohiro, walking up behind me. "It is by Hiroshige. Some say he was the greatest of all the Japanese ukiyo-e painters." His voice changed when he pronounced the Japanese word; it became softer, I thought, and more musical.

"Ukiyo-e? What does that mean?"

"Pictures of the floating world; of the real world," he said. Then he smiled. "Does it remind you of your visit to Père-Lachaise?"

I looked to see if he was mocking me. But there was no hint of that in his face. What I thought I saw was some kind of understanding or recognition. Of what, I wasn't sure. I looked back at the print.

Maybe, I thought, there *is* something in its quiet stillness, in its indifference to change, that does remind me of Père-Lachaise. Still, I was quite puzzled as to why Naohiro had made a connection between the two things.

"These prints are very fugitive," he said, as we walked through the house. "The color must be protected from the light or it will die."

It was an odd choice of words, his description of the prints as fugitive and capable of dying. But Naohiro, I was starting to see, expressed himself differently than westerners; particularly western men. He spoke English in a way that was both original and direct. I liked it.

By early afternoon the inside of the house had grown crowded and warm; it seemed a good time to retreat to the cool shade of the Japanese water garden. For a long while I stood with Naohiro watching the water lilies float under a small, green, wisteria-covered bridge. The sun filtering through the trees scattered tiny dots of light, like facets of a diamond, across the water's surface. I noticed that where the arc of the bridge met its reflection in the water, a green circle was formed: the real bridge at the top, its watery reflection at the bottom.

I wondered about my own garden. Were the daylilies blooming? Had the pots of geraniums survived? Was there new growth on the old lilac tree I'd pruned back almost to the ground? Not too many years ago I'd charted the changing seasons by my sons, by their growth and their blossoming. Now, with both of them far from home, it was azaleas and snowdrops that signaled such changes.

From a tiny island in the center of the pond, a mourning dove cried out from the hollow of his nest. As I looked down, I saw two faces reflected in the water: mine and Naohiro's. A small gust of wind abruptly shattered the image into ripples; our faces became puzzlelike pieces that moved apart and then together again, his floating across the surface with mine.

"What do you think of?" Naohiro asked.

I pointed to our faces, moving over the water. "Ukiyo-e," I said stumbling over the word. "The floating world."

He laughed. "You are a quick student. I shall take care in what I teach you." But I could tell he was pleased by my response.

I found something to like in his response, too, hinting as it did at a shared future.

We left Giverny and arrived in Paris just after six. I knew that Naohiro was staying at a hotel near the Eiffel Tower and wondered if he had friends waiting for him. It was Saturday night; I had no plans and was on the verge of asking him to have a drink with me when he asked if I had dinner plans.

We agreed to meet later at Tan Dinh, a Vietnamese restaurant that served, he said, some of the best food in Paris.

Although I'd never eaten at Tan Dinh, I knew of the restaurant. It was near my hotel on the rue de Verneuil, an old and captivating street I'd discovered the day I arrived here. I walked there often, using it as a shortcut to the Orsay Museum or just to enjoy its charm. A narrow street of small shops, a few fine restaurants, and old but expensive apartments hidden behind large wooden gates, it captured the Paris I loved best.

After leaving Naohiro, I returned to the hotel, where I found a letter waiting. It had been forwarded from the newspaper to my home in Baltimore and then to Paris. Sent by a reader in response to the last column I'd written before leaving—one in which I explained my hopes for the year—the note wished me good luck on my journey. The writer ended with a line from Eudora Welty: "All serious daring starts from within."

I sat thinking about how once I was daring not only on the inside but on the outside as well. In my adolescent years, after my father died, I feared nothing. Or at least I pretended to fear nothing. I made dangerous choices in those years, thinking myself bold and adventurous. Later I would come to understand I hadn't been daring at all, just driven by confusion and hormones. The person capable of true daring, I knew now, possessed two admirable qualities: curiosity and courage.

Given that definition, I guess in my adult years I had committed some daring acts. Not anything like living among Amazon tribes, as a friend of mine, a writer, had done. But a few years back I did go head-to-head in interviews with the likes of George F. Will and William F. Buckley, Jr. That, I decided, was daring enough for me.

As I showered and dressed, I thought of Naohiro; of how little I knew about him. Coming back from Giverny on the train I did learn a few things: that he worked in Tokyo in the electronics industry, lived in an apartment there, traveled a great deal, and had studied as a young man in California. He said little about his personal life and I did not press him for details.

But I wanted to. Most of all I wanted to know: was he married and did he have a family? Still, I did not ask. What lay at the bottom of my unusual reticence, I suspected, was a wish to avoid the disappointment I might feel if his answers were not the ones I wanted to hear.

I slipped on the black silk dress I'd bought at the small shop in Saint-Germain. Around my shoulders I draped the antique shawl—

thin cut-velvet the color of a ripe tomato—I'd picked up in a thrift shop on the rue du Bac. Looking in the mirror I fancied myself—with excessive generosity—quite the chic Parisienne. Already, fantasies were flitting like butterflies in my head. About Naohiro and me.

Oh, God, I thought, walking from the hotel to the restaurant. Is this what I left my job and home for? To become gripped by an intense infatuation? One with no possible outcome except disappointment? The feeling depressed me.

But the truth is, it exhilarated me even more. I thought of Doris Lessing's observation that "A woman without a man cannot meet a man, any man, of any age, without thinking, even if it's for a half-second, 'Perhaps this is THE man.' "

If ever there was living proof that Lessing had scored a bull's-eye with that one, I was it.

When I arrived, Naohiro was there waiting for me. Tan Dinh was a small, elegant restaurant with exquisite food and an impressive wine list. Naohiro asked if he could order for both of us. I said yes. Wine appeared; a Bordeaux. Then one by one the elegant dishes arrived: Saigon chicken rolls, steamed ravioli with smoked goose, lobster prepared with ginko leaves, and a mysterious, delicious dessert flavored with hazelnuts.

As the evening progressed I grew more and more comfortable with Naohiro. The wine, no doubt, helped. We talked of books and movies, of the pleasures and pains of traveling, and finally of ourselves.

Naohiro began by telling me about his two children, a son and a daughter, both in their early twenties. His daughter lived with him; his son was away at school. He spoke of them with great affection. And with humor, too, as he described his daughter's attempt to curl her straight hair with a permanent.

"I think," Naohiro said, "she was trying to look like Cher." We both laughed. But I think he knew what I was waiting to hear.

"Their mother," he said, "died two years ago."

Something in the way he said this suggested I should not ask any more about the matter. Still, I felt he had confided something that was painful for him.

I told him about my family, then about my job and why I had left it to come to France. He asked me to tell him about my work.

"It's never the same," I said. "That's one of the things I like about it. One week I'm doing a story on Siamese twins and the next I'm interviewing Jeanne Moreau over lunch at a fancy hotel."

To my surprise, he was eager to know what Jeanne Moreau was like. *Jules and Jim,* it turned out, was a favorite film of his.

"She's one of the most intelligent and charming people I've ever met," I said. I told him how impressed I was with the way she expressed herself in English. "Her images were poetic. But precise in the way that poetry is. And her face . . . It's endlessly fascinating." I laughed. "She told me that at twenty she was considered 'unphotogenic' and that it hurt her to read such a description. But as a woman in her fifties, she had stopped—and this is the way she put it—'looking into the mirror that others hold up to me.' "

As I told this to Naohiro, it occurred to me that Moreau's declaration of independence from "looking into the mirror that others hold up to me" was a deft description of what I was after on this trip.

Naohiro was a very good listener. He nodded his head as I talked, as if to encourage me to continue. So I did, telling him a bit more about my job. When I stopped talking, however, he said nothing.

It still unnerved me a bit, this habit he had of not jumping in immediately to offer his opinions on another person's thoughts. I started to say something to break the silence, but stopped. Maybe it was I who needed to learn how to be quiet instead of cluttering the moment with too many words.

After dinner we walked along the rue du Bac until we reached the Seine. We turned onto the quai Voltaire, and headed toward the lights of Nôtre-Dame. Near the Pont-Neuf a tall, thin man dressed in jeans and a black turtleneck sweater was bent over a guitar, singing "As I walked out on the streets of Laredo . . ." His voice was pure Texas.

Naohiro asked me to explain what "streets of Laredo" meant. Was Laredo like concrete? he asked. I explained—as tactfully as I could—that Laredo was a city in Texas. He laughed at his mistake, a warm, open laugh that, like the Bordeaux we'd shared, sent the blood rushing to my head. A dizzying sense of closeness enveloped me. I started to take his hand. Then I stopped. It seemed too forward a gesture. If Naohiro noticed this small, canceled movement on my part, he said nothing.

We walked along in companionable silence, stopping at the edge of the Seine to watch the *bateaux-mouches* glide up and down the river. Inside the lighted boats, people were eating dinner as Paris drifted by. A feeling passed through me, one I couldn't quite identify. Not happiness, exactly; more like the absence of worrying about finding happiness.

When we arrived at my hotel, Naohiro asked if I had plans for the next day. I had none. "Then I would be happy if you would visit Sainte-Chapelle with me," he said. I agreed.

That night before I fell asleep I studied the family photographs I'd brought along on the trip: of my sons, of my brother and sister-in-law, and of my parents, both dead. I was particularly drawn to a photograph of my father as a young man, sitting in a rickshaw in China. He was an adventurer, my father, and almost all the pictures I have of him were taken in some exotic locale: standing near the top of Sugar Loaf Mountain in Rio de Janeiro, patting an elephant's trunk in India, posing with my mother on a foggy Edinburgh street.

He died when I was eight.

Before my brother and I were born, my father had taught at a university. But it was not the life he wanted. His love of the sea and of the places it could take him drove him to maritime school, and then to a life at sea. His family and friends didn't understand this choice; his brothers never stopped their campaign to draw him into the family business. Always, my father listened politely; always he politely declined the offer.

In the years after his death, it grew harder for me to hold on to the memories of my father. Not just those that had to do with the relationship between the two of us, but his physical appearance as well. Then one day when I was about twelve I realized I no longer remembered what he looked like. Even now, when I tried to picture him, what I saw was the man in the photographs, the one who always looked utterly at home, no matter how foreign the background. He had a gift for that, I thought. Fitting in.

My father had a gift for spontaneity, too. Like a child, he always seemed ready to do anything that turned up, go anywhere that beckoned. When he returned, there would be presents for my brother and me; wonderful dolls from Brazil dressed in swirling samba skirts and, from India, carved ivory elephants crossing a bridge.

In his spare time my father wrote short stories. About places with exotic names like Bitter Creek and Silver Bow. They were adventure stories, he told me, set in the West. I think he sold a few of them to some magazine or another. Once he let me use his typewriter. I'd never seen one up close before and it was as exciting as anything I'd ever done, pecking out my name on the little round keys with letters in the middle.

I fell asleep that night thinking of my father: the explorer, the man who embraced the world so warmly, the man whose face I could never quite remember but kept searching for anyway.

It was midmorning when Naohiro and I arrived at Sainte-Chapelle. We climbed the winding stone steps from the lower chapel, designed as a place of worship for the royal servants, to the upper chapel, reserved for the kings of France.

Naohiro walked to the center of the chapel. I followed. "Stand next to me," he said.

And I did, trying to see what it was he saw. There, beneath the chapel's soaring, vaulted ceiling, surrounded by towering walls of glowing stained glass, it seemed that light and glass had conspired to form a new element: one composed of ice lit from within by fire.

I have no idea how long we stood there, Naohiro and I, in the light of Sainte-Chapelle. Finally I turned to look at him. His head was bowed slightly but his eyes were open.

"Thank you," I said, "for bringing me here."

He nodded but did not answer or turn to look at me.

But I continued to look at him. And as I looked a great tenderness sprang up in me; a tenderness for the spirit of the man standing by my side. Finally, he turned to me. In silence we stood together in the light, looking at each other.

I no longer felt self-conscious; I felt only my need to share this moment with him.

"I feel our spirits have met," I said.

He nodded. "I feel it is so."

"It is a good feeling."

"Yes," he replied. "It is a good feeling."

I looked at Naohiro's face to see what was there. He met my eyes with a steady, open gaze, one that evoked in me many different feelings.

In the days ahead, Naohiro and I would come to know a great number of things about each other. Still, of all the moments we shared, none, I think, was more intimate than the day we stood together in the light of Sainte-Chapelle.

PARIS

4

FELLOW TRAVELERS

Dear Alice,

    Do not forget the woman in gold lamé shorts, the Ritz, the sound of the leaves in the Tuileries, the veiled hats that reminded you of Mother, the light pouring out of the shops along the rue du

Bac, the lavender skies, the smiling dog, the people you encoun-
tered on this day. Do not forget the last time you saw Paris.
Love, Alice

It was after ten and I was on my way to Montmartre for a late breakfast with Susan, an American friend living in Paris, when suddenly it hit me: I didn't want to see her. This feeling puzzled me. After all, it was I who had called Susan to arrange the visit.

Like me, Susan was a woman who decided to take a detour from the life she'd spent a decade carefully constructing. "A year in Paris and then I'll be back," I remember her saying when she took a leave from her job at a Washington design firm. The year had turned into two, then three, and by the time I arrived, Susan—now a successful commercial artist—was entering the fourth year of her "stay" in Paris.

I found it surprising, the way she'd disconnected so easily from her past. True, she was divorced, her only daughter now in her mid-twenties and living in London. But Susan had left behind what seemed an extremely satisfying life: a circle of loyal and familial friends, a successful career, and a deep affection for the city in which she'd grown up. Although I didn't quite understand her reasons, I admired her ability to accept in midlife the challenge of reinventing herself.

But then Susan had a habit of reinventing herself. When I first met her at an embassy party in Washington she was thin and blond and quite vivacious. We struck up a conversation that night, one that resulted in our having dinner together the following week. When she walked into the restaurant I hardly recognized her. Her hair was carrot-colored and her makeup very dramatic. Somehow, it suited her. She liked to change her appearance, Susan told me; it was a way of expressing her artistic talent.

Our friendship, I suppose, was built on mutual loss. She was newly divorced; I was newly separated. We were both in that strange passage from married life to single-mother-looking-for-love-in-all-the-wrong-places. But Susan was also wickedly funny, a quality I valued in a friend. Once when I complained about being at an age that required never looking at yourself in full sunlight, Susan's riposte was immediate. "You know what can age you twenty years overnight?" she asked. "If all your friends got face-lifts the day before."

As I climbed the steep streets to Susan's apartment, I wondered if my reluctance to see her was simply anxiety about revisiting a time that, for both of us, had been confusing and painful. Five years had passed since I'd seen her, at a party to celebrate her move. She arrived with the man she was about to dump; I arrived with the man who, I knew, was about to dump me. We consoled each other with the contemporary maxim "a woman without a man is like a fish without a bicycle." But neither of us really believed that. We left the party—without our dates—and went on to a jazz club, where, slightly tipsy, we promised we'd always be friends.

But were we still friends? I wondered. Or just former friends facing an awkward reunion?

Although Susan's directions to her apartment—"Past the windmills on rue Lepic and you're practically there"—had seemed clear enough on the phone, the steep, narrow Montmartre streets had a life of their own. After thirty minutes of confused wandering I arrived finally at an address that matched the one I'd written on a scrap of paper. Situated on a quiet, rural-looking lane, the small apartment building seemed a world away from the tourist-jammed streets around the place du Tertre. Here, there was an air of a country village. An apricot-colored cat sat on top of a fence, bathing himself in the sun. A woman entered a courtyard, her face veiled behind a huge bunch of lilies and baby's breath. The sounds of Mozart drifted down from a window. It was a pleasant surprise; I hadn't known such neighborhoods existed in Montmartre.

I rang the bell. Immediately the door opened. "I was watching for you from the window," Susan said, hugging me. She led me into the large, airy room behind her. I recognized the furniture at once: the white sofas and black leather chairs, the faded Turkish rugs, the Matisse print on the wall, the old, burled-maple table Susan and I found together at a flea market. It was as though I were back in her Washington apartment. Even the placement of the windows was similar, except the view through them now was of Paris, not the Potomac.

"My God," I said, "this is like entering the Twilight Zone." We both laughed. She understood my shock at seeing the way she'd recreated her Washington home in the Paris apartment.

"I believe in change," she said, laughing again, "but only when it's for the better."

I laughed again, thinking of her chameleonlike appearance when I first met her.

She led me into her bedroom. It, too, was just as it had been in Washington. It was strange, I told her, but all the old furniture looked even better here.

"I know," she said. "It's as if all these things have finally found the place that suits them best."

I followed my friend into the small, sunny kitchen, where she set out fresh orange juice, croissants, butter, raspberry jam, cheese, and coffee. I watched her pour coffee and warm milk into large white cups. She was thinner than I remembered and her hair, dark now, was cut very short, like Audrey Hepburn's. But other than that she looked the same.

We sat at the table and talked. We talked about family and friends. About ex-husbands and the pleasures and trials of being single. About the excitement of Paris. We laughed and interrupted each other and exchanged wry congratulations on how gracefully we both were aging.

Finally I asked Susan about her decision to remain in Paris. "I don't know all the reasons why," she said. "Mostly I think I felt I'd outgrown my life in Washington. Not my friends—I still miss them. But every day I would get up and do exactly what I'd been doing for twenty years. And one day I just didn't want to do that anymore." She paused. "And then when I got to Paris, I fell in love."

So that was it, I thought: a man. *Cherchez l'homme.*

"Not with a man," Susan said, as if reading my thoughts, "but with Paris. With the life here."

I was curious about Susan's new job, which I knew, in terms of money and prestige, was several notches below her Washington one. True, she was successful in her new profession as a commercial artist but in letters to me she'd described herself as someone who still loved her work but was no longer obsessed with it. This was quite a change.

When I first met her, Susan was the most openly ambitious of all my friends; a woman who made no attempt to hide the fact that, after her daughter, work was her life. But even then I suspected that Susan, like me, occasionally found herself reversing the order, putting her work before her family obligations. At least temporarily.

Certainly it was true for me. In my most honest moments I recognized that earlier in my career, when the push to success was all uphill, my own children had sometimes taken a back seat to my work. Or, more bluntly, to my ambition.

Now, here we were, sitting in Paris, two women who had seemed to be on some kind of straight track to a planned destination but now found themselves somewhere else. "Do you remember those early days?" I asked her. "How naive we were? And how ambitious?" I laughed. "It's almost embarrassing to think about."

"Well, I'm still ambitious," Susan said. "Just in a different way. And I suspect you are, too."

She was right. I *was* still filled with ambition. More mellow, perhaps, but ambition nevertheless.

We sat talking about how your expectations change when you move into your fifties: about work, about love, and about a future that didn't seem as endless as it once did. At a certain point in one's working life, Susan and I agreed, the question becomes: what ultimately is one working toward? Personal achievement? Contentment? Wisdom? Retirement?

"For me, it's finally all about the work and nothing else," I said. "Not money or prestige." I made a face. "Although I wouldn't mind a bit more money."

Near the end of our conversation Susan asked: "What is the one emotion that you would like to feel for the rest of your life?"

I thought about it for a few minutes. "Hope," I said. "With it, I guess anything's possible. But without it . . ." My voice trailed off. I suddenly had thought of Naohiro. Hope? Or no hope? It occurred to me to tell Susan about him, but I didn't. Something inside me wanted to protect the relationship from outside opinions or advice. At least for a while.

I looked at my watch; it was almost two. I rose to go, telling Susan how much fun it was to see her again. We hugged and said good-bye, promising to get together for dinner the following week.

As I walked along the narrow lane from Susan's apartment toward the center of Montmartre, I heard my own footsteps following me like a carefree playmate on the first day of summer vacation. I listened as a small, buoyant voice said *School is out and I'm in Paris!* Halfway up the tree-lined path I stopped to watch a small gray turtle crawl beneath a bush edged with tiny yellow flowers.

It reminded me of the turtles Grandmother and I used to see at Woolworth's five-and-ten when I was little. Their shells painted in bright colors, these tiny turtles, perhaps fifty of them, crawled around in a glass tank. For about twenty-five cents you could buy one and they'd paint your name on it. I longed for a turtle named Alice, but no matter how pathetically I begged, Grandmother refused. It was cruel, she said, to paint living creatures; and, besides, the thrifty Scotswoman in her could not see spending money for something you could likely find in your own backyard.

The sun came out. It filtered down through the leaves, creating a playful pattern of light and shade that danced before my eyes. The air smelled of lilies of the valley. As I walked beneath the canopy of trees, wrapped in the delicate fragrance, caution fell away. It didn't matter that I had no idea which street led to the place du Tertre or to my Métro stop. Destination no longer ruled. My only map was that of free association: I would follow each street only as long as it interested me and then, on a whim, choose a new direction.

Such was my happiness that only my poorly accented French prevented me from saying to a formidable-looking woman sweeping down her sidewalk, *Très jolie, madame!*

A chilly morning had turned into a warm, humid afternoon and the tourists crowding Montmartre's streets looked wilted. It was time, I decided, to slip into a café for a cool drink.

From the outside, the café on rue Saint-Rustique looked quiet and slightly mysterious. When I peered through the door I could make out very little in the dark interior. Although I had seen a number of bright, lively outdoor cafés along the way, somehow the slightly dangerous look of this place attracted me.

I stepped inside and stood near the door, waiting for my eyes to adjust to the dark. It was cool, and the smell of beer hung pleasantly in the air. Squinting, I saw a long bar to my right and beyond that a large room. Music spilled out of it: the sound of an accordion and the voice of a woman singing. Probably a jukebox, I thought, heading toward the sound. But the music was not from a record.

Standing there on a tiny stage, dressed in gold lamé shorts, a top hat, and tails, was a heavily made-up woman singing in French to an inattentive group of beer-drinking German tourists. The woman in the gold lamé shorts appeared to be in her early forties. Her hair was dyed the color of a marigold, and two deep lines placed her Cupid's-bow mouth between parentheses. A small dog, almost obscured by the clouds of cigarette smoke in the café, sat near the stage, patiently watching her every move, his ears cocked to the sound of her voice.

"I love Paris in the springtime," sang the woman into a micro-phone, "I love Paris in the fall." Her voice rose and fell dramatically as she moved across the stage, a small figure caught in an unflatter-ing, blue-white spotlight. I looked at my watch. It was after three. In Baltimore, I'd be sitting in the cluttered newsroom at the paper, drinking bad coffee and writing my Thursday column. I thought of my friends back at their desks, phones ringing, rushing to meet their deadlines, agonizing over a lead for their stories. Suddenly that life seemed strange to me. Being in a café in Paris in the middle of the afternoon did not.

From the bar I spotted a woman sitting alone at a table. I pointed to the empty chair next to her and she motioned back that I could sit there. The woman, who was drinking wine and smoking a Gauloise, looked very French. Dressed in a pleated skirt and tailored white blouse, a black-and-white silk scarf artfully arranged around her neck, she epitomized the kind of simple elegance I associated with the women of Paris. I was surprised when she spoke to me in English.

"I see you're American, too," she said. I turned toward her, wondering how she had identified me as an American. She seemed to know what I was thinking, and glanced down at my feet. I fol-lowed her gaze. She was looking at my black leather Reeboks, which, we both knew, were not the sort of shoes any Frenchwoman over the age of thirty would ever wear.

"Only in America," she said, smiling.

We fell into conversation. Her name was Anne. She was a film producer from Los Angeles who, after a business trip to Cannes, had decided to spend a few days in Paris. Anne had some interest-ing observations about Frenchwomen.

"Have you noticed how affectionate they are toward one another?" she asked. In fact, I had. It was not unusual for Frenchwomen to walk along the street, arms linked, heads tilted together in close conversation. In cafés, they greeted each other with kisses and parted with embraces. I liked the way they were able to express affection without being self-conscious about it.

I told Anne about the sad-looking middle-aged woman who performed on the street across from Deux Magots, the legendary Saint-Germain-des-Prés café. Small crowds would gather around her while she danced the can-can, wearing a black-and-gold dress, short black boots, and a cheap red wig fashioned into a topknot. Stark white makeup covered her sagging face; her mouth was a slash of purple. Midway through the performance, when she stopped to change from boots to high-heeled silver sandals, you could see the bandages wrapped around her swollen feet and toes.

"It's a hard way to make a living," I said. "I found it painful to watch."

Anne nodded. "It's a bit too close to what all women fear deep down, isn't it?" she said. "Especially single women."

I knew what she meant. It was the fear that, through bad luck or illness or having no one to lean on, a woman might wind up alone and poor. I'd discussed this fear with my friends. Of course we always laughed when we talked about it. But the image of ourselves as old women living in a rundown hotel was always there, in the backs of our minds. Far off in the distance and unlikely, but there nonetheless. After such talks we always parted with the promise that, when the time came, we'd buy a large house and move in together.

It was Anne's first visit to Paris in ten years. She and her husband had celebrated her thirty-fifth birthday by staying a week at the romantic L'Hôtel on the Left Bank. They had divorced three years after the Paris trip. She had no children.

I told her that it had been almost ten years since I had visited Paris.

"It's changed a lot, don't you think?" she said. "And not for the better." Now she found Paris too crowded and the food not as good as she remembered. Even the most beautiful square in all of Paris—the place des Vosges—had diminished in her eyes.

"I wonder if it's really Paris that's changed," I said, "or if it's us."

Anne shook her head. "I don't think I've changed that much at all." Something about the way she said it suggested she considered this an accomplishment. And perhaps for her it was.

Anne told me she was anxious to get back to Los Angeles and her work. She'd been gone for almost three weeks and was beginning to feel nervous about her absence from the action. "Out of sight, out of mind," she said, explaining how competitive it was in the film industry. She asked me how long I intended to stay in Paris.

When I told her that I was on a leave of absence from my job as a newspaper reporter, she shook her head in disbelief and, I thought, disapproval. "But don't you worry about what could happen to your job while you're gone?" she asked. "If I did that I'd practically have to start all over again."

Her attitude annoyed me, although I didn't know why. Perhaps it aroused my own fears of losing my place at work.

Then, to my complete surprise, Anne said, "It's a bold thing to do. But maybe you're used to doing bold things."

I assured her I was not. But her remark secretly pleased me. It was the way I wanted to be seen, if only mistakenly so.

The thought put me in a good mood. I turned to Anne. "You know what I'd like to do? I'd like to go to the Ritz bar and have a drink."

"I'm up for that," she said. "I've always wanted to get a look at the inside of the Ritz."

As we walked out of the café, we saw the woman in the gold lamé shorts sitting at a table, surrounded by admirers. She was smoking a cigarette through a long silver holder and signing autographs for the German tourists, the dog perched on her lap. Who did she imagine herself to be? Marlene Dietrich? Edith Piaf? Was that the image that sustained her when she examined the realities of her life?

It made me wonder: who did I imagine myself to be? Since arriving in Paris, I was less sure of the answer. Yes, of course, I was still a mother and a reporter and a person who missed her friends. But from time to time I seemed to glimpse another woman trailing along behind me. I noticed this woman was quite curious about everything, and adventurous to the point of going alone to the free wine-and-cheese art gallery openings held on Thursday nights along the rue de Seine. And as if that weren't daring enough, one day she inquired at a *salon de beauté* about tinting her hair from brown to the color of a bright copper penny.

Anne was dressed for the Ritz. I was not. So we hailed a taxi and stopped off at my hotel, where I changed into a white silk blouse and navy crepe pants.

At the Ritz we ordered martinis. Anne made a toast. "To Hemingway," she said, "who opened up the Ritz Bar on the day of Paris's liberation in 1944."

I responded: "To Proust, who always wore lavender gloves when he visited the Ritz."

We went on to toast Coco Chanel, who had lived at the hotel, and were about to raise our glasses to Colette—for no reason other than being Colette—when a man approached us. An American who'd overheard our distinctly non-French accents, he invited us to join his group for a glass of champagne.

The group consisted of three married couples from California who were on their way to Egypt for two weeks of sightseeing. The women spoke of their eagerness to tour the Egyptian monuments and sail the Nile. The men, looking at their watches, spoke of calling their stockbrokers back in California. Paris was a one-day rest stop for them; they had spent most of the day shopping along the rue du Faubourg St.-Honoré.

The Californians were pleasant people who genuinely seemed to enjoy traveling as a group. That impressed me. "I guess I'm too selfish to travel well with other people," I told Anne later. "Except for my sons, I'd rather travel alone."

Somehow a journey taken alone seemed more of an adventure to me. Had I been traveling with a companion, I thought, I probably would not have met Anne or been here at the Ritz sharing a drink with the Californians.

"I envy you, your traveling alone for so long a time," said one of the women in the group, breaking into my thoughts. But she said it in a low voice, while the others were engaged in conversation, as though she didn't want them to hear.

"And I envy you," I replied, "for being able to find so much pleasure traveling in the company of others."

She seemed puzzled by this. "It's funny," she said, "but I never thought of it that way."

At about 9:00 P.M. Anne and I left the Ritz. It was a fine evening with still about an hour's light remaining. The sky over the place Vendôme was beautiful: pale blue, very high and filled with fast-moving white clouds. We said our good-byes in front of the Ritz and parted—Anne to her hotel a few streets away on the Right Bank and I to mine on the Left Bank. I decided to walk the mile or so back to my hotel, so I headed for the rue de Rivoli, about five blocks away. Halfway there I passed the Lotti, where, early in my marriage, I had stayed with my husband. On an impulse I decided to go in.

My only memory of the hotel was of the massive, antique furniture in our room, a room I had found dark and oppressive. Now, standing in the lobby, I could retrieve no other memories. It was as though I'd never been there before. I took comfort in the fact that, while the memories, along with the marriage, did not survive, the relationship did. After a few years of working out our post-divorce anger, we became loyal friends, my ex-husband and I.

From the Lotti I walked the half-block to the rue de Rivoli. The arcaded shopping street was bustling with tourists, who stopped to price the Rolex watches and fake Gucci handbags displayed in the windows. A few stopped to give money to the North African women begging under the arcade, their ashen, sad-eyed children sprawled on the ground next to them. I thought of the elegantly coiffed women I'd seen earlier emerging from Carita's, a famous hair salon a few blocks away. So glossy and perfect, they seemed to come from a species unconnected to these dirty, untended women begging along the rue de Rivoli.

Across the street in the Tuileries I could hear the wind moving through the trees; it made a rustling sound, like that of a woman waltzing in a taffeta dress.

In a few minutes I reached the turnoff to the Pont Royal, the bridge that would take me across the Seine to my hotel. I walked on. Past the Louvre and across the bridge; past the small cafés and brasseries; past the closed butchers' shops, and the patisseries still redolent with the scent of fresh-baked bread.

Near my hotel I stopped to examine a display of stylish hats in a millinery shop, some with veils as gossamer as spiderwebs. Suddenly I saw myself reflected in the window, peering out between the expressionless faces of two mannequins wearing small tilted hats with veils. Perhaps, I thought, I should buy a hat with a veil. Like Liliane's.

Just then I spotted an elderly woman walking toward me. She was carrying something. As she moved into the circle of light spilling out from the window, I saw she was cradling a small, smiling dog in her arms. Wrapped in a heavy woolen scarf, the dog looked at me quizzically. The woman, however, never lifted her eyes from the narrow sidewalk. As she passed, the air filled with the familiar scent of gardenias; it was the same cheap perfume adored by my grandmother.

I closed my eyes, breathed deeply, and pretended it *was* my grandmother passing by. Suddenly Grandmother's voice sprang out from the corners of my childhood: *Och, Alice, that canna' be you?* she asked in her achingly familiar Scottish accent.

I began to list all the women whose lives had intersected with mine that day. My friend Susan. The singer in the gold lamé shorts. Anne, the film producer. The women at the Ritz on their way to Egypt. The North African women begging on the rue de Rivoli. And now, turning the corner and passing just out of sight, the elderly woman cradling a dog.

How, I wondered, did we become the women we are? Was it just the accident of birth that ultimately placed some of us at the Ritz, drinking champagne, and others on the streets, begging? Or was it the fragility of permanence—the stunning ease with which an entire life can be broken and changed, in minutes, on an ordinary day. And why was it that I could imagine myself being any one of these women, doing whatever I had to do to make my way through the world?

Women do that, I thought. They learn to adapt. I watched my mother do it, and my grandmother too. Through marriage and divorce, through too little money or too much, too many children or too few, through sorrow and joy and all the longings that were not and never could be named, women, I learned, adapted.

At first the lives of women frightened me. They seemed so fragile, so dependent on fathers and husbands and brothers and lovers. Gradually, though, I noticed how supple their lives were beneath the surface. Then I realized it was this flexibility that enabled them to survive. I saw, too, that sooner or later, by choice or by chance, most women faced the task of adapting to a future on their own. When at my most optimistic, I thought of it as independence; in darker moods, as survival. Either way, women had to do it.

But now as I approached my hotel I left behind both past and future. I was here in Paris, alive, feeling only the simple pleasure that comes from entering the moment. The night air on my bare arms, the lamps from the nearby café punching holes of light into the darkness, the elegant, veiled hats arranged in a shop window, the skies overhead changing from pale lavender to deep violet: this was what existed for me.

In my hotel room, the bed had been prepared for sleep, its soft, cream-colored sheets neatly turned back. I opened the large French windows to let in the gentle night air and then sat down at my desk.

I began to write:

Is it possible to change your outer geography without disrupting the inner geography? The travels within yourself? Today I traveled back to my past and forward to a future shaping itself somewhere at the edge of my thoughts. But I also traveled to a place less often visited: the childlike purity of the ticking moment.

5

FIVE EXTRAORDINARY DAYS

Dear Alice,

Yesterday I had a big breakthrough, one that made me feel like a true Parisienne: I entered the Café Flore as though I belonged there. Instead of moving awkwardly, like a timid outsider, through the crowded terrace, I strode to my table with all the icy hauteur and conspicuous self-regard of Simone de Beauvoir. It seemed to work, this new attitude. Within minutes I assumed my new role as one of the café insiders, passing judgment on all who *entered. Is belonging that simple? A matter of attitude? Or is attitude just another form of self-deception?*

Love, Alice

For several days the spring rains had moved back and forth across Paris with enough force to send even those with raincoats and umbrellas scurrying for cover beneath café awnings. "So much rain means Paris will be very green this summer," said Monsieur Jacques one day while I waited out a sudden storm inside his tiny newsstand. Still, despite his prediction, I was totally unprepared when a week later on a fine, fresh morning I walked out of my hotel to find lush green grass covering all the narrow sidewalks. For a moment I thought I was hallucinating.

I looked around to see if people were walking on the grass. They were. In fact, no one was paying much attention to what seemed to me quite an extraordinary event. Gingerly, I stepped out from the hotel doorway and onto the green that carpeted the sidewalk. I bent over to examine it. Just as I was about to pluck a blade of grass, an elegantly dressed woman passing by said, "It is carpet, madame. Green carpet put down by the art and antiques galleries to celebrate *Les cinq jours de l'Objet Extraordinaire.*"

She pointed to the nearby corner, where the rue de l'Université met the rue des Saints-Pères. "See, madame, the hanging trees?" I followed her gaze upward to the overhead wires. Small, decorative trees—boxwood and holly and some flowering white plant that I couldn't identify—hung upside down from the wires. "They mark the streets of the celebration," she said. "What we call the *Carré Rive Gauche.*"

Without waiting for a reply the woman nodded and walked on, her high heels sinking ever so slightly into the green of the carpeted sidewalk.

Although I was grateful for her explanation, it raised more questions than it answered.

As I walked toward the Musée d'Orsay—navigating the green carpet with far less aplomb than my French counterpart—I struggled to translate the phrase *"Les cinq jours de l'Objet Extraordinaire."* Five days. Five days of something. Five days of the extraordinary object. That was it. But what did it mean? And who was celebrating whatever it meant? And what was the *Carré Rive Gauche?*

It was strange, the feeling that suddenly seized me: here I was, on a tiny ancient street in Paris, a grown woman embarked on a real-life adventure, yet all I could think of was Nancy Drew. As I grew up, I had helped her solve The Clue in the Crumbling Wall and The Secret of the Old Clock; now it was she who walked beside me, ready to tackle The Mystery of the Five Days of the Extraordinary Object. It was a pleasant feeling, perhaps because it connected the two parts of me: the woman and the girl I once was.

The girl gave way to the woman, however, when I turned the corner and saw Naohiro standing in front of the museum, waiting for me. He had not yet seen me. Impulsively, I stepped into the shadows of a café doorway so I could observe him without being seen. *He is waiting for me,* I thought, studying him. In his black, open-necked shirt and black pants he looked like a dancer, his body lithe but powerful, his stance gracefully relaxed. *He is waiting for me,* I thought, *and it is all I can do to keep from running across the square to his side.* But I didn't. I wanted to prolong the anticipation.

Suddenly a voice interrupted my excited daydreaming: *This is the good part,* it whispered in my ear. *Enjoy it while you can. You know it won't last.*

I knew this voice well. But I was not about to let it ruin my day. *Nothing lasts forever,* I shot back. *In fact, most things that threaten to last forever often become quite annoying.*

And with that, I hurried across the street and up the museum steps, thrusting myself into the powerful orbit of Naohiro's glance.

"Hello," he said simply, moving quickly to close the distance between us.

"Hello," I said, slightly out of breath, although perhaps not from climbing the steps.

As we walked toward the museum entrance, he took my hand. By now, being with Naohiro seemed easy and natural. Why this should be so was as puzzling to me as any mystery that Nancy Drew was ever called upon to solve. The difference was that I could live without solving this mystery. At least, I liked to think so.

Although our original plan had been to spend the afternoon in the museum, Naohiro and I agreed the day was too beautiful to waste indoors. Besides, we had picked a bad time to visit the Orsay; tourist buses were arriving and long lines had formed at the entrance. But the decision pleased me for another reason. I wanted nothing to intrude upon my time with Naohiro, not even the great paintings in the Orsay.

I suggested we have lunch on the Île Saint-Louis, a small island filled with glorious seventeenth-century architecture and quiet, narrow streets lined with tiny shops and elegant residences. He agreed, asking if I wanted to walk or take the Métro to the island.

"Let's walk," I said.

It amazed me that I, who at home traveled even short distances by car, no longer thought of a forty-five-minute walk as more than a pleasant stroll. In Paris I walked almost everywhere, as most Parisiennes do. By the end of a month I understood why so few French people are overweight. My own weight, despite a hearty appetite, was lighter by five pounds.

The fact is, I hadn't walked this much since I was a child. In those days, walking was my chief form of transportation. Mother refused to learn how to drive the family car and my frugal Scottish grandmother didn't believe in spending money on streetcars when one had "two pairfectly good feet to tread about on." Distance, it seemed, was not a factor. At least not if Grandmother was in charge. I remember she and I once walked from our house to that of her friend, a distance of about seven miles. Naturally I complained all the way, suggesting to Grandmother that it would cost a lot more to replace my worn-out shoes than to spend twenty cents for a streetcar ride.

Now, of course, I look back on those walks as a time of profound sharing. As we walked, we'd break into laughter at the posturing of some conceited neighborhood cat or another; try to spot the first snowdrops or last rose; comment, sometimes wickedly, on the outfits worn by innocent, unsuspecting pedestrians; pick out the houses we liked best and least (we favored designs, though that word was never used, incorporating large bay windows and façades of whitewashed bricks); all the while listening to the sounds of dinner plates being set on tables inside kitchens, radios tuned to afternoon soap operas, and children practicing scales or playing some easy beginner's tune like "Who-o Goes the Wind."

And so it was with Naohiro as we walked along the Seine, laughing and talking and stopping to look at the view or examine the antique postcards and used books peddled by *bouquinistes* from their zinc-topped boxes. I could feel it: the same subtle casting of lines between us, the same kind of connection I remembered from childhood.

Finally, we reached the Pont Saint-Louis, the tiny bridge just behind Nôtre-Dame cathedral that connects the Île de la Cité to the Île Saint-Louis. We walked over it behind a tall, dark-haired girl carrying a cello. As we reached the other side we passed an elderly woman accompanied by an overweight bulldog, a package wrapped in bloody butcher's paper clamped between his teeth.

Naohiro and I exchanged glances. "His dinner?" I wondered aloud.

"Or her dinner?" said Naohiro. Either way, we decided, it was a unique French twist on the concept of carry-out food.

We reached the café—Le Flore en l'Île—and took a table over-looking the Seine. It was quiet and uncrowded on the small island, one of the few areas in Paris with no Métro stop. Only six blocks long and two blocks wide, I'd always thought of Île Saint-Louis as a lovely floating village, moored to the banks of the Seine by ropes of bridges. Always in past visits to Paris—hectic visits, during which I tried to cram six centuries of culture into a week's stay—the day eventually arrived when I needed a brief vacation within a vacation. And always I'd head for an afternoon on the island.

Naohiro and I had just ordered a bottle of wine when we heard the music: the sounds of a cello, soft and pure, hanging in the air, then drifting out over the Seine toward the Left Bank. It was the young woman we'd followed across the bridge. Seated at the corner of the long, narrow street that runs through the island, she was playing, head tilted down, her black hair spilling like ink over her shoulders. Back and forth she drew the bow, releasing a sound of sweet innocence, like that of a child singing a nursery rhyme.

As she played, I suddenly heard the high, childish voices of my sons saying good night as they did so many years ago. *Good night, Mommy,* they'd sing down from their rooms. The sound echoed in my head—*Good night, Mommy, Good night, Mommy*—until I heard the last note reverberating from the cello into the air, where it echoed briefly before disappearing.

I sat silent, ambushed by love for my sons. And by regret. Regret for the past, when I didn't or couldn't give them the nurturing they needed, and regret for what they—and I—could never have back. The irony was that now, when my sons no longer needed it, my love for them was unconditional. But the past, I knew, still had the power to cast its long shadow. Sometimes, when either of my children came up against a thorny problem, I found myself worrying: did I give him what he needs to deal with this? Could I have done better? *I could do better now,* I thought. *Now that it's too late.*

"What do you think of?" Naohiro asked, moving his chair closer to mine.

"Of my sons. And of my regrets about the things I'd like to do over again as a mother."

"But when you speak of your sons it is always with admiration. Is it true you would like to return and do things that might change how they are?" Naohiro asked, smiling.

I laughed. He was right.

But so was I. There were quite a few knots I wished I could go back and untie. Still, it helped to remember how honest and funny and decent my sons were and how fortunate I was to have had them as traveling companions for so much of my life's journey.

But I also thought of the next part of my life, and wondered if I would travel it alone.

It was not a question about Naohiro, although I didn't doubt that the closeness between us had nudged it to the foreground. It was really a question about me. Sometimes I feared I'd grown too comfortable with my independence to relearn the give-and-take that intimacy demands.

I liked being in control of my life; of where I went and what I did, of going to bed late and getting up early, of eating meals that suited me when it suited me. Sometimes when I looked back at the days of being a wife and mother, one of the things that most amazed me was that every day I was the one who made the decision as to what three other people would eat. It tired me out now just to think about the effort it had taken over the years to come up with the thousands of meals that would meet the different requirements of my husband and sons. And while I knew that the care and feeding of children was behind me, my fear was I'd grown too selfish—when I was in a better mood I thought of it as having become "set in my ways"—to sustain a life with even one other adult.

But lately another thought kept presenting itself. I'd begun to wonder if my enjoyment of the independent life was more complex than just a matter of selfishness. Perhaps, this line of reasoning went, I was simply a person who, because of age and inclination, had changed her idea of what constituted a satisfying life.

Naohiro and I spent the rest of the day walking. To the busy, trendy Marais district, where the scent of baking bread and spiced meat from kosher delicatessens followed us down the street. To a unique Art Deco synagogue designed by Hector Guimard, the man responsible for the sinuous Métro entrances. To a locksmith museum that featured iron chastity belts and Roman door knockers. To a pawnshop, where we witnessed a sad auction of wedding rings and engraved silver baby bracelets and heart-shaped necklaces complete with pictures of once-loved faces. And finally to the oldest and most beautiful square in Paris: the place des Vosges.

"It is one of my favorite places," Naohiro said, as we strolled beneath the sheltering arcades that line the square's pale, salmon-colored brick mansions. "The first time I came, many years ago, as a student, I was thinking of studying architecture." He laughed. "Instead I went to business school and learned how to build corporate structures."

Beneath the laughter, however, I detected a note of regret. I asked if this was so.

"I do not believe in regret," he said, somewhat curtly. "Regret is an illusion. It depends on what might have been. And that is a waste of time."

The sharpness of his reply surprised me. It also annoyed me. Surely he must remember that earlier in the day, when I'd expressed to him some regrets about my sons, he had responded in a sympathetic way. Was his pronouncement that regret "is a waste of time" a subtle rebuke directed at me? A tiny surge of doubt crackled through my thoughts about Naohiro. Had I misread him? Or was it simply the first sign of reality intruding into our idyllic relationship?

We lingered in the place des Vosges late into the afternoon, sitting in the park, wandering in and out of its shops, stopping to peek into the inner courtyards whenever someone entered or exited through the large wooden doors hiding them from view. We spent a long time gazing in the window of a classy real estate office, studying the photographs of exquisite apartments for sale.

"Which do you like best?" Naohiro asked.

"That one," I said, pointing to the picture of a spacious, beautifully decorated living room with high ceilings, honey-colored parquet floors, and extraordinary floor-to-ceiling windows that overlooked the city of Paris. It cost in the millions of francs.

"What about you?" I asked, turning to look at him.

"It also is my favorite." He paused, then in a wry voice asked, "Shall we buy it and live happily ever after?"

"Yes, let's," I said, trying to match his wry tone. "But we'll have to get rid of all those tacky Oriental rugs. Maybe replace them with tatami mats."

He laughed. Then without warning he took my face in his hands and gently brushed back my hair. He repeated the delicate movement several times, his hands fluttering like doves about my head. Dizzy, I leaned against him; his body was surprisingly strong and muscular. He leaned back. For several minutes we stood like that, under the arcade of the place des Vosges.

For the second time that day I felt something shift between us. But whatever it was, now I liked it.

When we left the Métro at the rue du Bac, the sun was already moving west, past the Eiffel Tower. We had just passed Deyrolle—an incredible museum of a shop where earlier we'd spent a long time studying hundreds of pansylike butterflies so exquisite that even Nabokov would have been ecstatic—when Naohiro stopped. "Look at that," he said, pointing. "What is it?"

Immediately I saw what Naohiro had spotted: the green carpet lining the sidewalks at the corner where the rue du Bac and the rue de l'Université meet. I had forgotten to tell him about my discovery that morning of the mysterious *Les cinq jours de l'Objet Extraordinaire.* When I told him now what had been told me, he was as puzzled as I.

I looked at my watch; it was just 7:15, a time when most shops would have locked their doors for the day. Instead, we noticed that visitors were streaming in and out of the small galleries along the streets. The mood was festive. Outside, silk banners bearing the words CARRÉ RIVE GAUCHE fluttered in the breeze, and gardenia plants and pots of flowering jasmine scented the moist evening air. Inside the shops, people drank champagne from sparkling glass flutes, laughing and chatting, underlining their remarks with the typical Gallic hand gestures and shrugs.

We stopped on the rue des Saints-Pères, in front of a gallery that featured a huge, ancient-looking urn in its window.

"Shall we go in?" I asked. "It seems to be open to everyone."

Naohiro nodded. We walked in. Immediately someone handed each of us a glass of champagne. Naohiro turned to me and raised his glass: "To the future."

I was about to return the toast when a Japanese couple approached us. The woman was quite striking. Dressed in a tailored, ivory silk suit, her dark hair held back by two carved ivory combs, she presented an interesting combination of modern western couture and ancient eastern allure. The man, bowing slightly to both of us, turned to Naohiro and began speaking in Japanese. The two conversed for a few minutes—occasionally, the woman would join in—and as they spoke, I studied Naohiro. His presence here in the real world—as opposed to the one he and I had created for just the two of us—only confirmed my estimation of his grace and intelligence, of his desirability. He dazzled me.

Of course, I knew what lay beneath the dazzlement. Or at least the sensible, no-nonsense, feet-planted-firmly-on-the-ground part of me was wise to what was going on. *It's all romantic idealization and adolescent infatuation,* this part of me said.

Yes, yes, I know. Now go away, I replied, eager to be reunited with my dazzlement.

Naohiro turned and introduced me to the Japanese couple. They had been explaining to him, he said, the significance of *Les cinq jours de l'Objet Extraordinaire.* Every year, apparently, the art and antiques dealers of the area—known as the *Carré Rive Gauche*—hold a celebration for five days and nights, during which time they place in their windows one rare item relating to a chosen theme.

"This year, the theme is 'Extraordinary Gardens,'" said the woman. She explained that this was the third time she and her husband had been in Paris during this festive, open-house event. "It is one time when everyone feels free to walk into the galleries, even when you cannot afford to collect such beautiful pieces." Her English was close to perfect and her voice charming: soft and sibilant, it reminded me of water splashing across pebbles.

We accepted an invitation from the Japanese couple to join them in visiting other galleries along the neighboring streets that formed the *Carré Rive Gauche.* Passing La Villa, I suggested we stop in to listen to some jazz and have a drink. Immediately, everyone agreed. Later, sitting at a table, I couldn't help but think about my visit here with Liliane and Justin. Being with a man, I decided, *did* change a woman's responses to the world. Sometimes it just made life more fun.

When the four of us exchanged good-byes, it was close to midnight. I could see an indigo sky spilling down into the spaces between buildings at the end of each long narrow street. Naohiro and I walked slowly along the rue Jacob. At this time of night, men and women were returning to their apartments from an evening out, from a good day or a bad one, from whatever routine guided their daily lives. As lamps were lit, small halos of light appeared on the sidewalks, guiding us like stepping stones to some unknown destination.

As it turned out, our destination was a café on the boulevard Saint-Germain, where we sat on the terrace watching Paris go by. Happy and relaxed in a way I hadn't experienced for a long time, I thought again of how fortunate I was to have this chance to take a detour from my normal life.

I blurted out my thoughts to Naohiro. "I feel so lucky to be here. It's like a fairy tale."

His response was immediate. And once again to the point. "No," he said, "it's not a fairy tale. This is real."

In the days that followed I had a mantra: "Let tomorrow come tomorrow." It was a quote I'd come across a few years back, one I'd never been able to put into practice.

"Let tomorrow come tomorrow," I thought, waiting at the hotel for Naohiro, trying not to count the days left to us. So far I'd done a pretty good job of it, letting tomorrow come tomorrow. But it was difficult, this living in real time only, and not diluting it by looking back or skipping forward. No wonder it's never really caught on with most people, I thought. It's just too hard.

We had arranged to meet at one o'clock, after Naohiro's final meetings with a group of French businessmen. But he arrived almost an hour late, looking exhausted. He apologized, telling me the negotiations took longer than he'd anticipated. Our plans were to visit Père-Lachaise, a trip I'd looked forward to all week. But he seemed so tired I suggested we postpone our visit and instead have lunch at Madame Cedelle's *salon du thé* just a few blocks away on the rue de Beaune. It was a place we had taken a fancy to: the food was excellent and the ambience an interesting combination of coziness and elegance.

Naohiro did not resist my suggestion to abandon the visit to Père-Lachaise. I took it to be a sign of how tired he was.

Outside, a damp wind blew down the streets and fast-moving gray clouds traveled past a barely visible sun. By the time we turned the corner into the rue de Beaune, a few raindrops were hitting the green carpets on the narrow sidewalks. It was the next-to-last day of the five extraordinary days in the *Carré Rive Gauche* and, against all reason, I found myself wondering if the rain would make the carpets grow.

When we arrived at the café, Naohiro immediately ordered tea. His face, even in the flattering rosy light of the tearoom, looked pale. I wondered if he was getting sick. The tea, however, seemed to revive him, and throughout lunch he seemed his usual self. With one surprising exception: he allowed himself to be more vulnerable than he had been in our past meetings.

"You know what is hard for me to accept?" he asked halfway through the meal. We had been talking about some of the advantages of age. "That the future will come and I will not be in it to see my children and their children grow into old age."

He told me of once sharing a taxi in Tokyo with a stranger—a man in his fifties—who, for some reason, reminded Naohiro of his son, then twenty. "It is difficult to explain, but I felt myself to be in the presence of my son as he will be thirty years from now. It was a very real feeling—that I was riding in the taxi with my fifty-year-old son." Naohiro looked away for a moment. "I have never forgotten that experience. It made me both happy and sad."

I was moved by his words and the longing expressed in them. His willingness to reveal himself stirred in me a similar desire to speak openly of private thoughts.

"Has it ever occurred to you," I asked him, "that we are shaped more by our sorrows than our joys? When I look back, it's not the happy times that still have power over my life. It's the places where things went wrong."

Naohiro said nothing. But I didn't really expect a response. It was enough to express such thoughts out loud, without feeling guarded or awkward.

"Sometimes I wonder if that's all I add up to," I said. "The sum of my sorrows."

"And is that so bad? To be the person of your sorrows?" Naohiro asked. He paused for a long time, but I could see he was not finished. "I grew up near Hiroshima fifty years ago," he said finally, "and I do not forget the person of that sorrow. I bend still to him with respect."

It caught me off guard, this particular reference to his past. For some reason—perhaps because of my son's lively young friends in Japan—I tended to connect the Japanese people with the prosperous, influential Japan that now existed, not the ravaged, postwar country of fifty years ago. This glimpse into Naohiro's life moved me.

I put my hand on his arm, looking into his face to see what was there. What I saw was not what I expected; not the fatigue or illness so visible earlier in the day. What I saw was longing. I recognized it because I felt it, too.

"Let's go home," I said. "Let's go back to the hotel."

Late in the afternoon, after Naohiro had fallen into a restless sleep, I sat in a chair at the window and watched him. *Now what?* I thought. Tomorrow had become the next day and then the day after that and the day after that. Soon—tomorrow in fact—we would be down to our final day together.

I needed a way to think about this, about Naohiro. Just a small adventure, perhaps? I was well aware that traveling alone was the perfect setup for brief, intense encounters of both the romantic and platonic kind.

But even as I tried to dismiss, or at least downgrade, what I felt for Naohiro, another voice from some place deeper down said, *Face it. This man awakened in you a feeling you've been denying. A longing for closeness, the wish to be known and loved.* But had I really seen that in Naohiro? Or just imagined it?

I sat down on the bed next to Naohiro. Instantly he awoke.

"Hello," I said. "How do you feel?"

"Happy," he replied. "How do you feel?"

"Ready to buy that apartment on the place des Vosges."

"Even with the tatami mats?"

"Especially with the tatami mats."

I dreamed that night of the birth of my older son; of the intense bond I felt when he was put into my arms for the first time. Looking down at his face in the dream, I said, *Hello. I was wondering when we would meet.*

The next morning I awoke feeling that someone was in the room with me. I sat up in bed and looked around. No one was there. Still, the feeling of someone standing close by me was so real that it took several minutes to convince myself I was, in fact, quite alone.

London

6

THE SLOANE STREET CLUB

Dear Alice,

    I came across this postcard of the three Brontë sisters at the National Portrait Gallery. Immediately I thought of three new friends I've acquired in London. They love the Brontës' writing, and Jane Austen's, as much as I do. It is one of the strongest

bonds, I think, that can spring up between people: sharing a pas-
sion for certain books and their authors. Alas, my friends are not
Nabokov-lovers. Ah, well, you can't have everything.

Love, Alice

I arrived in London in early July, just after the hot dry weeks of Wimbledon, when the summer had turned rainy and cool. Cold, actually. The shops up and down Sloane Street were filled with tourists buying sweaters and wool blazers. "First the heat and now the cold," said an American woman trying on jackets in Harvey Nichols, the fashionable department store. Everyone, including me, had been hoping to put off purchasing anything until the mid-July sales, but it was just too cold.

Why was it, I wondered, searching through racks of coats, that no matter how carefully I packed for a trip, I never had the right thing? It was only my second day in London, but already I knew my unlined raincoat wasn't going to work, no matter how many layers I wore beneath it. What I needed was a heavier coat. But a quick look at the price tags stopped me in my tracks; clearly this was not the store for bargains.

Actually, most of the shops along Sloane Street were out of my price range. Chanel, Gucci, Armani, Valentino, Hermès—many of the pricey one-name designer shops were located here, just south of Knightsbridge. Still, it was fun to window-shop.

As I neared the Hermès boutique I passed a young Japanese couple. Immediately my thoughts went to Naohiro. He was in Tokyo now, probably going to bed or waking up; I wasn't sure which. In Baltimore I knew how to calculate the time difference so that I avoided waking my son with a phone call in the middle of the night, but here in London I was slightly confused about the arithmetic involved. I decided to picture Naohiro the way I had last seen him: waking up to the Parisian morning sun.

When I reached Hermès, I decided to go in on the pretense of actually intending to buy something. It was a device I used occasionally to check out shops that were way beyond my price range. I considered it my duty as a reporter to observe how the Other Half lives so that, when the occasion arose, I could report on their lives with accuracy.

"I'd like to know the price of the gray snakeskin bag in the window," I said to the formidable-looking saleswoman standing guard over the locked-up Hermès handbags. She looked me over, always a decisive moment between clerk and client in shops such as this. But I had taken care to dress for just such a situation, in what I liked to think of as my "I'm so wealthy I don't have to wear clothes that scream MONEY" outfit: a ten-year-old pale gray silk suit, pearls, and a soft, pleated-leather Fendi handbag I'd bought secondhand at a Paris thrift shop.

I stood my ground. The moment passed. Or more precisely, *I* passed the moment.

"Ah, yes, one of our most popular items," she said, unlocking the case to remove a bag similar to the one in the window. "It comes in a variety of leathers and colors. But I must warn you, there is a waiting list for some of the bags."

I asked the price. She told me they ranged anywhere from £1,200 pounds to £5,000. I made a mental effort to convert £1,200 pounds into dollars. Eight hundred dollars? Eighteen hundred dollars? Either way, I wasn't walking out of the shop with any bag other than the one I came in with. After telling the saleswoman I needed the bag immediately so a waiting list would not suit, I

thanked her and left. Outside I headed for a store where I planned
to do some real shopping: the Safeway supermarket on the King's
Road.

I had taken a flat in nearby Chelsea, a few blocks from the
King's Road and Sloane Square. Although I'd been told of a charming "villagelike" shopping area just minutes from the flat, I knew
there were cheaper supermarkets dotting the King's Road. I even
had a specific market in mind.

Actually, I knew the neighborhood around my flat quite well.
Twenty-five years earlier, along with my husband and our two-year-
old son, I had lived in an apartment on the other side of Sloane
Square. My mother had joined us for a time, renting a separate
apartment in the same house, making it very much a family affair.

By the time I neared the square at the bottom of Sloane Street,
a light rain was falling. All along the street umbrellas began unfurl-
ing, their bright colors dotting the gray day like flowers in an urban
meadow. At the corner I spotted a familiar sign: THE GENERAL TRAD-
ING COMPANY, EST. 1920. I remembered this shop well. It was filled
with sumptuous English-country-house furniture and floors brim-
ming with fancy culinary equipment and antique silver. When we
lived nearby I had spent many rainy afternoons there poking
through rooms of antique tables and expensive bed linens. I also remembered it had a delightful café. On a whim I decided to go in,
look around, and have lunch.

After a quick tour through the gift department, I headed downstairs
to the small café on the ground floor. At the café entrance a line had
formed; about a dozen women stood waiting to be seated by the

hostess. This could take a long time, I thought, trying to decide whether or not to wait.

Suddenly the hostess's voice called out: "Anyone single?"

Caught off guard, the question puzzled me: I was uncertain whether this meant single as in not being married, or single as in dining alone. However, since I fit into both categories, I raised my hand with confidence. "Would you mind sharing a table?" the hostess asked. "Not at all," I said, following her into the café.

She led me to a table where three women were seated. Two of them seemed to be together; they were engrossed in conversation and barely looked up. The third woman, seemingly a "single" like me, was sitting with a book, waiting to be served her lunch. I looked at the menu, ordered lasagna and salad, and, feeling uncertain about the proper etiquette in such a setting, turned my attention to a map of London.

Within minutes the waitress reappeared to ask if I'd ordered hot tea or iced tea. "Iced, please," I said, looking up from my map and, in the process, locking eyes with my "single" lunch-mate.

She smiled. "You're on holiday?" she asked, nodding in the direction of my map. Her voice, in just three words, conveyed a confident, lively attitude. Her accent was resonant with British history.

"Yes, I am."

"So am I." She hesitated. "In a manner of speaking." She told me she had come down from Scotland, her home for the last twenty years, to visit her daughter. "She's thirty. Just received her degree in economics. But now she's decided to go into publishing." She laughed. "But then that's the way nowadays, isn't it? Young people spend most of their lives gathering up degrees in one field only to end up doing something entirely different." Her son had done the same thing, she said: "Started mathematics, then went into veterinary medicine." He was twenty-eight and now lived in Australia.

I told her about my sons, adding that the one in Japan, who was now a translator, had just decided to go to law school. "It seems to me we didn't have so many choices at that age, especially as women," I said, launching into a bit of a lecture about women and choices and the kind of work that was hospitable to us then.

She nodded, seeming to agree. "It's the same with marriage and motherhood. It was simply what was supposed to happen in a woman's life. Quite likely though, it was that way for men, too. Something expected of them."

"Do you think you'd make a different choice today?"

The woman smiled. "No. But that's beside the point, isn't it?"

I laughed. I liked her directness, the way she said what she meant. I also liked the look of her, her expressive face and mischievous eyes.

Her name was Victoria and she was in town alone, staying for the month at a nearby residential hotel. She explained that her husband was away on business and she preferred a hotel to staying in her daughter's small apartment. "We like each other better with some distance between us," she said, smiling.

Victoria was an interesting woman with interesting opinions and we stayed, talking about our lives and politics and the differences between British and American newspapers, until the café was almost empty. After paying the bill we walked outside together, where we stood talking about what was going on in the London theater. Finally, we said our good-byes. Then, just before she turned to leave, Victoria asked if I'd like to join her for lunch later that week. "I'm meeting an old friend. I think you'd like her. She's a writer, too. Does pieces on gardening for magazines, mostly."

"That sounds like fun," I said. We agreed to meet back at the café on Friday, and, finally, I headed for the supermarket.

It was a short walk from the supermarket back to my flat. Still, the two bags filled with bottled water, All-Bran cereal, skim milk, tea bags, coffee, yogurt, packaged biscuits, and paper goods seemed quite heavy. It had been a long time since I'd walked home from a supermarket carrying all my groceries. It reminded me of the daily treks I made as a child to the neighborhood store, Mother's hand-written list tucked away in a purse along with a two-dollar bill.

I was eager to settle into my flat. Although I'd spent only one night there, I liked everything about it—the tree-lined neighborhood, the gracefully proportioned white limestone building, the pleasantly decorated living room and bedroom, and, most of all, the tiny balcony overlooking Cadogan Street and Sloane Avenue.

I'd found this gem of a place quite by chance, while reading the classified ads in *The New York Review of Books*. A call was put in to the telephone number listed, a quite reasonable rent was quoted, photos were sent. And although I'd learned the hard way that photos of real estate often bear little resemblance to the actual property—I'd once taken an apartment in Paris owned by a Harvard professor who sent me glorious pictures and glowing descriptions of what turned out to be two tiny rooms in an attic overlooking a hotel service area—I immediately engaged the London flat.

Finally, I thought as I approached my new digs, *all those years of reading* The New York Review of Books *has paid off.*

When I entered my building a porter inside greeted me, then took my shopping bags and placed them in the elevator. "Seventh floor, is it?" he said, pushing the button before I could answer. The elevator was one of those old, slow numbers that took forever to get from one floor to the next. But who cared? I had nothing but time. When it finally lurched to a stop, I stepped off, turned the corner, and unlocked the door to my flat.

The late afternoon light was coming in through the kitchen- and living-room windows. Instantly I put down the groceries, walked to the balcony, opened the door, and stepped outside. Below me was Cadogan Street and to my left, tree-lined Sloane Av- enue. I hung out as far as I could over the railing, looking first in one direction, then the other. After a few minutes of this I returned to the living room and turned on the lamps. The room was as pleasant as I remembered: the furniture stylish and comfortable, the white walls softened with framed prints and drawings.

I put away the groceries and fixed myself a drink. A special- occasion drink: Cutty Sark, with ice. I carried the glass with me into the bedroom, where I set out the family photographs I'd brought along on the trip. Then back to the living room, where I kicked off my shoes and sat down to watch the evening news.

How nice, I thought, sipping my drink, to hear the news in a language I fully understood.

When I arrived at the café on Friday, Victoria was already there, queued up. With her was a tall, attractive woman whose face, tanned and mapped with fine wrinkles, suggested a life spent out- doors. Victoria spotted me and waved me into the line next to her.

"So nice to see you again," she said, holding out her hand. She then introduced me to the woman next to her. "I'd like you to meet Sarah Davies. Sarah and I went to boarding school together. Met there when we were eleven and have been friends ever since. Which means we've been friends for about a hundred years."

Sarah and I laughed as we shook hands.

"Sarah's in town for a few months doing a piece on Mrs. Some-body-or-other's gardens," Victoria continued. "She's left her hus-band behind in Kent. Where, I suspect, he is busy with his roses and his dogs."

Sarah laughed again. She didn't seem to mind at all Victoria's running commentary on her life. "But, Victoria," she said, "the two of us being here without our husbands will make it just like the old days."

Victoria was about to answer when the hostess beckoned us to a table. We sat down and after ordering salad and iced tea, Sarah asked about my stay in London. "Victoria said you wrote for a newspaper but were taking several months off. It sounds quite ex-citing." She turned to Victoria. "Do you remember our plans to travel around the world when we turned eighteen?"

Victoria nodded. "Yes. But it never happened, did it? As I re-call, you fell quite madly in love with Stephen and had to have him. And that was the end of it."

A skeptical look crossed Sarah's face. "Funny that, because I remember it the other way round. *You* fell in love with a stuffy old professor and had to have him. And *that* was the end of it."

The two women exchanged private glances, then burst out laughing.

I liked the easy rapport between Victoria and Sarah. At home I had friends like this, women with whom I could exchange in bold shorthand strokes whole parts of our shared history. It was what I missed most on this trip: my women friends. I could always count on them to boost me up or take me down a peg when I needed it.

Sarah began asking questions about my trip. Where I was going. Where I had been. How I chose my flat in London. She seemed genuinely interested. Then Victoria joined in, asking me what had prompted me to do what I was doing.

"I needed an adventure while I still had the legs for it," I said, only half-joking.

"Yes, well, they say the legs go last," Victoria replied.

"And what do your children think about all this?" Sarah asked.

"They're all for it." I laughed. "Actually, I think they were pretty impressed that I, their *mother,* would do such a risky, spontaneous thing."

"Quite the thrill, isn't it, having your children give *you* a pat on the back instead of the other way round?" Sarah said, lifting her iced tea in a small salute.

I asked Sarah how she came to write about gardening.

"My family was quite keen on gardening. And from very early on I had my own corner to plant. It grew into a passion." She said she'd kept a gardening diary since she was eight or nine and, after marrying, began sending in columns to various garden publications. "I do quite a bit of freelance now. It's a wonderful way to snoop around strangers' houses."

"Yes, but it has its dangers," Victoria said. "Remember, Sarah, how we got locked in that potting shed down in Sussex?" She turned to me. "Alas, we had to break a window to get out."

In my mind I suddenly saw the two of them as Nancy Drew characters: smart, fearless young women, traveling about England in a snappy blue roadster, trying to solve The Secret at Larkspur Lane. Naturally I said nothing of this, saying instead, "It must be exciting to explore such wonderful gardens." I mentioned that every time I visited England I promised myself a trip to the famous gardens created by Vita Sackville-West and Harold Nicolson at

Sissinghurst Castle in Kent. "I've never managed to get there. But I'm determined to do it on this trip."

"Oh, you absolutely must," Sarah said. "The White Garden alone is worth the trip. Although the whole place is pretty much a paradise as far as I'm concerned. How do you plan on getting there?"

"Well, I don't . . ."

Before I could finish, Victoria interrupted. "I've a lovely idea. Why don't we arrange an outing? Sarah here can beguile us with her arcane knowledge of plants, and I'll bore you with all the gossip about Vita and Harold." She turned to her friend. "What do you say we ring up Angela? She's a great one for impromptu affairs. And besides, she's got that big old car. The one that looks like a cab."

"A Bentley, I think," Sarah said.

Victoria explained that Angela was also an old friend, although not from boarding-school days. "We met her when we were all young marrieds, before Sarah and I moved away from the city," Victoria said, launching into a chronology of their friendship that I couldn't quite follow. But I gathered that Angela was considered the "sophisticate" of the group. Widowed twice—the second time after only two years of marriage to an Italian actor—her only son married and living in Wales, Angela remained single, devoting much of her time to fund-raising for the arts, particularly theater and dance. When not doing this, they said, she traveled.

"Particularly to Scotland to fish salmon," Victoria said. "Although I can't think why anybody would want to do that, can you?"

Angela sounded quite fascinating and, frankly, I was dying to meet her. However, throughout Victoria's soliloquy, Sarah remained noticeably silent. Was this a polite way of indicating she had no interest in the Sissinghurst trip? Clearly Victoria was a person who liked to bring people together, to mix and match them. But

Sarah, perhaps, had not counted on a lunch date with a stranger turning into a moveable feast. I noticed Sarah looking at her watch. Not a good sign, I thought; she's figuring out how to leave gracefully, without having to turn down Victoria's plan.

Then Sarah looked up and said, "I don't think Angela would be home right now. But I could ring her tonight. It sounds like something she might fancy doing."

When we parted outside the café an hour or so later, Sarah and Victoria took my phone number with the understanding that one of them would call me about the trip.

I decided to walk over to Chelsea Green, the "village square" that had been recommended to me as a great place to market. Only two blocks from my flat, Chelsea Green did indeed prove to be both charming and useful.

There, clustered together around a small square, were vegetable markets, delicatessens, gourmet food and wine shops, florists and dressmakers, restaurants and carry-out shops. At The Pie Man, which offered everything from homemade carrot-and-orange soup to Thai beef salad, I selected my dinner: roasted red-leaf salad with pancetta and tarragon, and a chicken breast cooked in lemon and ginger sauce with broccoli florets. A few doors down I stopped at the greengrocer and bought fresh fruit and a bunch of flowers—clear yellow irises mixed with spikes of pale green foliage.

I didn't mind eating alone in London, whether in a restaurant or in my cozy flat. In Paris it had bothered me, but by now I'd grown less sensitive to dining solo. In fact, I rather liked it. If I ate out, it gave me a chance to observe the scene around me; if I ate in, it gave me a chance to brush up on my cooking skills. Once I'd been an accomplished cook, but long working hours and living alone had eroded both the desire and the ability to turn out a proper meal.

Lately, though, I'd seen flashes in my small London kitchen of the woman who used to enjoy cooking so much that she'd taken classes in everything from bread-making to classic French cuisine. I remembered how much this woman had liked *suprême de volaille farcies, duxelles*—or, in plain English, chicken breasts stuffed with mushrooms minced and sautéed in butter. I recalled liking it, too. To my surprise, I knew the recipe by heart and one night decided to give it a try. After serving myself dinner on the balcony of my flat, I decided the chicken was even better than I remembered.

As I walked back from Chelsea Green with my groceries, I noticed a little girl wearing a flower-sprigged blue-and-white dress furiously pedaling her three-wheel bike along the sidewalk of a quiet neighborhood street. Pausing to watch her, I saw a pattern emerge: every few minutes, after a burst of high-energy pedaling, the girl would lift both hands from the handlebars, put her arms out to either side, and allow the bike to steer itself. As she did this, she made whooping noises of unleashed exhilaration.

Aha! I thought, a fearless woman in the making. But then the bike suddenly swerved into a large pot of red geraniums and the girl tumbled off. Immediately, however, she picked herself up, righted the bike, and somewhat more cautiously pedaled on.

Life's like that, I thought, as I turned the corner to my building. Freedom has its dangers as well as its joys. And the sooner we learn to get up after a fall, the better off we'll be.

That night I went to a play at the nearby Royal Court Theatre on Sloane Square. It was a long-winded, lecturing piece written by an American. I left at the intermission, a luxury I would never allow myself if I weren't alone. On the way home I celebrated my new-found independence, theatrically speaking, by having a beer in a nearby pub. *Here's to you, old girl*, I toasted myself, lifting the heavy glass to my lips, *and to the Queen Mum.* I wasn't sure why I threw in that last bit until, on the walk home, I remembered how much my grandmother had adored her.

I had barely closed the door to my flat when the phone rang. It was Victoria, calling about our trip to Sissinghurst. We were on for the following Wednesday, she said. And Angela was joining us. They would pick me up at ten, in front of my building.

At precisely ten o'clock on the following Wednesday I spotted a large maroon sedan making its way through the Sloane Avenue traffic. Where Sloane and Cadogan intersected a waving arm appeared through the car's back window. It was followed by Victoria's face. The car pulled up in front of me; a door opened and Victoria said, "Been waiting long?" She laughed and moved over, making room for me in the back seat.

"Good morning," Sarah said, turning around. "Quite the fresh day, isn't it?" I noticed she and Victoria wore almost identical outfits: dark tailored slacks and sweater sets, one yellow, the other pink. "This is Angela Martinelli," she said, introducing me to the woman at the wheel of the car.

Angela turned and held out her hand. "So you're the American I've been hearing about. How nice to meet you." Something about the way she said this, the warmth and wry tone of her voice, made me like Angela. Angela was not wearing slacks and a sweater set. Angela, looking as sleek as a greyhound with her white hair pulled back and tied with a black ribbon, wore what looked like khaki jodhpurs and a crisp white cotton shirt.

"Well then, ladies, we're off," she said. Then, affecting a Bette Davis voice, she added, "Fasten your seatbelts, it's going to be a bumpy night."

Bette Davis! From *All About Eve*, one of my favorite movies! Now this is a woman after my own heart, I thought, as the big boxy car moved soundlessly out from the curb and into the stream of traffic.

Although the drive to Sissinghurst took about two hours, it seemed much shorter. But then time always telescopes when you put four women together who are eager to share what's on their minds.

On the way Sarah talked about the creation of the Sissinghurst gardens. "They were really designed to function as outdoor rooms, walled in by hedges and enclosures. And the White Garden was where the family dined." But it was the garden's creators—Sir Harold Nicolson, a diplomat, and his wife, writer Vita Sackville-West—that interested me most.

"It was a most unconventional but remarkable marriage," Sarah continued, explaining that Vita had engaged in passionate affairs with a number of women. But despite this, the marriage held. "Restoring Sissinghurst, I think, played a large role in keeping Vita and Nicolson together. You might say the gardens became the object of Vita's passion."

"Well, not *completely*," Victoria broke in. "Wasn't there something in that biography of Virginia Woolf about an affair with Vita before the war? One that ended when Vita grew tired of Virginia?"

"Well, I guess gardens can only go so far in the passion department," Angela said.

"And how would you know?" Sarah asked wryly. "It's not as though you've ever gardened."

"No. But we've all got our Sissinghursts, haven't we? Our secret gardens that replace some lost passion in our lives. My Sissinghurst, I suspect, is salmon fishing."

I was struck by Angela's honesty. And by her willingness to share such an intimate observation. It seemed very brave. What was my Sissinghurst? I wondered. The answer was not difficult: my writing. The search for an elegant way to explain something in words—what I thought of as the physics of writing—still thrilled me.

At the gardens Sarah acted as our guide, leading us through the breathtaking estate that had been nothing more than a series of deteriorating sixteenth-century buildings when Vita and Harold purchased it in 1930. Now there were lawns, orchards, and a lake. And, of course, the famous gardens. The Rose Garden. The Sunken Garden. The Cottage Garden. And the one everyone came to see: the White Garden, known for its flowers and fragrances.

"Quite likely it's the most copied garden in the world," Sarah said, leading us through a landscape of drifting, fragrant whiteness. White snapdragons. White roses. White peonies. White irises. White geraniums. White lilies. White poppies. It was like walking through a field of snow flurries.

We strolled through the garden more or less in silence, four women, each with her own thoughts. But later, as Angela and I followed the other two women back to the car, she asked me what I thought of Sissinghurst.

"I was trying to imagine what it would be like to live here and walk through the White Garden in moonlight."

"Quite lovely, I suppose, in a ghostly sort of way," Angela replied. "I know you'll think me mad, but standing in the garden I was thinking about my last fishing trip."

"And what did you think?" I asked.

"Oh, that standing in a stream always gives me a feeling of connection."

"Connection to what?"

"To myself, I suppose. To the person inside who's been there for as long as I can remember."

I was intrigued and wanted to know more about the person inside Angela. But by this time we had reached the car, where Victoria and Sarah stood waiting.

It was about seven o'clock when the maroon Bentley glided to a stop in front of my apartment building. "It was a marvelous day, wasn't it?" Victoria said. "But I'm dead tired."

We were all dead tired. And comfortable enough with each other to admit it, thereby eliminating any halfhearted suggestion about going on to dinner. But tomorrow was another day, and Victoria, the Scarlett O'Hara of the group, always planning something, came up with an idea.

"I've heard of an absolutely fantastic production of *Pride and Prej-*

udice going on in London this month." A theater company in town, she told us, was presenting an adaptation of Jane Austen's book in various historic houses around London. "It will be like watching the Bennets in their own drawing room," Victoria said.

The idea appealed to all of us immediately. It was just a matter of finding out when and where the performances were scheduled, a task Victoria eagerly accepted.

Two days later, she called to ask if the following Thursday suited me. It did. "We're going to have a light supper over on Walton Street before the play," Victoria said, referring to a charming street tucked away behind the Brompton Road just near my flat.

"That sounds lovely," I told her, parroting the phrase that by now was etched into my brain.

The performance of *Pride and Prejudice* took place at an historic house near Greenwich Park in the southeast section of London. Victoria had been right; listening to the drawing-room conversations between Elizabeth Bennet and Mr. Darcy in such a setting engaged the imagination in ways not possible in a regular theater. The production was delightful and I was thoroughly enjoying myself when, near the end of the play, a sharp, throbbing headache appeared. Ten minutes later, a queasy feeling began to come and go.

The cause of my distress puzzled me. I'd felt fine at dinner and had not eaten or drunk anything likely to account for my symptoms. I tried to concentrate on the play, telling myself the feelings would pass. But they didn't. Later, when it was suggested we have a drink, I said nothing to the others about feeling ill, saying instead I was way behind in my letter-writing and would pass on the drink.

It was a wise decision. By the time I unlocked the door to my flat, the headache was so bad I could barely see. I turned on one small light in the foyer—any light brighter than that made me feel dizzy—and managed, just, to undress myself, take some aspirin, and crawl into bed. Automatically, I turned on the radio on the nightstand. It had become a habit to fall asleep listening to the "chat" shows that ran throughout the night on London radio. And, I figured, if ever I needed someone to help get me through the night, this was it.

I slept fitfully, waking every hour or so to the sound of disconnected bits of conversation coming from the radio. *Pruning of flowering shrubs is best done after the blooming season. . . . Your puppy should be spayed at eight months. . . . Having sexual relations twice a week is not unusual for couples in their seventies. . . .* In between, I dreamed. Jumbled-up, nonsense dreams that patched together bits and pieces of my life, past and present, into surreal vignettes.

When I heard a phone ringing I wasn't sure if I was dreaming or if I was awake. Slowly, though, I realized it wasn't part of a dream; someone really was on the other end of the line, trying to reach me. But did I have the strength to answer it? With great effort I rolled over in the direction of the night table and picked up the receiver.

It was Angela. She was calling to say, in a voice shot through with wry amusement, that I should be on my guard, that Sarah and Victoria had discussed dueling schemes after dropping me off the night before. "Sarah wants to go to Hidcote Gardens and Victoria's keen for Bath. What do you think?"

I tried to sound as normal as possible, telling Angela I was a little under the weather and would have to take a rain check. But my voice, so weak that it was almost unintelligible, did not fool Angela.

"You sound awful. I'm coming over," she said, brushing aside my halfhearted protests.

The truth is, I was relieved to know she was on her way. And very glad that it was Angela who was coming.

"You look ghastly," Angela said when she arrived, skipping any polite pretense about my appearance. Ordinarily, I considered such things important—keeping up appearances, no matter how difficult, affecting an attitude of self-sufficiency, not letting on when I was feeling ill, etc., etc., etc. But when the body fails as mine had, regression seizes the opportunity it's been waiting for: to push aside the adult and let the child—in my case the sick child—take over. I yielded to Angela's ministrations.

To my surprise, she knew her way around a sickroom. She took my temperature—"Up, but not too bad," she said, dispensing a dose of aspirin—then moved me to the other twin bed while she changed the sheets. Then she handed me fresh night clothes and a cool washcloth, crushed some ice, pouring it over the Coke syrup she'd brought with her, darkened the room and, finally, checked the medicine cabinet and pantry to see what was there.

"I'm calling Victoria to bring over some things from the chemist and the grocer. You should try to get some sleep," Angela said. She left the bedroom, leaving the door behind her slightly ajar. Exhausted by the morning's activities I quickly dozed off.

I awoke to the low, musical sound of women's voices in the living room. As I listened through the half-open door to the soft, blurred conversation, its slow cadences as reassuring to me as a cool hand on my brow, I thought of Mother and Grandmother, talking at night on the porch just beneath my window. I looked at the clock; a little after one in the afternoon. I checked myself out by trying to sit up in bed. But even raising my head required more energy than I had. It also produced a wave of dizziness that sent me scurrying back to my pillow.

"Ah, I see you're awake," a cheery voice said from the door. It was Victoria. Angela stood behind her. "How do you feel?"

"Like a cat on a hot tin roof," I said, without the slightest clue as to what in the world prompted such a totally inept description of my physical state.

"Can you drink some tea?" Angela asked. "Maybe eat a dry biscuit or two?" I said I'd try.

A tea tray was brought in and the two women sat on the bed opposite mine, pouring tea and offering sympathy.

They stayed most of the afternoon, seeing to it that I drank fluids, took aspirin, and rested.

"Sarah will pop in tonight with some soup," Victoria said as they were leaving. "And we'll see you tomorrow."

Over the next few days, a three-shift schedule went into action. Someone on duty in the morning, usually Victoria; then Sarah in the afternoon; and in the evening, Angela. Each woman stayed for an hour or two, and each had her own approach to the task at hand.

Victoria arrived bearing two or three newspapers, from which she would read aloud after fixing me tea and toast. Sarah brought flowers and wholesome things to eat such as chicken-and-rice soup and delicate puddings. She also brought flowers and watched television with me. We particularly enjoyed a show called *The House of Eliott*, a story of two sisters who become fashionable London dressmakers in the 1920s.

But it was Angela's evening visits that I looked forward to most. What Angela brought was: herself.

Like Scheherazade, she told me stories; tales about her life as an only child and as a slightly reckless young woman who longed to be an actress. She told me of her first marriage to a barrister, a happy union that produced a son; and of her second one to an aging actor she'd met while living for a year in Italy. She talked of her son, of their closeness, even though he lived in an isolated part of Wales. And she talked of what she wanted in the years ahead: "The life I have now, plus my health," she said. "And maybe one grand surprise every year or so."

On one such evening Angela brought me a book titled *The Journey's Echo.* "It's a selection of travel writings by Freya Stark," Angela said, explaining that Stark, who'd died just three months earlier at the age of 100, had spent most of her life exploring Arabia and the Middle East. "She was an extraordinary woman who traveled alone at a time when women simply didn't do such things. I thought you might enjoy it."

I was touched by Angela's thoughtfulness. And flattered, too. I had come to admire her very much.

Later that evening, while thinking about how I had let myself depend on the kindness of these three women, I suddenly bumped into a new thought: the realization that something in me had loosened, the way a knot loosens, and I had allowed myself to lean on someone else. Over the years, without noticing it, I'd subscribed to the notion of independence as a condition that dictated complete self-sufficiency. That I should let go—even temporarily—of such a ridiculous idea came as something of a surprise.

That night I had a dream: *Mother and I are sitting on the back porch in the sun. I am a little girl and she is washing my hair in a white enamel basin. Later she dries it with a towel and begins to braid it. I love the feel of her hands in my hair and I lean back against her body, overcome with happiness and contentment.*

Three days after the onset of my illness I awoke at five in the morning. Immediately, I knew something was different. For the first time in several days, I felt hungry. *I'm well*, I thought. *Whatever I had is gone and I'm well.* I sat up and looked through the window. Outside, the stars were growing pale. I pulled on a robe and stepped onto the balcony.

Daylight was just starting to color the sky. London was not yet awake. But the birds were. From somewhere above me a dozen speckled birds appeared, flying through the sleeping sky in tight formation, passing near enough that I could hear the *flap, flap, flap* of their wings rowing the cool morning air. As they moved away, they called to one another, their shrieking cries trailing behind them. Seagulls? I wondered, remembering I'd read somewhere that on windy days, the gulls can be blown inland to London. Were they heading for the ocean?

Wide awake now and caught up in the euphoria of feeling well again, I imagined myself an adventurer, flying solo like Amelia Earhart through the night skies, through the stars, into daylight. I thought suddenly of the book Angela gave me. It seemed the perfect time to start it.

I carried a cup of tea and a scone with me out onto the balcony and settled into a chair. Opening the book, I turned to the first page and read a passage written from Baghdad by Freya Stark in 1929, when she was thirty-six years old. It began:

To awaken quite alone in a strange town is one of the pleasant sensations in the world. You are surrounded by adventure. You have no idea of what is in store for you, but you will, if you are wise and know the art of travel, let yourself go on the stream of the unknown and accept whatever comes in the spirit in which the gods may offer it.

Immediately I felt the little thrill I always get upon opening a book and finding inside the voice of a kindred spirit. It happens some-times in life, too, that immediate sense of kinship. I felt it when I met Victoria. And Sarah. And Angela. Particularly Angela.

Of course, I knew that the kinship of strangers, particularly those met while traveling, is often a temporary kinship. But who's to say length is the yardstick by which to measure such encoun-ters?

I decided I would take Freya and my three new friends with me when I moved on. I could see it now, Freya leading the four of us through the gardens of Baghdad. Or Freya crossing the desert on camelback, followed by four women, in matching sweater sets, rid-ing behind in a boxy maroon car. But she wouldn't be scornful of us, not if she's the Freya I think she is. She would understand some of us are more comfortable walking in the foothills of adventure than climbing to the summit.

And Freya would understand that even though I wasn't scaling mountains or crossing deserts in this, my Year of Living Danger-ously, I was in my own way wading into the stream of the unknown, accepting whatever the gods had to offer.

7

LOVE LETTERS

Dear Alice,

 I wonder if there will ever be another event that brings people together as the Second World War did. Not in my lifetime, I suspect. The truth is, the world has changed so much I'm not sure any event could produce the "home front" mentality that existed then. We Americans had it and so did other Allied countries. But none so much, I suspect, as Great Britain. You still *cannot walk here in London without sensing the presence of Britain's "finest hour."*

Love, Alice

One morning while having breakfast on the King's Road I suddenly realized how foreign my life as a reporter now seemed. When I thought of it now—the deadlines, the constant search to find material for a story or column, the compulsive need to read three newspapers daily, the fear of getting something wrong or not getting the whole story—it was like imagining a country I hadn't visited in some time.

Just how far I'd strayed from the newspaper mentality, however, was driven home that morning when my café au lait arrived and I settled in to read the papers. As usual I was armed with the *International Herald Tribune*, which I bought every day but didn't always read, and the *Kensington & Chelsea Post*, a neighborhood newspaper that I always read. Instead of focusing on world news or politics or what might loosely be described as important-issue reporting, I found myself avidly reading a front-page story in the Kensington-Chelsea paper about a cat.

Under the headline, HUNT CONTINUES FOR MISS ARIELLE, the article began:

A Kensington woman has been overwhelmed by the response to appeals to find her missing cat.

The white pedigree chinchilla silver-tipped cat Miss Arielle disappeared two weeks ago, leaving three tiny kittens.

After printing 1,000 leaflets asking for help, she has been inundated
with callers thinking they have seen the cuddly creature. Some have even
called at the house with cats which look like Miss Arielle but so far no-one
has found the real thing.

Next to the story was a photo, larger than the entire article, of a
man holding a rather plain-looking white cat. "Pictured with the cat
is the owner's husband, John," read the caption beneath.

I ordered another cappuccino and sat thinking about Miss
Arielle's disappearance. I thought about the people who took the
time to show up with Arielle look-alikes, about the thousand
leaflets put up by Miss Arielle's owner and about what seemed—
judging from the photograph—a totally romanticized and inflated
description of the missing cat. Soon, a short story began taking
shape in my head. Fortunately, before I reached the point of making notes on my napkin, my second cappuccino arrived, and I
turned my attention to the *Trib*.

After glancing at the front-page headlines and passing over articles on the Treaty on European Union and Alan Greenspan's position on inflation, I paid my check and left.

In the old days—the days before this trip—articles about lost
cats would have passed quickly through my system, leaving me free
to digest the meatier opinions of know-it-all politicians and pundits
on the state-of-the-world-and-all-those-problems-that-threaten-it.

Not anymore. I'd given myself license to assume the world and
its problems could struggle on without me, at least for the rest of
the year. I was reminded of E. B. White, who commented, after
leaving *The New Yorker* for a simpler life in Maine, that he hadn't been
able to keep up with the papers because he was "building a mouse-
proof closet against a rain of mice."

As I headed up the King's Road toward the Underground

station—keeping an eye out for a pedigree chinchilla silver-tipped cat—I spotted a few mice, along with two black cats, a gray tabby, and one unusually big furry creature that may or may not have been of the feline persuasion. I also saw a man who looked like my personal idol: John Cleese, the great British actor and comedian of *Monty Python* fame. Upon closer inspection, however, I decided that, like all those faux Miss Arielle copycats, the handsome charismatic man on the King's Road was not the real thing.

When I reached the Sloane Square station I had to run to catch my train. Halfway down the steps I could hear it rumbling onto the tracks below; the sound set everyone into motion. Like a herd of wildebeest startled by a hunter's shotgun, we stampeded down the stairs and onto the platform. I hopped aboard just as the doors were closing and quickly moved to a seat at the window.

I looked at my watch. It was about eleven. By this time my brother, Shelby, and his wife, Pat—who was like a sister to me—would have arrived in London after an overnight flight from Texas. The thought of seeing them during the next few days put me in a good mood.

But first, before meeting Shelby and Pat and a group of their friends for dinner that night, I was on my way to read some love letters. The letters were on display at, of all places, the Imperial War Museum.

At first I'd thought it odd, a war museum mounting what the guidebook described as "an exhibition about the special nature of romance in wartime, featuring true stories of happiness and heartbreak, illustrated by love letters, keepsakes, poems and telegrams." But the more I thought about it the more it made sense. What, after all, heightens the intensity of love more than separation? Particularly when that separation involves danger and uncertainty. And what more intimate way to transcend the terrible, aching apartness than through the writing down of words that carry in each pen stroke the physical presence of the absent one?

At the St. James's Park tube stop, a well-dressed young man took the seat next to me. After a minute or two he pulled from his briefcase a thin sheet of airmail stationery and began to write in small, precise, straight-up-and-down strokes. As I watched the words take shape, I thought of my father's handwriting and remembered how as a child, after he died, I would trace the handwriting from his letters over and over again onto onionskin paper, trying to make it my own. *Dear Children,* I would trace carefully with a finely sharpened pencil, *I have just arrived in Brazil, which is a beautiful country. . . .*

Of course what I desperately wanted to trace were not his letters to Shelby and me but the ones he wrote to Mother. She would not allow it. "They are private," she would say in a firm voice, one that suggested whining or pleading wasn't going to change her mind. Sometimes, however, I would write down from memory the words I had seen in those letters: *My darling Nancy . . . My dearest wife . . . How I miss you.*

Now, as the darkness rushed by outside the train's window, I allowed myself to think of another letter, one I'd received earlier in the week and was trying *not* to think about. But the mind has a will of its own, and I managed to get around the self-imposed prohibition by thinking of Naohiro's letter as though I were watching a play:

A woman, dressed in a slightly wrinkled gray silk suit and in dire need of a haircut, is leaving her flat one morning when the porter hands her a letter.

*As soon as she looks at the postmark she turns around and takes the lift
back to her flat, where she sits on the side of the bed and, still holding her
purse, opens the ivory-colored envelope. The letter consists of two short para-
graphs, which she reads over and over again. The first paragraph begins, "I
am on the bullet train, thinking of you"; and the second one ends, "I will be
in Paris in October. Where will you be?"*

In Italy, I thought, trying not to feel sad. But walking the few blocks
from the Underground station to the War Museum, I let myself feel
the sting of missing Naohiro. Then suddenly the geography of
hope kicked in: *it's only an hour-and-a-half by plane from Paris to Venice,* I realized, feeling as elated as Penelope must have at the prospect of
seeing Ulysses upon his return from Troy.

As I turned onto Lambeth Street and the Imperial War Museum
came into view, I thought of the building's origins. A large, archi-
tecturally elegant structure set in the middle of a park, the museum
had once been a hospital for the insane. It was the last site of the
notorious Bethlem Hospital for the Insane. Or Bedlam, as it came
to be known. From insane asylum to museum. The building's cur-
rent name struck me as the perfect metaphor for the insanity of our
time: war.

On my first visit to the Imperial War Museum I had been surprised to see that, despite its dated name, the museum's approach
to keeping alive the horror and sacrifice of the two world wars was
quite modern. On the lower level of the building one could partic-
ipate in a striking re-creation of what it was like to live through the
London Blitz, from the warning sirens to walking through the

smoky rubble after a raid. There was also a re-creation of what trench warfare was like in World War I. After seeing it I began to understand, for the first time, the horror of life in the trenches. I seldom visited London without stopping by the War Museum to pay my respects and look around.

When I reached the entrance, a museum guard pointed out the location of the exhibit I'd come to see: "Forces Sweethearts." To get there I passed through the glass-domed hall, where Spitfires from the Battle of Britain and a Sopwith Camel from World War I hung from the ceiling like mobiles over a child's crib. Then, after passing a huge German V-2 rocket of the kind used to pound London in 1944 and a frighteningly small one-man German submarine, I turned into an enclosed space at the back of the center hall.

Inside this softly lit room there were no weapons or terrible recreations of trench warfare. Instead a woman's voice sang "We'll meet again, don't know where, don't know when . . ." It was the voice of Vera Lynn, the "sweetheart" of British and Allied forces during World War II. Her plaintive words drifted over the 1940s-style vanity dressing tables set with silver hairbrushes and small blue-and-silver perfume bottles of Evening in Paris. They drifted over the pictures in heart-shaped frames of young men in uniform, of wedding dresses made from parachute silk, of pin-up photos of Rita Hayworth and Betty Grable. It was like stepping onto a movie set, one built for a romantic war film starring Teresa Wright as the girl at home waiting for her GI to return.

But it was in the love letters and pictures of the laughing young men who wrote them that I found the script for this movie: *Dearest, how I miss you . . . My darling girl, it seems so long since we held each other . . . Darling, do you remember the night . . .*

I stopped before a photo of a dark-eyed young sailor with a wide grin. A British submariner, he had asked his sister to send the letter to his girlfriend, Betty, if he "should not return." His submarine was lost in May 1941. The letter began:

18.4.41

Dearest Betty,

 Betty—my darling—I think that you wouldn't mind me calling you that for the last time, as I expect by now my sister has informed you that I have died in fighting for our country. . . . But I may say, looking down, that my last thoughts were of my family and you, and I will love you while there is breath in my body.

I looked again at the photo of the young sailor, imagined him hunched in his bunk under a tiny light, scratching out shaky words of love as the small submarine moved silently beneath the great weight of the ocean. How brave to face one's own death, I thought. And how kind to write such comforting words to the one you love.

Then I imagined Betty, her face ashen beneath the rolled pompadour of her long hair, sitting at the dining-room table reading and rereading the shattering words meant to comfort her. I can see her rise and, after bracing herself against the back of a chair, walk to a desk, where she places the letter in a quilted satin box, next to other letters tied with blue ribbon.

And now, after all these years, here was the letter, in the Imperial War Museum—*Betty—my darling—I think you wouldn't mind me calling you that for the last time* . . . Leaning forward, I touched one of the blue-and-silver perfume bottles on the table, wondering if any of the sweet, heavy fragrance remained inside. As I straightened up and took a step back, my large tourist's handbag sideswiped a woman standing just behind me.

Before I could apologize, the woman spoke to me. "My husband courted me with a bottle of that perfume," she said, calling to her side a man standing nearby. "Harry, do come and have a look at this, won't you?"

"Right-o," the man said, putting down a brochure he was read-ing. As he drew near, she pointed to the Evening in Paris perfume bottle. The man—I judged him to be in his mid-seventies—glanced at his wife and smiled. He was tall, tall enough to have ac-quired a permanent forward tilt of the head that brought to mind a gooseneck lamp. That's what years of making eye contact with shorter people does to you, I thought.

"It brings back memories, doesn't it?" the woman said to the man. Then she turned to me. "Are you a Yank, then?" She laughed when she said it, a pleasant laugh that made me think she had rea-sons to like "Yanks."

"Yes, but how did you know?" I asked, a little confused, since I'd not yet spoken.

"We were at the entry when you came in and heard you asking about the exhibition." Actually I'd noticed them, too: the tall man wearing a V-neck sweater, shirt, and tie under a tweed jacket, and the short, ruddy-faced woman dressed in a bright red jacket, white shirtwaist, and dark pleated skirt. "It's quite touching, isn't it?" she said. "All these heartbreaking letters. But in those days we all lost someone in the war."

I wondered whom she had lost. Obviously not Harry. A brother, perhaps. An uncle. Maybe even her father. World War II, after all, was not a war fought exclusively by the young.

The three of us moved through the rest of the exhibition at the same pace; not exactly together but close enough to remark occa-sionally on this letter or that diary.

"I remember starting a diary when the buzz bombs began com-ing over Kent in 1944," the woman said. "I remember we'd go down into the bomb shelter and a lot of the girls would knit or darn socks.

But not me. I'd be writing words from the songs my husband and I used to dance to." She put up her arms and pretended to dance, her purse jiggling from her hand. Seeing this, Harry smiled.

After staying another half-hour or so we left the exhibition and walked together through the main hall. Suddenly Harry stopped in the middle of the room and pointed to a small plane hanging from the ceiling. It was a very basic-looking plane, except for the torpedo-shaped appendage above its tail. "That's a buzz bomb," he said. "But everybody called them 'doodlebugs.' "

I was surprised; the buzz bomb looked completely different from the way I'd imagined it. "I've always pictured it as looking like a rocket," I told Harry. "Like that one," I said, pointing to the huge V-2 rocket rising ominously out of the floor like an evil stalagmite.

Harry, who hadn't talked much before, warmed to the subject, explaining the differences between the two rockets in power and speed. But it was the distinct sound of an approaching doodlebug that had left the most indelible impression on him. "It was not like anything I'd ever heard. First off, we'd hear this sputtering engine noise—*putt, putt, putt*—like a plane in trouble. Then the noise just stopped and there was this frightful silence for a few seconds. Then, an explosion."

"Yes," said the woman, "its a noise one never forgets." She told me about hearing it one night and knowing there wasn't time to get to the bomb shelter. "So we snatched up the baby and ran out into the fields." Later she was told it had exploded in an open space, not too far from where they crouched.

I wanted to hear more and invited them to join me for a cup of tea in the museum's café.

"What do you think, Harry? Shall we nip in for some tea?"

"Right-o. I could do with a cup of tea," he replied. "And a bit of cake, as well."

For the next hour or so the three of us sat at a corner table and talked. Or, rather, they talked and I listened. Listening, I had learned in my job as a reporter, was just as much of a skill as asking the right questions. And I sensed that Harry and Helen had stories, like many who visited this museum, that they needed to tell.

Harry, who had worked near Dover as an engine fitter for the RAF, recalled watching Spitfires chasing the doodlebugs, trying to shoot them down before they reached London. "One clear night when it was fairly quiet I went out to get some air. Just a bit after that, I saw our lads coming in after one of the 'D's,' firing at it." It seemed to be headed in his direction, he said, but he couldn't move. "Frozen to the spot, I was. Kept thinking I should run. But which way?" After a few suspenseful moments, the doodlebug passed over him, crashing and exploding just past some large trees. The next day, Harry said, he went to church for the first time in years.

Helen nodded as Harry talked, the way people do when they know exactly what the other person means. Then she said, "You know my husband flew alongside the Yanks on some of their bombing runs. In an RAF plane, as an escort. I've never forgotten something he wrote in one of his last letters, about watching your chaps take off in their Flying Fortresses. Dozens of them. Said it was like watching a great migration of cranes flying across the sky."

Helen's remark stunned me. Among other things, it meant Harry was not her husband. And now I knew who it was she'd lost in the war. I tried to process in my mind the information on which I'd based the assumption that she was married to Harry. But I was too flustered to do anything more than nod my head as Helen talked of her husband's letter.

For some reason—I suppose to cover up my shock—I started telling Harry and Helen of my interview with a famous British neurologist who'd grown up in London during the war years. I was writing a profile of him, pegged to the publication of his book about the fascinating, sometimes bizarre, patients he'd treated. About halfway through the interview, he told me of being sent at the age of three from London to the countryside to escape the Blitz. As he described the physical and emotional abuse he'd suffered at the hands of his "caretakers," he grew sad, then angry. My sense was he'd never forgiven his parents, two prominent London physicians, for what he saw as their "abandonment" of him.

"Alas, such things did happen," Helen said. "I suppose war upsets all the normal things, doesn't it? Tears families apart and all that. Life is never quite the same after as it was before."

"Yes," Harry said, "I believe that for the lot of us who lived through it, we'll likely always mark our lives by before the war and after."

We talked some more and then rose to leave. When Harry went off to the coatroom to fetch his umbrella, I summoned up my reporter's nerve and asked Helen how she met Harry.

"We met here at the museum a few years back," she said. "Sat next to each other in the café and just started talking. It seems we had a lot in common—the war and growing up in Kent, that sort of thing."

I wanted to ask more, but didn't. It was none of my business really. Instead, we said our good-byes and left.

Well, that answered one question, I thought, watching Harry and Helen hug good-bye and walk off in separate directions. They were not a couple; just friends. And yet, in a way, they shared something that made them a couple. Not their lives before the war or after the war, but the experience of what went on during the in-between years. I suspected a lot of Brits, the ones who lived

through the war years, had the same invisible bonds. It struck me
that it must be like the bonds that spring up between soldiers.

Once the long bony hand of War and Death touches you, I
thought, its presence never leaves. War and Death. I understood
that. Or I thought I did.

Before going back to my flat to change for dinner I set out to buy
some shoes. The dinner with Shelby and his friends promised to be
a rather grand affair and my wardrobe by this time was looking a bit
forlorn. After going through my closet that morning, I decided a
pale beige silk skirt, paired with a blouse of the same color, would
do fine for the dinner. But the narrow skirt that stopped just above
the ankles required a certain style of shoe, a style not in my closet.

I headed for Sloane Street and began browsing the shop windows. The sales were on in full force and the stores were jammed
with bargain hunters. I was tired and about ready to give up when I
spotted what I thought might work: a pair of beige silk espadrilles
with high rope-soles and laces that tied round the ankles. Although
such shoes were all the rage in London, I knew they were way too
hip for me and I'd probably look ridiculous wearing them.

But what the heck, I thought. Why not? It was time to let go of
worrying about such things as whether or not I looked foolish in a
pair of trendy shoes. The shop had my size. I bought them.

As I walked back to my flat, I wondered if Freya Stark, whose
book had become my bedtime companion, was ever lured into buying clothes when she traveled. Some garment in Turkey, perhaps,
that seemed quite flattering at the time, but once out of its native

habitat looked ridiculous. The night before, to my surprise, I'd learned that Freya had an interest in and a theory about clothes: "Nothing is more useful to a woman traveller than a genuine interest in clothes; it is a key to unlock the hearts of women of all ages and races," she wrote, describing a subject that had enabled her to connect with women from very different backgrounds. "The same feeling of intimacy is awakened, whether with Druse or Moslem or Canadian. I wonder if men have any such universal interest to fall back upon?"

Reading this made me like the intrepid, no-nonsense Freya all the more. It also made me ponder her question as it might relate to men. Were sports the male equivalent of a universal interest? It was the only thing I could think of that might be comparable, although I knew many men who had little or no interest in gamesmanship.

But right now another, more pressing question faced me: would I be able to walk in my new shoes? Or, for that matter, even stand in them for any length of time without falling flat on my face? I imagined my apprehension to be similar to what Freya must have felt when she mounted her first camel and set off to cross the desert atop that ridiculous-looking creature.

My brother and sister-in-law were staying at the posh Lanesborough Hotel at Hyde Park Corner. Shelby is all the family I have left from my childhood. He is the last person who shares with me family secrets and the realities of who we were before we remade ourselves into the adults we are. Sometimes it was hard for me to connect the boy I knew—the skinny smart kid who collected lead soldiers and pursued Boy Scout merit badges—with the phenomenally successful man he'd become. But sooner or later, when we were together, some remark would inevitably trigger childhood memories and then we'd be off, zipping down a path that existed now only for the two of us.

After all, who else remembered the ten-year-old boy who, trying to keep the battery from dying, regularly started up the car Mother never learned to drive? And who but Shelby could retrieve the memory of his three-year-old sister being rushed by ambulance to the hospital in the middle of the night when her appendix ruptured?

We were the repository, he and I, of our family's history and its secrets. Together we held on to the memories of Father returning from a trip, loaded with surprise gifts; the taste of the plain, sometimes peculiar, Scottish food we ate as children; our exciting visits with an aunt and uncle to the exotic Algerian Room, a nightclub in the Baltimore hotel where they lived.

But mostly when we were together Shelby and I lived in the present and concentrated on having a good time. This visit was no different. For the next several days we talked over long, leisurely breakfasts, visited the sights, shopped, went to the theater, had late-night suppers, and always closed down the day by gathering with his friends in the cozy hotel bar for champagne. In between, there were massages and facials for the women; lunch at the club and business appointments for the men.

It was quite a departure from my usual routine and I welcomed its brief appearance. It was fun to have someone else do all the planning and, at a deeper level, to have someone looking after you. It would be easy, I thought, to grow used to having another person take care of you.

The truth is, I had lived alone for so long I sometimes forgot that the responsibility for running my life was solely mine. There was no sharing of duties and decisions in the life I'd chosen. Whether it was taking the car to the repair shop or hanging the screen door, it was up to me. Most of the time I liked being in charge of my life, thrived on it, in fact. But occasionally, when I was tired or unhappy, I'd find myself thinking how nice it would be to let someone else run the show, at least for a while.

On the morning of our last day together in London, Shelby and I lingered over coffee, talking about our plans. He and his group were on their way to Scotland, where Shelby planned, among other things, to do some research on our family's Scottish heritage. I was staying on in London, but within a week or so would leave for Oxford.

Toward the end of our talk, Shelby leaned forward and said, "You know, you look more and more like Mother."

"And you look more and more like Father," I said, laughing. "So that's what it's come down to, has it? We've become our parents." This time we both laughed.

But beneath the laughter I was thinking something else. I was thinking that, despite what I'd told my brother, the truth was I didn't have a clear memory of what my father looked like.

What I did remember were like errant pieces of a puzzle waiting to be fitted together into a whole. The way my father tilted his head. The amused expression in his eyes. The pith helmet and white summer suits he wore. His youthful manner and easy laugh. I think he was handsome. At least he looks that way in the tailored white officer's uniform he is wearing in the photographs kept by

Mother in a leather album. Were the pictures taken before he went off to serve at sea in World War II? Or after? I had no idea.

I wondered: is what we remember more important than what we forget?

I could remember so little of that day when two men in uniform—or was it only one?—came to the house. They had with them a blue leather box that contained a medal of some kind. If I stirred the memory, small bits and pieces of that afternoon—or was it morning?—rose to the top:

I was in third grade and we were home sick with the flu, Shelby and I, when the men arrived. The two of us, wearing pajamas, stood in the living room with Mother and Grandmother, listening—but not understanding—the words being said: "His ship torpedoed . . . German submarine . . . only four survivors . . . we regret to tell you . . ." When the men left I went to my room, frightened, not sure of what it all meant: the way Mother put her hand to her throat as if to hold it together; the tears rolling down Grandmother's cheeks; the brave look on Shelby's face that threatened to dissolve before he could run out of the house and down the back steps.

At least that's how I remember it.

What I do have a clear memory of, however, is going to my desk to retrieve a piece of paper. I see myself sitting down to trace some words from it: *Dear Children, Brazil is a beautiful country . . .*

After saying good-bye to Shelby and Pat, I decided to walk through nearby St. James's Park. It was lush and green and very pleasant, and when I reached the lake that divides the park in two, I walked along its banks.

A man unintentionally fell into step beside me. I glanced at him. He resembled Harry, I thought, the man who'd been at the War Museum with Helen. Tall, sweet Harry, whom I would always think of as a young man standing outside on a clear night gazing at the stars; a sight that could have been, but wasn't, the last thing he'd ever see. Thinking this, I stole another look at the man still walking beside me. This time, however, I couldn't see the resemblance. It was as though I had imagined, not remembered, what Harry looked like.

I thought of the letters I'd read at the War Museum. Love letters. *Betty—my darling . . . my last thoughts were of you . . . I will love you while there is breath in my body*. I thought of how I'd imagined Betty, her face ashen, reading and rereading the words, trying to grasp the awful reality that lay beneath them, trying to break through her numbness.

I understood that. How many times I've tried to recast that day the officers came to our house with the news of my father's death; to put some feeling into it, to cry or be angry, or tell God I hated him. To feel anything but the thick numbness turning me into stone.

I have a theory that women like me, women who had fathers for only a short time, never give up the search to have back what was lost too soon. We look for some trace of the lost father in the faces of our brothers, our sons, our husbands, our lovers. Sometimes even in the forward tilt of a tall man's head.

Lately, however, I thought I detected a change in my attitude. There were signals coming up from some deep-down place that made me think I might be ready to start letting go of the imaginary father I'd been searching for. That meant, of course, I'd now have to start looking for the real one. But where? To my surprise, it was Dostoyevsky who answered my question. One good memory, he'd written somewhere, especially one from childhood, could give even the hopeless something to hang on to.

Okay, I thought, I'll start with one good memory of my father. I let my mind go blank and soon enough, just as though I were back on the analyst's couch instead of sitting on a lawn chair in a London park, I saw us together, my father and me.

We're in the family Plymouth, just the two of us, taking a ride down a country road, looking at the scenery. It's a hot day and the windows are down, blowing the smell of fresh-cut hay into the car. We pass some black-and-white cows in a field and my dad leans out the window and goes moo . . . mooo . . . moooo. I crack up and lean out my window, imitating my dad imitating the cows. On the way home we stop at an ice-cream stand and have chocolate shakes. I spill most of mine down the front of my sundress. But my dad doesn't care. He just lifts me up and carries me to the car. I fall asleep.

As I was thinking about this, I saw a man sitting on the grass in the park, next to the lake. I seemed to recognize his face: the brown eyes, the cleft in the chin, the high cheekbones.

I know who he looks like, I thought, standing alone on a summer's day in a park far from home, and even farther from my childhood: *he looks like my dad.*

8

Ladies of Small Means

Dear Alice,

It was Jane Austen, wasn't it, who said that everything happens at parties. True enough. But equally as true, at least for me, is the admonition by somebody or another to "Have fun and go home when you're tired." I think this is one of the wisest bits of advice I've ever heard & I plan to put it into effect im-

*mediately in my life. Not just at parties, but in ways more pro-
found and necessary.*

Love, Alice

The woman behind the information counter at the Finchley Road
Underground was visibly perplexed. "So you're looking for Maresfield Gardens, are you?" she said, answering my question with a
question.

"Yes. The exact number is twenty Maresfield Gardens. I was
told to get off at Finchley Road."

"*Twenty* Maresfield Gardens, is it? I've not heard of it. Is it in
Hampstead?" She consulted a map tacked up on the wall. "Wait
here, dear. I'll just go have a talk with someone else and see if he
knows of its whereabouts." She disappeared around the corner of
the tiny desk.

I stood waiting, my right foot tapping out my impatience. The
trip had taken longer than expected and I was not pleased to find
myself lost and, possibly, nowhere near my destination.

"Well, here we are, dear," said the station attendant, returning
with a uniformed man. He proceeded to ask me the same questions. *Maresfield Gardens? . . . Are you sure it's in Hampstead?* As he was
talking to me, a light bulb seemed to go on over the woman's head.

"Are you going to Freud's?" she asked in a cheery voice.

I told her I was. "Well, then you just go up the street outside to
Trinity Walk and take a left. Then at the top of the hill, take another
left. And that's Maresfield Gardens."

The directions sounded quite simple, but I wrote them down
anyway. After thanking her I made my way out to Finchley Road, a

commercial street lined with shops and offices. Of course, it being Sunday, everything was closed, giving the area a deserted, melancholy feel. As I walked along Finchley Road, the only pedestrian on the abandoned street, I felt like a character in an Edward Hopper painting. *The Sunday Blues*, I called it, this sad feeling that sometimes came over me on the seventh day of the week. It could hit particularly hard if I was on the road, traveling alone.

In Paris I'd handled the problem by buying the London *Sunday Times* and reading it at the Flore over a long, hearty breakfast. I found that once I got through the morning the rest of the day seemed to fall into place. I hadn't been able to find a London antidote to my Sunday Blues. Certainly there was nothing around here, I thought, looking along the deserted street.

But maybe that was appropriate. After all, I was on my way to pay my respects to Sigmund Freud who, were he alive and waiting for me, would expect me to examine such feelings from the depths of his famous couch. Freud was right, I thought, when he compared analysis to archaeology, implying that the task of both was to unearth a hidden past. I knew my Sunday Blues went back pretty far; as far back, actually, as I could remember.

The problem is that the past is never past; it lives on, directing us like an undercover traffic cop. Freud, of course, said it a little differently. But that's what he meant.

I loved interpreting Freud. Turnabout is fair play, after all. And besides, it took my mind off the Sunday Blues.

After climbing the perilously steep Trinity Walk, I emerged on a quiet, leafy street. I walked a short distance, reading the house numbers until I came to number twenty. The house where Freud lived turned out to be quite elegant, a three-story brick dwelling surrounded by well-kept gardens and hedges. What struck me most, however, were its many windows. A fitting touch, I thought, for a man who spent his life looking through the windows of other people's minds.

I walked inside, bought my ticket, and signed the guest book. Then, bypassing Freud's re-created study, I headed right for the video room to see the films I'd been told about. They were said to include intimate scenes of Freud with his family, friends, and beloved dogs.

When I arrived in the darkened upstairs viewing room, the films were already flickering across the faces of the dozen or so viewers who'd gathered there. I took the first seat I could find, nodding to the woman who looked up as I sat down next to her.

At first I couldn't make sense of what I saw on the screen. Freud was sitting in a beautiful garden, the center of attention at what seemed to be a party. As people looked on, a parade of dogs marched by the psychoanalyst. The dogs—chows, I thought, with perhaps one jumbo Pekingese thrown in—were dressed in collars with bows. Then a sweet, disembodied narrator's voice explained this was a film of Freud's birthday party, and that attached to the dogs' collars were congratulatory messages.

"That's Anna Freud's voice," whispered the woman next to me. "Freud's daughter." I nodded, remembering how it was my ex-husband's desire to train with Anna Freud that had brought my family to London twenty-five years earlier.

The film continued with fascinating glimpses of Freud and his family in Paris and at their villa outside Vienna. Always the psychoanalyst was accompanied by his dogs, saying of one chow, "My Jofi is a delightful creature; recuperation after most of the human visitors." Upon hearing this the woman next to me snickered loudly.

When the film was over, I turned to the woman and asked if I'd missed much by coming in late.

"Not much at all," she said. Then in an amusing way she summed up the five minutes or so I'd hadn't seen. Her rapid-fire delivery of the material was punctuated by sharp, funny observations, more like that of a stand-up comic than a sit-down analyst: *dog comes in, dog goes out . . . Freud relaxes in Paris with famous analyst Marie Bonaparte, who is sans Napoleon . . . Dogs on parade offer congratulations to doting Dr. Freud . . .*

Between laughs, I listened, trying to place her accent. South African? Australian? I couldn't tell. I took a chance and asked if she was Australian. She was.

Jean Gillespie was a psychoanalyst from Sydney. In almost one breath she told me she had studied years ago at the Hampstead Clinic founded by Anna Freud, but that she now practiced in Australia and was thinking of moving to New York although she'd heard it was tough to crack the New York Psychoanalytic Society and anyway she might possibly give up private practice. At the end of her soliloquy, she asked, "Are you an analyst?"

I was tempted to say yes. After all, I had raised two children—a task Freud himself compared to the "impossible" profession of analysis—along with playing housemother to countless narcissistic cats. But I told her the truth instead. "No, but my ex-husband applied to study at the Hampstead Clinic. We actually moved to London, but his plans fell through."

She asked me what I did. I told her I worked as a newspaper reporter, which in my opinion also qualified me to declare myself, at the very least, a lay analyst. She laughed. It was a loud, booming sound, one that came without warning. It must have alarmed her patients, I thought, when it came at them from behind the couch. Indeed, there was a raw quality about her whole person that ran counter to the image of the analyst as quiet cipher. I found it re-freshing. But I wasn't sure I'd want her to be my therapist.

We spent the next hour or so walking together through the house, paying special attention to Freud's study and library. The large room was a replica of his consulting room in Vienna, furnished with belongings transplanted from 19 Berggasse, his home for forty-seven years. For the last year of his life he worked here, sur-rounded by the familiar past. I was reminded of the way my friend Susan had managed to re-create her Washington apartment on a hill in Montmartre, bringing along a bit of the past with her into a new life.

In the study, Jean and I paused to contemplate the famous couch. It was roped off from the rest of the room.

"Probably to discourage any homesick patients from taking a lie-down on it," Jean said.

"It looks pretty uncomfortable to me," I said, eyeing the short, heavy-looking couch that roller-coastered down from the head end and was covered with a scratchy-looking Oriental rug. I told Jean of my observation that the decor of an analyst's office seemed always to be one of two styles: either sleek, leather-and-chrome minimal-ist with the obligatory Miro print, or a mismatched, just-hauled-up-from-the-beach-cottage look accessorized with a Käthe Kollwitz print.

Jean laughed. "Well, I'm afraid I fall into the second category. What about your analyst?"

"Definitely beach cottage," I said. "On humid days his office even had a musty seaside smell. Actually, I don't think I'd feel com-fortable with an analyst who had a leather Mies van der Rohe couch."

"I hear the Mies couch is popular with New York analysts. Which is another good reason not to move to New York."

Before leaving, Jean and I stopped at the gift shop. "I wonder what Freud would think of being merchandised this way," I said, browsing through the notecards, posters, mugs, commemorative stamps, and replicas of the Greek, Roman, and Egyptian antiquities he so famously collected. Some of them weren't cheap.

"I suspect he'd be amused and not at all surprised," Jean said, handing over thirty pounds to the cashier for a pair of nondescript silver earrings. She explained to me the design of the earrings was taken from a doodle by Freud on one of his manuscripts.

When the clerk handed Jean her change and the boxed earrings, she immediately unwrapped them. "The way I look at it," Jean said, guiding the silver posts through her earlobes, "it's like wearing a little piece of Freud's unconscious."

Jean and I took the Tube back to Green Park together. She told me she was staying in Mayfair with some rich Australian friends who, several years earlier, had made their fortune in mining. "Tin, or something like that. In South America, I think. They're out of town this weekend so I've the whole place to myself."

It was getting close to dinnertime and the thought of eating alone on a Sunday evening was bothering me in a big way. Without hesitating, I asked Jean if she had plans. I figured I'd had good luck so far in the friends I'd made on this trip and Jean, my instincts told me, was someone I'd enjoy having as a pal in London.

Meeting people on this trip, I'd come to see, was not difficult. I was good at being thrown into situations with total strangers and finding a way to connect, at least temporarily. That's what reporters do all the time. But developing a real relationship, even a temporary one, was far different from being shielded by a reporter's notebook. Reporters, I'd come to think, were not unlike analysts: their anonymity—that is, their ability to not insert themselves into the interview—was an important element in drawing out the other person. Not that reporters shouldn't be smart and charming and know more about the subject than the subject himself does; no, it is all a matter of not forgetting who exactly the subject of the interview is.

But meeting people on this trip, I realized—although initially easy—required going beyond the one-sided reportorial encounter. It required revealing yourself. And it also required a willingness to not be offended when the object of your attention did not respond to you. I was getting better at both aspects of the travel relationship.

Jean, however, did not reject me. She immediately said yes to my dinner offer, suggesting that we eat at a Chinese restaurant in Mayfair. We walked through Half Moon Street, ducking briefly into Shepherd Market for a quick look around, and then crossed Curzon onto Queen Street.

The restaurant, which struck me as quite chic, overflowed with fashionably-got-up people waiting to be seated. I was about to suggest we go back to an Indian restaurant in Shepherd Market when the headwaiter motioned to Jean. We left the line and followed him to a table. I was impressed.

"Did I miss something?" I asked her. "Are you some sort of celebrity or did you just slip the headwaiter a twenty-pound note?"

"Oh, it's probably just my undeniable glamour and conspicuous charm that accounts for it." She laughed. "Either that or my fake Gucci handbag." She then told me that her hosts in London—who lived nearby in the Chesterfield Hill area—frequently dined at the restaurant. "I've been their guest here several times, so I have status. It's one of the perks of hanging around with rich people, you know."

Over dinner Jean and I talked about our lives; at least the *Reader's Digest* versions. When she was growing up, Jean said, she dreamed of going into veterinary medicine. "I'm animal crazy and the idea of treating large animals—horses, cattle, sheep, that sort of thing—appealed to me." She switched her focus to psychiatry after her father fell into a deep depression. She was in her teens at the time. "My father never fully recovered and somehow I was the one in the family best able to cope with him." Her mother and sisters, she said, quickly allowed her to take over this role. She read a lot about the illness and by college was fixed in her decision to become a psychiatrist.

"It's worked out well except I seem to be attracted only to men who have depressive tendencies. Something I don't seem to have worked out in my own analysis." Jean said she'd been married and divorced twice, once to and from a fellow analyst. Her month-long stay in London, she said, was prompted by the breakup of her most recent relationship. "With another analyst," she said, letting out a mock sigh.

None of this seemed to have depressed Jean. She struck me as an outgoing, optimistic person with a keen interest in everything around her. An ardent horsewoman, scuba diver, and trekker, she'd been around the world several times and seemed to have a large capacity for adventure. Her appetite for food and wine, I noticed, was also large. Although I liked Jean and enjoyed her company, her loud unpredictable laugh, which sometimes drew attention to our table, made me uncomfortable. I decided to write it off as part of her raw, bigger-than-life personality.

I noticed a second wave of diners—probably the after-theater crowd—was starting to arrive. When I looked at my watch I saw it was close to eleven. Jean and I paid the bill and, after a short stroll along Curzon Street, prepared to part company.

Just before saying good-bye, Jean mentioned a party her hosts were giving the following weekend. She asked if I'd like to come.

"Sounds like fun. I'd love to."

"I'll call you." She took down my number and handed me a card printed with the phone number of her London hosts.

My trip to the Freud Museum had left me with a strong urge to visit our old house near Sloane Square, the place where I'd lived as a young wife and mother. So after breakfast the next morning, I set out on a pilgrimage. As I walked toward the row of houses on Sloane Gardens, I imagined my husband and elder son as they were twenty-five years ago: a studious-looking man, slender and blue-eyed, with the high forehead of an intellectual, and a blond, blue-eyed two-year-old, running from one end of the square to the other, chasing pigeons.

If I looked hard enough I could see, off to the side, a dark-haired woman in a pink silk coat buying flowers—big bunches of pale apricot roses—from the vendor in front of the Underground stop. It was my mother. She'd made it a habit, while in London, to fill up her apartment and ours with fresh flowers.

The neighborhood was so familiar to me that it was tempting to continue reconstructing the past. So I did.

There is Bliss's chemist shop, I thought, where we bought cold remedies and Band-Aids. And there's the Peter Jones department store; we all bought raincoats there. And, oh, look! There's W. H. Smith's bookshop, where my husband bought books and I bought toy trucks for our son.

But I knew enough to be parsimonious with such memories.

They still had the power to ambush me. I knew that lurking in the dark corners of such memories was an unwanted thought: the possibility that the most important part of my life existed in the past. Most of the time I knew this was not so, but occasionally, when trapped by memories, I would mistake change for loss, and grieve over the marriage that dissolved, the mother who died, the boy who grew up, and the young woman I was when I lived on this street.

But which house was it we lived in? Suddenly I couldn't remember the exact number. Was it 15? Or 17? Looking at first one, then the other, I drew a complete blank. Then a door opened and a pleasant-looking woman of about forty, wearing a chador but with her face uncovered, stepped out.

"Are you looking for someone?" she asked in a way that suggested a wish to be helpful.

"Well, I was," I said. "A family that used to live here. But they've moved away."

When the woman turned to walk back into the house, I saw a flash of high-heeled silver sandals from beneath her chador. Watching her close the door to Number 15 Sloane Gardens, I wondered if she ever got homesick for a garden in Persia, one with a fountain splashing in the courtyard. I wondered if she, too, might have returned there once, searching for the person she used to be.

It was still early, so I decided to visit a museum I'd heard about: the quaintly named Museum of Garden History. One of my English friends had warned me not to miss the museum or its special exhibition celebrating the 150th anniversary of Gertrude Jekyll's birth.

"Gertrude Jekyll?" I had said, pronouncing the last name Jeckul, as in Dr. Jekyll and Mr. Hyde. "The name sounds vaguely familiar but who exactly is she?"

"First off, it's JEE-kill, not JECK-ul." She smiled. "The ladies at the museum get quite cross when you mispronounce the name of their gardening heroine." She went on to explain that Gertrude Jekyll was probably the most important garden designer of the century, and that most of today's gardens were influenced by her ideas.

What my friend forgot to tell me, however, was that the museum was housed in a former church. After passing the Church of St. Mary-at-Lambeth several times, searching the almost empty streets for the right address, I was ready to give up. Then I spotted a woman who looked as though she might be a gardener: tweed suit, pleasantly weathered face, brisk stride. "Excuse me," I said. "Do you know where the Museum of Garden History is?"

She nodded. "It's just over there," she said, pointing to a small, lovely church directly behind me.

It was cool and quiet inside the thick walls of the museum-church. Straight ahead I saw a gift shop, as cozy as a kitchen nook, where volunteers in plaid skirts and sweater sets gently presided over garden books, botanical watercolors, and assorted gifts. The museum's collections of garden tools, historical exhibits, and fascinating photographs and sketches tracing the evolution of garden design were displayed in what was the nave of the church. There was also a space set aside for a tearoom.

I felt completely at home in this combination church and museum. It was as though the great noise of the world gave way to the soft buzzing whirr of childhood memories: of Sundays spent in church dozing off, with the thick smell of lilies in the air; of visits to Mr. Moore's hardware store with Grandmother to buy small packets of seed with names like poetry. *Heavenly Blue Morning Glory. Sweet*

Pea. Golden Marguerite. Black-eyed Susan. It wouldn't have surprised me to find Grandmother there in person, wearing her pith helmet and rubber boots.

Instead I turned around and bumped into another extraordinary woman: Gertrude Jekyll. Right away I knew we were kindred spirits; knew it from the moment I heard her voice—her lucid, wry, *thinking* voice, that is—that was transcribed straight from her head into articles and notebooks:

"Throughout my life I have found one of the things most worth doing was to cultivate the habit of close observation," wrote Miss Jekyll.

And: "Near my home is a little wild valley, whose planting, wholly done by nature, I have all my life regarded with the most reverent admiration."

And: "There is always in February some one day, at least, when one smells the yet distant, but surely coming summer."

But it was the voice of the woman, now sixty years dead, expressing her still-strong connection to the child inside her that sealed the deal:

"Well do I remember the time when I thought there were two kinds of people in the world—children and grown-ups. And I think it is because I have been more or less a gardener all my life that I still feel like a child in many ways, although from the number of years I have lived I ought to know that I am quite an old woman."

By the time I left the exhibition I was in love with Gertrude Jekyll.

But then, who would not fall under the spell of a woman who, herself well-to-do, designed for no fee the gardens and interiors of the Home of Rest for Ladies of Small Means. Set in the woods of Surrey, the home was open to working women, mainly nurses and teachers, in need of a holiday. She decorated the common room of

the home with ladder-back chairs, an oak table, and country orna-
ments. Simple things were used, she said, to keep the interior har-
monious with the "simple truth and honesty" of the house's
timbered construction.

Her life struck me as reflecting the same qualities: simple truth
and honesty.

I trudged back to my flat, loaded down with books by and
about this extraordinary woman. I was tired but excited. More and
more I saw how complicated my own life had become; how over-
grown it was with thickets of worries and regrets, unearned vanities
and silly insecurities. Somehow Miss Jekyll had found a way to simplify, simplify. Perhaps I could, too.

That night Jean Gillespie called to give me details about the party
her friends were giving. "Saturday night. Drinks around eight-
thirty. Dinner at ten. There'll be wonderful food and great wine. So
come hungry and thirsty."

My attempts to find out what I should wear proved futile. "Oh,
dress any way you want," Jean said. I asked what she was wearing.
"I'm not sure yet. I'll see what strikes me at seven-thirty on Saturday night. Ring the buzzer marked Robert and Olivia Morgan."

My English friends were more specific with their advice. Dress
up. Arrive at least a half-hour late. Take a gift. The last two sugges-
tions were easy. I would take flowers and arrive at nine—after eating a light supper, of course. There was no way I could hold out
until ten to eat dinner.

But their suggestion to "dress up" still didn't solve the dilemma
of what to wear. For some reason I wanted to look good. Really

good. My guess was I had something to prove: that I could fit into this group of people described by Jean as "high rollers." Fit in for one night, anyway.

At precisely nine o'clock, wearing the black silk dress bought in Paris and carrying an armful of pale yellow roses, I rang the buzzer to the Morgans' apartment. A butler opened the door. Inside, I could see the party was in full swing. "Allow me to take your flowers, madam," said the butler, who then whisked them away, never to be seen again. So much for arriving late and bearing a gift, I thought.

I stood there, surrounded by a roomful of strangers engaged in animated conversation, wondering what to do next. A waiter passed by with a silver tray of tulip-shaped glasses filled with champagne. He seemed to have no intention of stopping, so I hailed him as I would a taxi, and took one. Then, just as I started to make my move toward a cluster of guests, I heard a booming laugh erupt behind me. I knew immediately it was Jean and turned around to say hello. Her appearance stunned me.

Jean looked like a movie star; a *large* movie star but a movie star nonetheless. She looked the way I imagined Geena Davis might look if she put on twenty pounds. Slowly I took in Jean's appearance. The woman who didn't know what she was going to wear was dressed in a draped red chiffon gown held up by two ribbons of red silk. Her dark hair was swept back into a French braid and her lips rouged the exact red of her dress. The perfection of all this—and her pretense about throwing herself together at the last moment— would have put me off were it not for one thing: her earrings.

"Remember these?" she asked, putting her hands up to the dopey-looking silver earrings she'd bought at the Freud Museum. They looked totally out of place with her getup. "These are to remind me that I don't really belong here. That I'm just an analyst sponging off some very rich friends." We both laughed, a conspiratorial laugh that suggested our awareness of being outsiders at this soiree.

"C'mon, love, let me take you around," Jean said, taking my hand and pulling me through the crowd. Each time she stopped to introduce me she would add on after my name, without pausing, "a reporter from America." Her need to identify me by what I did didn't bother me; everybody at the party had an identification added onto their names. *Gerald, a commodities trader . . . Fiona, a theater producer . . . Russell, a land developer . . . James and Terry, the horse breeders. . . .* I found myself thinking of Naohiro, of how pleasant it would be to have him sitting next to me. But would he even enjoy a party like this? I wondered.

It was a warm night, but a breeze coming in through the floor-to-ceiling windows made the temperature in the spacious drawing room seem almost pleasant. Jean suggested we work our way over to one of the open windows, where a man and woman stood talking. Seeing the two of them, I instantly thought of *The Great Gatsby.* He was wearing a white dinner jacket that accentuated his dark hair and slanted eyes. She was also dark-haired and wearing white—a simple silk dress, its only adornment a strand of pearls. They were talking face-to-face near a Steinway piano, holding each other's hands in a friendly yet intimate way.

"Oh, there's our host and hostess," Jean said. "Let me introduce you." I was anxious to meet this couple described by Jean as "self-made, salt-of-the-earth millionaires."

She was right. Despite their glamorous looks, Robert and Olivia Morgan turned out to be nothing like Jay and Daisy. For one thing, Olivia's voice was not "full of money." It was filled instead with curiosity and intelligence and the rhythms of a native Australian. Robert was more difficult to read. Clearly he was a hard-driving man with a razor-sharp mind. But there were hints also of a

thoughtful, poetic nature when he discussed with Jean a book by
William Trevor that they both were reading.

A butler appeared to announce that dinner was served. Jean and
I walked behind the host and hostess into a large dining room,
where five round tables, each seating eight people, were set with
sparkling crystal and gleaming silver. The whole room was lit by
candles that flickered from the movement of the guests entering. I
consulted the card I'd been handed. I was to sit at Table Number 5.
"My table, too," Jean whispered.

Two guests were already at the table when Jean and I sat down.
She introduced me to her friend Edward, a psychoanalyst, and to
Georgia, a ruthlessly fashionable woman who bore a striking resemblance to the late Diana Vreeland, the famous fashion editor. Arriving next was a young, attractive couple from Australia. "He's in
business with Robert," Jean whispered, leaning across the empty
seat between us. Finally, I was pleased to see the host and hostess
take their places at our table.

Almost immediately Georgia asked if anyone had read the
piece in the *Herald-Tribune* quoting John Updike on Ernest Hemingway. "He delivered an absolutely delicious line," she said. "Updike
pointed out that living wasn't what Hemingway did best, that we
should remember him as a writer." She laughed. "Quite the put-
down, isn't it?"

Edward, the analyst, weighed in with his opinion. "Perhaps.
Perhaps not. Maybe it wasn't a negative judgment but simply a
statement of fact. Hemingway's life was rather a mess, wasn't it?"

"Yes, but that's not the point," Robert said. "Who's to say that
Hemingway wouldn't prefer to be remembered for his writing and
not for what he did when he wasn't writing?"

Edward laughed. "Bob, you're starting to sound more like an
analyst every day."

"Well, *I* certainly wouldn't want to be remembered for the way I live," Georgia said wryly. "I want to be remembered for the way I dress." Everyone laughed.

"Well done," said Olivia, standing with her wineglass raised to make a toast. "And may none of us forget that dressing well is the best revenge."

"I don't think it's funny," Jean said suddenly and loudly. "Hemingway was a depressed man. He killed himself. Remember? Just like his father. Is that funny?" Her speech was noticeably slurred.

An awkward silence followed her outburst. It was hard to know what to say. I couldn't help but think of all the depressed men in Jean's life, including her own father. Finally, Robert came to the rescue, changing the subject to a play just opening in London. I saw Jean shoot him a grateful look.

The waiters appeared and began to serve the food. It was just before eleven and, despite my earlier dinner, I was ravenous. As soon as I saw my hostess lift her fork, I dug in.

At the end of the evening Georgia suggested we move the party—at least the one at our table—over to her place in Chelsea.

"Smashing idea," said Jean, whipping out a mirror to add a fresh coat of red lipstick, one that only approximated the actual shape of her mouth. Everyone agreed it was a capital idea and we began preparing ourselves for the short journey to Chelsea. Outside, I looked at my watch; it was a little before two.

It was just before dawn when we left Georgia's apartment. A few minutes later, when I stepped out of Robert and Olivia's car to enter my building, Jean leaned out of the window to call after me:

"Don't forget. Lunch at one. At the Connaught." She looked exhausted but also wired. Did I look like that, I wondered? One thing I knew: the muscles in my face hurt from too much animation over too long a period of time. Having fun really takes it out of you, I thought.

"See you then," Olivia chimed in, before letting her head drop back onto Robert's shoulder.

Although I'd already decided not to meet them for lunch, I said nothing. Later in the morning I'd phone and make my apologies.

It had been an exciting night, but I'd had my fill of life in the fast lane, at least for now. I liked the Morgans and their friends, but they were people who lived big, sprawling, complicated lives; lives that involved drivers and butlers and houses on more than one continent and partying around the clock. It suited them. And as long as I only had to do it once every five years or so, it suited me, too.

I undressed, took a shower, and put on a pair of soft cotton pajamas. It was Sunday and my plan was to sleep through the afternoon. But first I needed to unwind with a cup of tea and something to read. I reached for the small book of essays that celebrated the life and work of Gertrude Jekyll.

One essay, a personal recollection written by a horticulturist, described a visit to Miss Jekyll in 1931, the last year of her life. He wrote of the simplicity of Miss Jekyll's "modest and charming home amongst the trees on the sandy rising ground. Our tea was brought and we had it on occasional tables near the sunny windows, thin white bread and butter and a preserve (I do not remember what) and some little cakes. Her mellow voice floated on through the words of wisdom she imparted and I came away deeply moved by all I had seen and heard."

She found the life that suited her, I thought, closing the book. Work that interested her, a house she loved, good friends who came for tea and, of course, the company of her cats, Pinkie, Tavy, Tittle-bat, Tabby, and the ever-excitable Blackie. It was a simple life but by no means an unsophisticated one.

Remembering the candlelit glamour of the night before, I found myself comparing its luxurious excess with the elegant economy of Miss Jekyll's life. There was little doubt which suited me best: I was much more Jekyll than Hyde.

Still, turning off the lamp, I had to admit that every once in a while it was quite exciting to travel up front, in first class.

9

UP AT OXFORD

Dear Alice,

  Going back to school is like going back in time. Immediately, for better or for worse, you must give up a little piece of your autonomy in order to become part of the group. And every group, of course, has its hierarchies and rules—spoken and unspoken. It is like learning to live once again in a family—which, of course, is the setting where all learning begins.

                              Love, Alice

Driving up to Oxford from London on a clear Sunday morning, alone, and with no traffic on the road, the air still fragrant from Saturday's rain, singing along with Ella Fitzgerald on the radio, I felt like a sixteen-year-old who's just been given permission to drive the family car. And like an adolescent, I felt up to the challenge of whatever lay ahead.

Even the act of driving, which I usually found boring, took on an edge of pleasure. I shifted into overdrive and, still singing out loud with Ella, purposely passed a silver Jaguar. It was a move, I realized, that allowed me to relive simultaneously two of my adolescent fantasies: one, to be a singer like Ella, and two, to own a souped-up convertible and cruise the highways leaving startled but admiring drivers in my dust.

The souped-up car thing never worked out, but I actually pursued the Ella thing. At the Miss Henrietta Freedenberg School of Music in Baltimore, to be exact. Once a week, armed with my Rodgers and Hart songbook, I took three streetcars to Miss Henrietta's studio for a private singing lesson. There, Miss Henrietta would accompany me on the piano in her living room—or "studio" as she called it—while coaching me on how to properly breathe and "emote." Words to be "emoted" were penciled on my score in all capital letters by Miss Henrietta.

Although I had every reason to doubt my singing talent, I had no fear of failure. Not even when I got to the part in "My Funny Valentine" that begins "Is your mouth a little weak" and then rises precipitously to the phrase "When you open it to speak, are you SMART?" I still remember my excitement as I vocally climbed, or thought I climbed, the octaves to the summit where the word "SMART" stood alone, waiting to be conquered.

I do not remember when I wised up to the fact that my only musical talent lay in listening, not singing. Still, for the year or so that I sang Rodgers and Hart and the occasional Cole Porter tune in Miss Henrietta's living room, my adolescent optimism made the illusion of a career in jazz singing seem possible. Other illusions followed and, adolescence being what it is, they all seemed possible.

That's it, I thought, driving up to Oxford. *That's exactly what I'm feeling: the return of adolescent optimism.*

I don't know why I felt this way. Perhaps my excitement had to do with driving alone in a foreign country, where every road is an unknown one and every turn holds out the promise of an adventure. Perhaps it was the idea of returning briefly to the academic life; I was going up to Oxford to take a course in the history of the English village. Or perhaps it had to do with something I was learning about myself: that I was a naturally optimistic and curious person.

The funny thing is, I knew, that most of my friends would describe me in just such a way. But, to be honest, I'd never been sure it wasn't an act I was putting on—not to fool other people, but to fool myself. The world, I'd always thought, was much more welcoming and much less threatening if a person approached it with curiosity and optimism. It was an approach that had worked well for me, in both my personal and professional life. But sometimes I wondered if this really reflected my true nature, or whether I'd shaped my personality to fit some perceived notion of what it required to successfully navigate life.

But there was no one to please or not please on this trip. I could be as inward or as outward as I felt; I could be an observing person or an experiencing person; I could be optimistic or skeptical. And I was learning each day that, depending on the occasion and my mood, I had in my arsenal of feelings all of these responses.

Still, the dominant person I saw emerging was genuinely optimistic and curious. She really did love to meet people and explore new places. And, best of all, when things didn't work out, she moved on.

What can I say? She was plucky and, most of the time, not a whiner. Except for the occasional and sometimes expensive preoccupation about what to do with her not-so-manageable hair, I found her quite an agreeable traveling companion.

Friends in London had told me the drive to Oxford was an easy one, and they were right. What was not easy, however, was finding my way, once in Oxford, to Brasenose College, where those enrolled in the course were to stay.

I had been given a map of Oxford and directions to Brasenose, which was located in historic Radcliffe Square. I was also given instructions on how to gain access for my car into the gated and locked square: I was to leave the car at the entrance to Radcliffe Square, walk to the porter's lodge at Brasenose, pick up the key to unlock the gate to the square, walk back to my car, unlock the gate, drive into the square, park my car, and then get out and relock the gate before proceeding to the heavy, wooden doors of Brasenose. There, theoretically, a college porter would allow me to enter the college's interior courtyard and give me further instructions as to where to go.

What followed was a two-hour fiasco. To begin with, nothing

on the Oxford street map I had corresponded with reality. Most of the streets, it turned out, were one-way and to my annoyance always seemed to go the way I didn't want to go. For the next hour I found myself driving around the center of town in ever-widening circles. At one point I wound up on a road out in the Oxfordshire countryside.

The narrow, cobblestoned, tourist-filled streets were hellish enough, but the directions given by pedestrians whom I judged to be locals were even worse. At one point, however, I actually found myself at the corner of Brasenose Lane. I was elated, thinking I must at last be close to my destination. And I was. But there was a problem: I was at the back of Brasenose College and in order to enter the front—which was on Radcliffe Square—I had to start circling all over again.

Somewhere in this last Circle of Hell I lost, temporarily, all my adolescent optimism and high spirits.

Finally, just as I was considering abandoning the car and setting out on foot, I came upon the gated entrance to Radcliffe Square. Parking the car was easy; opening the gate was not. The key handed me by the college porter, a surly, unhelpful man dressed in a tired, shapeless black suit, was a huge, ancient-looking thing attached to a large board. As I struggled to open the gate, small crowds of tourists gathered to watch. Help finally came in the form of a passing taxi driver. He opened the gate; I drove through and parked in front of the massive, sixteenth-century stone walls guarding Brasenose College.

From the outside it looked like a medieval fortress: forbidding, impenetrable, damp. The unwelcome thought crossed my mind: had I made a mistake? Should I have taken a room at some nice bed-and-breakfast where there might be heat to warm the cold Oxford nights and a tea kettle whistling on the stove all day long? I found myself wondering, as Elisabeth Bishop did in a poem, "Should we have stayed at home and thought of here?"

But once I passed through the outer walls, through the damp darkness of the porter's lodge, and stepped out into the light of the interior courtyard—a rectangle of perfect emerald-green grass surrounded by buildings whose casement windows blazed with trailing red flowers—my doubts vanished. It was as though I had stepped into the Middle Ages. And into the great history of all those who throughout the centuries have studied at Oxford. Now, in a small way, I was a part of that.

I was shown to my rooms in the "Old Quad" part of Brasenose by Albert, a tall, thin student at nearby Lincoln College. Albert, who was born in Sri Lanka, earned money during the summer vacation by looking out for off-season students like me.

"You're lucky," Albert said, as he lugged my huge suitcase up three steep flights of narrow, winding steps. "Your rooms have a private bathroom." His accent was very British, clipped and clear.

My "rooms" during the school year were occupied by an undergrad and they looked it. The larger of the two rooms contained an aging mud-colored leather chair and matching sofa, a threadbare Turkish rug, a small desk, and a wooden table with matching chairs. The walls were bare and the tilted floors creaked. The overall effect was that of a rundown hospital waiting room. The bedroom was tiny; just a chest with drawers that either stuck or fell on the floor when pulled out, a small night table, and a lumpy cot that could barely support my weight.

But as Albert pointed out again, there was a private bath. Even better, I had been assigned rooms with a view. A breathtaking view; a view in its own way that rivaled the glories of E. M. Forster's Florentine room with a view.

On one side of the living room was a row of wide casement windows through which I could see not only the green grass and flowering courtyard of Brasenose, but also the outlines of the medieval Radcliffe Square buildings: the massive dome of the oddly named Radcliffe Camera, home to part of the Bodleian Library's two million volumes; the fourteenth-century spires of the Church of St. Mary the Virgin, the spectacular towers of All Souls' College, where the legendary Lawrence of Arabia once studied.

I opened the windows and leaned out. No matter where I looked there was a spire or dome pushing its way into the soft, pliant backdrop of the Oxford sky. It looked unreal, like a stage set for a fairy tale.

I looked around the room, so stark and yet so full of the past. Who, I wondered, had lived here and studied here over the centuries? I knew that George Washington's great-grandfather studied at Brasenose, and so did the grandfather of John Adams; it was not inconceivable that one of them might have occupied these rooms. Of course, if I strolled farther down the road I would come across Merton, where T. S. Eliot studied, and St. John's, the college that was home to A. E. Housman.

I looked through the windows again. Oxford beckoned.

Oxford. The word rolled around in my mind, conjuring up the best of Britain. Not to mention several episodes of my favorite television show, *Masterpiece Theatre.* It thrilled me to know that the Oxford portion of *Brideshead Revisited* had been filmed right here at Brasenose. If I closed my eyes, I could see Sebastian Flyte leaning across the window box into Charles Ryder's room on the day they first met.

I couldn't wait to get out on the streets and walk among all that history. The Ashmolean Museum, established in 1683 and the oldest museum in Britain. Blackwell's bookshop, offering one of the largest selections of books in the world since 1879. The Sheldonian Theatre, the first building designed by Sir Christopher Wren, in 1663.

But there was something I needed to do before leaving my ivory tower to hit the Oxford streets: I needed to take a nap.

At dinner that night I met my classmates. There were eighteen of us, ranging in age from the middle twenties to upward of sixty. We took our first meal in the soaring, formal dining hall at Brasenose, where the regular undergrads ate. It was an evening of get-acquainted small talk, pleasant enough, but ultimately unsatisfying. Everyone was in their introductory, best-foot-forward mode; I longed for some real conversation.

Listening to the voices around me I found myself remembering my first meeting with Naohiro. How quickly, I thought, he and I passed from small talk to real talk. I could still hear his soft, musical voice telling me on the train to Giverny, *You must go to Sainte-Chapelle to stand in the light;* and my own voice responding, *And you must go to Père-Lachaise Cemetery to stand in the past.*

But it was unfair to compare this first meeting with my classmates to that encounter with Naohiro. It was also preemptory. As the candlelit dinner at Brasenose progressed, I found myself drawn to several people in the group.

After dinner I set out alone to explore Oxford. It was a cold, windy night and the streets were almost deserted. Within a few minutes I was shivering, my body tensed in knots against the strong wind. Common sense told me to turn back, but the magic of Oxford propelled me forward, into one narrow lane after another. Finally, the cold and the cobblestone streets, some so uneven that the stones hurt right through my shoes, became too much of a struggle. I decided to return to Brasenose.

The problem: I hadn't a clue as to where I was or how to get back to the college. I'd brought along a map—I learned early in my travels never to be without a map—but it was the same one that had led me in circles earlier in the day.

I looked up at the street signs. I was somewhere on a residential street called Holywell, which on the map appeared to be not too far from Brasenose. As I stood beneath a street light studying the map, a woman turned the corner and headed for one of the houses. She unlocked the door; a circle of light spilled out. I could see through the door the warm glow of lamps and pictures lining the pale yellow walls. An orange-and-white cat, back arched, tail plumed up into the air, suddenly appeared to greet her, rubbing up against her legs. The woman bent to stroke the top of his head; the cat leaned in to her caress. "Did you miss me?" I heard her ask in a voice flushed with affection.

A wave of homesickness washed over me. Standing on a strange street, a cold mist swirling in on top of the wind, lost and alone, I thought of the warmth of my own house, of my friends, and of Tasha, the cat who waited patiently for me to come home. Then I remembered the cold, spartan rooms that awaited me at Brasenose,

the lumpy cot with its unyielding pillow and scratchy sheets. A part
of me wilted.

Walking back to Radcliffe Square, I thought of something my
mother used to read to me. It was a passage from a book by her favorite naturalist, Wendell Berry. In it he offers advice to those about
to enter the wilderness. "Always in the big woods when you leave
familiar ground and step off alone into a new place," he wrote,
"there will be, along with the feelings of curiosity and excitement, a
little nagging of dread. It is the ancient fear of the Unknown, and it
is your first bond with the wilderness you are going into."

Eight years earlier my mother had carried his words with her
into the hospital. I'd found them neatly copied in her handwriting
on a piece of paper in her handbag, the one I took home from the
hospital after she died. She'd taken them with her to prepare for
the journey ahead of her. It was to be her last trip, one that would
take her into a new kind of wilderness, an unmapped territory
known only to those who entered it.

Still, I knew that every small wilderness we enter—even one
composed only of the unfamiliar streets of Oxford—offers a
chance to practice for the larger one that lies in all our futures.

The course on "The English Village and Cottage Life" focused on
the history of village life in England and how these small communi-
ties shaped the character of the English people. I found the lectures
to be mixed: some quite stimulating, others deeply boring. Lectures on England's land migration patterns, for instance, simply did
not do it for me. Still, others in the group seemed intensely interested in the same lectures I found dry and statistical.

At least, that's the impression conveyed by the fury of their note-taking and the number of questions they asked during such lectures. This kind of academic zeal often sent Ellen, a hip New Yorker with a sarcastic streak, into orbit. "What is it with this note-taking and question-asking?" she'd hiss into my ear. "Isn't there a statute of limitations on trying to be the smartest kid in class?"

The answer, I could have told her—but didn't—was: no, there is no statute of limitations. I knew this to be true because occasionally during a class I found myself listening not only to Ellen's mocking comments but to those of an inner companion as well: "Perhaps," this companion—whose name was Insecurity—whispered to me, "you're just not as smart as the others."

At such times I reminded myself that life was not a test and no one was grading me. Except my own superego, of course.

As the days passed and the group settled into the routine of lectures followed by trips out into the English countryside, I realized how much life at Oxford resembled life in high school. Small groups formed, hints of romance surfaced, complaints about the lodgings arose, rumors flew.

"Did you hear about Jane and Mike?" a classmate asked at breakfast one morning. "They're gone. Just up and left. No one knows why." But everyone had a theory. As the day progressed, several explanations emerged for Jane and Mike's abrupt departure, ranging from sudden illness to impending divorce.

I loved it. All of it. I loved being back in a learning situation surrounded by opinionated, smart, and complex people. I loved the political arguments that started at dinner and ended hours later in a pub on the High Street. I loved the rumors and the gossip. I even loved watching the way in which small circles formed and broke away from the group. I saw it as a valuable lesson in the psychology of how people select—often after an initial mis-selection—the company they prefer to keep.

All of it, even the occasional petty or snide observation made by one person or another, I found endearing. Endearing because it was so *human*. I viewed the group, myself included, with a lenient, familial eye, one that ultimately valued our connectedness over everything else.

Of course, caught up in the group dynamics of the situation, we were in fact functioning as a family. Although the hierarchy was blurred—sometimes one group seemed dominant, at other times not—we all had our roles within the family. There were the elders of the group and there were the young and the restless. There were the intellectuals and the practical-minded; the charismatic leaders and the uncertain followers; the sophisticates and the naifs; the winners and the losers; the fun-seekers and the complainers.

It was this last category that, ultimately, interested me most. I found myself observing each classmate from this angle, looking for signs—I gradually came to think of them as symptoms—that identified them as either fun-seekers or complainers. The fun-seekers, I noted, were spontaneous and flexible. They approached each day and each situation with a willingness to ride whatever wave came along, just for the experience of it. The complainers, on the other hand, would only catch a wave if it was exactly to their liking. Anything else drew loud protestations about how it was not what they expected.

I wanted to be a fun-seeker. Not only because I just plain wanted more fun in my life, but because intuitively I knew my energies were working in that direction. To my surprise, it was Albert who gave me my first lesson in how to seek out fun.

Albert, along with the rest of us, had been sucked into the vortex of this purloined family. He spent a lot of time with us, eating meals, going out in the evenings, acting as a sort of guide and concierge. His role was that of the Oxford insider; the one who knows the system and how it operates. My guess was that the insider role was not the one usually assumed by Albert, who seemed a reserved, almost shy young man. But as time passed he seemed to grow into it. And to enjoy it.

Albert, the son of psychiatrists, liked to tell stories about Oxford and, as he grew more comfortable with us, about himself. Although he was probably not aware of it, his personal stories often opened up a view, for those who cared to look, into the inner Albert.

One late afternoon while sharing a glass of sherry with a half-dozen of us, Albert recalled a temporary job he'd had in London, one ruled over by a difficult, demanding, never-satisfied boss. He commuted by train to London every day. One day his train was late. "By the time I arrived at the station in London I was already fifteen minutes late," Albert told us. "And I knew when I got to work I would be fired. So I thought about it for a few minutes. Then I thought, 'Why not turn this mishap into an adventure?' So I decided to go to Cornwall right from Paddington Station."

He never returned to the job. "But," he said, "I had a wonderful time in Cornwall."

For some reason I was quite taken with Albert's philosophy of turning a mishap into an adventure. When I returned to my rooms that evening I, who never took notes in class, got out my spiral binder and wrote, "Must experimentally test Albert's Theorem of M=EA (Mishap equals Excellent Adventure)."

However, I didn't realize fully how much it impressed me until several weeks later in Italy when I found myself, by mistake, on a train going to Assisi instead of Arezzo.

Dumped out of the train, standing in the station at the foot of

Monte Subasio, three miles below the Umbrian town of Assisi, I thought, "Why not turn this mishap into an adventure?" On an earlier day trip to Assisi I'd explored a charming small hotel that hung over the mountain's edge, thinking that someday I would return for a longer visit.

Fate, or so I convinced myself, had plunked me down in Assisi sooner rather than later for that visit. I decided to stay for a few days.

That night, as I sat on the outdoor terrace of the hotel, I silently toasted Albert, the man who turned a mishap into an adventure. And who not so incidentally made me realize how simple it is to do. How simple and how necessary. It seemed an important lesson.

As things turned out, it was not the only lesson I was to learn from Albert during my stay at Brasenose. It was through Albert that I met Barry, the Oxford instructor I would remember above all others.

10

A Cotswold Encounter

Dear Alice,

How odd that a chance meeting with a woman named Letty would add a large piece to the puzzle of how to enjoy life as you grow older. Letty's found the secret, I think, to staying young. How? By responding as a child does: seeing the world as it is, not as we wish it to be.

Love, Alice

The first field trip scheduled for the class was to the Cotswold village of Burford. For me it came just in time, this jaunt out of the lecture hall and into the actual countryside that gave rise to cottage life in England. I had already cut class one morning to travel on my own to the nearby village of Woodstock, and was really looking forward to visiting Burford.

It was a sunny, cool morning when we left Oxford for the hour-long drive to the Cotswolds. Through the windows of the bus I watched a gentle wind move the sun slantwise, like the beams from a lighthouse, across the sea of Oxfordshire meadows. Sheep grazed, streams gurgled, dales quietly rose into hills, tall grass bent before the wind. We had arrived in quintessential English countryside.

I got out my book on the Cotswolds and read the names on the map: Shipton-under-Wychwood, Bourton-on-the-Water, Moreton-in-Marsh, Stow-on-the-Wold. How I loved these quaint names. In my head I had a picture, formed long ago by seeing photographs in one of Grandmother's books, of what life was like in English villages such as these. The corner pub, the medieval church towers, the flocks of sheep driven to market through the village, the thatched-roof cottages and wild, blooming gardens, the square where everyone gathered: this was English country life as it existed in my head.

The drive from Oxford to Burford took us first through Witney. It was a village that seemed less idyllic and picture-perfect than many of the better-known Cotswold tourist attractions.

In Witney, the quick eye caught glimpses of real people living real lives. Housewives with hunched shoulders and weary expres-

sions carried their string-tied packages from the butcher shops. Elderly men sat in the sun, canes by their sides, caps pushed back to
reveal faces sculpted by hard work. Bored-looking teenagers gathered in front of a drugstore, flirting and puffing on cigarettes, their
schoolbooks lying in piles on the ground. At Angelina's Beauty
Shop a young shampoo girl with butter-colored streaks in her long,
dark hair stood daydreaming at the half-open door, a wet towel
slung over her shoulder.

I tried to imagine what it was like to be young in a place such as
Witney. Does growing up in a small town make for a smaller life? I
wondered. Or does it offer a more secure, less complicated one?

I knew from my conversations with the owner of an Oxford
bookshop—a smart, observant man who grew up in Oxfordshire—
that many young people from nearby villages, restless for adventure, emigrated at an early age. "I'm too old for that," he said.
"Oxfordshire is where I'll make my stand."

After talking to him, I thought of Grandmother, who moved to
America in her late fifties. Unlike so many younger people, she
moved out of necessity, not the desire for adventure. From her I
learned that the older emigrant feels something the young do not:
the deep sadness of leaving home. The "Old Country," she used to
call it, when telling me bedtime stories about her life in Scotland.
Occasionally, she would pull out from under the bed a cardboard
box. Inside, carefully wrapped in tissue paper, was a kilt woven in
the tartan of her clan. "It's from the Old Country," she would tell
me with pride and, I later realized, sadness, too.

For a long time I thought the Old Country was the name of an
ancient land, one that, like Atlantis, no longer existed. I pictured it
as a place of rolling green hills and deep glens, of cottages with
smoke puffing through chimneys; a place populated with kind

women wearing sturdy shoes and bright tartan kilts; a place that somehow, for no reason I could figure out, just disappeared one day.

When we arrived in Burford I set out to explore the town on my own. Positioned on a hillside, its main street rising dramatically from a small stone bridge spanning the poetically named Windrush River, Burford retains the unspoiled charm of the seventeenth-century wool town it once was. With its steep main street—the High Street—and its quaint, honey-colored limestone inns and shops, Burford emerges from the Oxfordshire countryside like a mirage bathed in golden light.

Standing at the low point of the town, looking up the long street that seemed to rise until it simply disappeared into the sky, I felt as though I'd stumbled across an English version of Brigadoon: a storybook village that existed somewhere out of real time. But it was not just the look of the village; even the friendly, sturdy locals out on their morning errands conjured up some primitive image of how life ought to be.

Earlier that morning I had been told by one of the Brasenose "scouts"—the name given to the good-natured women who clean the rooms at Oxford's colleges—that there were two things I should do in Burford. "You mustn't miss the church," my scout said as we chatted at the top of the perilously steep steps leading to my rooms. "Oh, it's a beauty, dear. And mind you, get a jar or two of the homemade lemon curd. There's nowhere you'll get better curd than Burford, I always say. It's quite lovely."

Her recommendations suited me. Not only do I, too, think lemon curd—a custardlike combination of lemons, sugar, eggs, and butter—quite lovely, I also think there is nothing better than having as short a list as possible of must-see places when you travel. A two-item list seemed about right. I decided to visit the church first. That, I reasoned, would open the rest of the day for lemon-curd shopping and creative wandering.

The Church of St. John the Baptist was just as my scout described it: a beauty. Left behind by the Normans, the church had changed and grown over the centuries—it was fairly large for a village the size of Burford—but care had been taken to preserve its splendid original architecture. I lingered for quite a while in the cool stone interior. The air inside was redolent with the smell of the damp, fertile earth seeping in from the surrounding countryside; it was like breathing in life itself.

Outside, on my way back to the High Street, I stopped to admire the stalks of purple lavender blooming along the pathway. I smiled, remembering all the handmade sachets Grandmother and I had filled with lavender from her garden. Months later the small, stitched-together squares of blue silk would be given away as Christmas gifts.

I squeezed the blossoms between my fingers, releasing their aromatic scent. Instantly, like a genie let loose from a bottle, Grandmother was there, standing beside me, in her no-nonsense pith helmet. The helmet was a gift from my father, who wore one himself during the summer months. Grandmother wore hers as a sun hat when she worked in the garden.

Suddenly a voice behind me broke into my thoughts: "If you put the crushed lavender under your pillow, you'll get a fine night's sleep."

I turned around and saw the voice belonged to a woman with wavy, reddish-gray hair, lively blue eyes, and fair skin that was papery and lined, like a sheet of parchment. She wore a well-tailored poplin raincoat and carried a smart-looking tan leather purse with a gold clasp. A tweed skirt peeked out from beneath her raincoat. She looked, I thought, as Mrs. Miniver might have looked in her later years. She also struck me as a woman who in her youth might very well have had a rose named in her honor.

"Yes, I've been told that about lavender," I said. "By my grandmother."

"Well, now, that's what a grandmother's for, isn't it? To pass on stories about lavender and such."

I was struck by the wry tone of her voice; it conveyed a sharpness that attracted me. Emboldened, I told her the story of the lavender sachets and my thrifty Scottish grandmother. I think I even mentioned the pith helmet. It pleased me that she laughed in all the right places. Then I told her about my mission to purchase some of Burford's finest lemon curd. For some reason she seemed interested in all this, so I took the next step: I introduced myself. She replied, saying, "And I'm Letty Thompson."

I liked Letty Thompson from the start. She had a responsive air about her, one that suggested she was an intellectually curious woman. I could see it in her blue eyes, in the half-amused way they studied whatever came to their attention. *She reminds me of someone*, I thought. But try as I might, I couldn't summon up the identity of the small shadow that, in my mind, accompanied Letty Thompson.

"Do you live in Burford?" I asked.

"Oh, yes, I do now," she said. She told me she had retired five years earlier to Burford—where she'd grown up—after spending her working life in London. "The thing I love about living in Burford," she said, "is that you can walk through the town and always meet someone you know."

"And someone you don't know," I replied. "Like me."

She laughed. "Well, now that we know one another, would you

like me to walk you up the High Street and help you find that lemon curd?"

"I'd love it," I said.

For the next hour or so, I walked through the village with Letty Thompson as my guide. Up the High Street we went, then on to Sheep Street and Priory Lane, circling back to the High Street. And as we walked we talked. Although Letty gave no hint of being bored with village life, I could tell she was eager to meet new people.

Letty told me about her life in London as a young single woman—"spinster" is the word she used—and later, as an older single woman. She told me about the dressmaker's shop where she had designed and sewn dresses for well-to-do ladies after giving up her hope of becoming an artist. She'd taken up painting again, she told me, since retiring to Burford.

"Watercolors," she said. "Landscapes and animals, mostly. I rather fancy painting the birds hereabout."

"In other words, you might be described as Burford's answer to Audubon."

"Yes, one could say that. Although perhaps just a bit more accomplished than your Audubon," she said wryly. I laughed, silently admiring the quickness of her wit. It was one of the things I most admired about the Brits, their sly but sharp humor.

Suddenly Letty stopped walking. She turned to face me. "Would you like to see some most interesting paintings?" she asked. "They're in a little gallery just near here. Quite captivating if you like the look of primitive art." The artist's name was Joan

Gillchrest, Letty told me. "She's seventy-five and lives in Cornwall, in a small fishing town called Mousehole. She's painted a long while. And with some success, too."

We turned off the main street onto Bear Court, a narrow, cobblestoned lane, then stopped before a small shop with the sign WREN GALLERY. Peering into the window, our heads close together, I caught the scent of Letty's perfume. It was fresh and light and smelled like orange blossoms floating on top of a sea breeze. It suited her, I thought.

"Let's go in, shall we?" Letty said, leading the way.

The paintings were wonderful. Charming and sophisticated, they were like something out of a child's book: tiny bold blocks of color painted without perspective onto the flat canvas. It was as though Brueghel and Grandma Moses had collaborated to bring to life the village of Mousehole. Tiny painted villagers marched by, leading their dogs along a frozen canal. Women wearing hats and mufflers stopped to talk by a seawall, gesturing as they exchanged the news of the day. Men in long dark coats and caps stood at the canal's edge, where boats were trapped like fish frozen in the icy waters.

As we stood there in the Wren Gallery, we saw spring come to the village, too: flowers bloomed, cats stretched in the sun, and crabbers sailed in bright red boats straight from the bathtubs of my childhood. Like Alice in Wonderland, I had fallen into a strange, captivating country: Mousehole. Even the name held the promise of remarkable adventures.

What made it more exciting, though, was that Letty Thompson had fallen with me into this Wonderland. Together we raced from painting to painting, pointing out a black dog here, a skating figure there, the slumped posture of a sausage-shaped dog on a leash, the tilt of a head in conversation, the single stroke of a brush that summed up a cloud or a wave.

Neither of us wanted the other to miss anything. And somewhere in the sharing and the laughing, Letty and I moved past the superficial barriers of age and background. Of time, too: I could see the young woman Letty had been and, beneath that, the adventuresome, fun-loving girl.

It was then I knew the identity of the shadow trailing Letty. It was my grade school chum, Ducky Harris, with whom I'd shared everything. It was Ducky who shared my preadolescent passion for swimming and tap dancing, for scouring thrift shops in search of exotic beaded evening purses, for putting on plays in Eve Blum's club basement.

And it was Ducky who taught me how to lighten my hair by dousing it with lemon juice and sitting in the sun. And it was from Ducky that I learned it was okay to wear navy blue with green. The two of us even had matching outfits—red beanies and white smarty-pants shorts—that we wore each Saturday to our tap-and-tumbling classes at the YWCA. For some reason—I wasn't sure why—Letty made me feel the way Ducky had: profoundly alive.

After an hour or so of Mousehole-watching, Letty and I decided to take tea at the Golden Pheasant Hotel. Seated in front of a window overlooking the street, we watched the townspeople go by. We talked without constraint, the two of us, the way travelers often do when they meet someone they like but know they'll never see again.

After asking me about my trip, Letty told me she regretted not having traveled more. "I always wanted to go to China," she said. "When I was a little girl I read about the Great Wall and the Forbidden City, and, oh, just the names caused quite the stir in me. Then there were the books later—what I call the Pearl Buck influence— that made it all seem so romantic." She laughed. "I was always sure if I went to China I'd meet an exciting foreigner who'd sweep me off my feet."

I told her that I thought Paris was my China; that for as long as I could remember Paris was the city I'd dreamed of making my home. "Maybe that's why Paris—even on my very first visit—always seemed familiar to me," I said. I described visiting Père-Lachaise to search, always unsuccessfully, for Proust's grave. "Maybe I don't want to find it," I said, as much to myself as to Letty. "Maybe I like the idea of having unfinished business in Paris."

Letty poured more tea into our cups. "I wonder if the tea in China tastes different," she said, lifting the white porcelain cup to her lips.

I laughed. "Oh, Letty, wouldn't it be fun if you could pop over to Paris when I'm there. It's not that difficult now, you know. And you could stay with me."

"Yes, being with you would be grand," she said, leaving it at that.

Later, when Letty and I walked down the High Street, our arms linked, to purchase the almost-forgotten lemon curd, we stopped again at the pristine rows of lavender outside the Church of St.

John the Baptist. It was almost time for me to board the bus back to
Oxford.

I began saying good-bye to Letty when suddenly she bent over
and broke off a stalk of the purple flowers. "There's lavender," she
said, handing me the blooms. "That's for remembrance."

Impulsively, I kissed Letty on the cheek. "I could never forget
you," I said. Then to lighten up the moment, I added, "We may not
have Paris, but we'll always have Mousehole," and we both laughed.

Later that night as I sat in my rooms writing in my journal and
spooning lemon curd onto a biscuit, I read the white paper wrapped
round the lid of the jar: "Specially prepared for Aubrey Newman at
Christmas Court. 94, High Street, Burford, Oxfordshire." Carefully, I flattened the paper and pressed it, like a flower, between the
pages of my notebook.

I thought of Letty, of her remark about how she loved living in
a town where you could walk about and "always meet someone you
know." In some ways, it was the opposite of what lay behind this
trip—my wish to break away from being a known entity. And yet in
London, from time to time, I'd felt the tug of familiarity and the
wish to belong somewhere.

It was a cold night and I sat wrapped in a quilt listening to the
wind outside. Distracted, I got up and walked to my window.
There, gathered in an adjoining courtyard, were a dozen or so
young people, some wearing frock coats and others in costumes
that had an Elizabethan look about them.

Despite the cold they seemed to be rehearsing something in a small amphitheater at the next college. I could see them gesturing theatrically as they entered and exited with great flourish, but even after opening my window I could not make out the words above the wind.

For a long while I stood watching at my window. *A Midsummer Night's Dream,* I decided, finally. That's what they're rehearsing.

I closed the window, and walked across the room to the view I loved most. I could see the majestic dome of the Radcliffe Camera and St. Mary's spire, both lit from below. The lights from the rooms surrounding Brasenose formed changing patterns on the emerald-green grass below. As people turned off their lights to retire for the night, pieces of the pattern disappeared. Then, as late-night concertgoers returned to their rooms, switching on the lamps inside, other patterns took their place.

I inhaled the air, deeply, as if to take it all in and make it a part of me.

But perhaps what I really wanted was to make me a part of it: of Oxford and its history, of this windy starry night, of these rooms in Brasenose College that for this brief time belonged to me.

That night I dreamed. One of those crazy, mixed-up dreams that if you were going to your analyst the next day, you'd spend the whole hour talking about—partly because you wanted to understand what your unconscious was telling you and partly because you wanted to experience again the feelings unlocked by the dream.

It is a sunny Saturday morning and Ducky Harris and I are walking along Clay Street, a small alley near the YWCA that is home to several wholesale florists. Suddenly Ducky bends over to pick up a discarded snapdragon stalk.

When she stands up I notice she has on a hat, a green plaid tam-o'-shanter, one just like Grandmother wore when we went Christmas shopping downtown at Hutzler's department store.

But Ducky doesn't look like Grandmother. She also doesn't look like Ducky. She looks like some movie star I'd seen on the posters outside the old Century movie house.

She says something to me, the red-haired woman who's wearing Grandmother's tam-o'-shanter. I try to make out exactly what the words are, but there's just too much unconscious dream static in the way. I can see her mouth moving, forming words, but the sound disappears before reaching me.

Then suddenly I could hear her. "Hello, it's me," she said, smiling. "I'm still here."

Brasenose College
Oxford

50P

11

THE DANCING PROFESSOR

Dear Alice,

    I think what I will remember long after I've forgotten rural England's economic history & patterns of settlement may be the lesson taught by Barry, an instructor in ballroom dancing. Not only did I learn the quickstep & cha-cha from Barry, but, more important, I relearned something I had forgotten: the pure joy of letting go & just having fun. Alice, try not to forget this again. Further down the road you may need this knowledge much more than English history.

Love, Alice

One night at dinner Albert asked if anyone in the group would like to take a lesson in ballroom dancing. Immediately a groan went up from one end of the table. Oxford was filled with concerts and plays and lectures, so why, the groan suggested, would anyone be interested in ballroom dancing? Particularly, as someone pointed out, when a Chopin concert was being offered at a nearby hall.

Often it was fun to go to one of the concerts or plays that seemed to take place in every church or hall in Oxford. But occasionally I liked to break away from the group and see what I could find on my own.

Sometimes I was lucky. The night, for instance, I watched a movie—*The Bodyguard*—with a group of American college students. They were spending the summer at Oxford, taking courses and quartered in a dorm on the other side of Brasenose in the New Quad—so named because of its recent arrival on the Oxford land-scape: circa 1878. I met the students on my way back from a visit with a friend quartered in the New Quad. After approaching them to ask where I could buy a soft drink, we began talking about what they were studying and what I was studying. Before long, pizzas arrived and the whole lot of us were watching a movie in a large room furnished with worn armchairs and sofas. I looked around at the boys sprawled barefooted across the sofas, taking huge bites out of pepperoni pizzas, and the girls sobbing softly when Kevin Costner and Whitney Houston were forced to part. It reminded me of home; I felt deliciously comfortable.

Sometimes, though, I wasn't so lucky. There was that night when I bumped into a couple from Baltimore who were in Oxford for one night. I knew them vaguely—we'd met at a large party given by mutual friends—and when they suggested dinner at a pub, it sounded like a good idea. Three hours later, after listening to a minute-by-minute rundown of every detail of their week-long tour of the Cotswolds, I yearned to be put out of my misery.

On the night that Albert suggested we try ballroom dancing, I had nothing planned. Several people, mostly couples, were quite enthusiastic about the idea. They asked me to join them.

"It'll be fun," Ellen said. "And, besides, I could use the physical contact."

My answer was immediate and not entirely honest. "Oh, I'm too tired for dancing," I said, although I wasn't. "I think I'll just take a short walk and then read a bit."

As I walked back to my rooms I wondered why I had dismissed the idea and why I'd felt the need to offer a phony excuse. Actually, I loved to dance. When I was sixteen, a girlfriend and I used to sneak out on weekends to a Latin American ballroom. Dressed and made-up to look like twenty-one—which was the age requirement at the ballroom—we'd sit at a table sipping 7Up, hoping that the silky-looking young men circling the room would ask us to dance.

Although I had no real idea of how to mambo, samba, or tango, I had learned, to my surprise, that I could follow anyone who did. I thought of it as a gift, this ability to follow such intricate steps without any instruction; a gift similar to playing the piano by ear.

I knew my mother would kill me if she found out about my

dancing at the ballroom, but frankly I didn't care. In these moments of dancing I saw myself as a sophisticated, independent woman destined for a life of adventure—probably as a writer living in some foreign land.

Secretly I prided myself on being a good dancer; it made me feel in control of my body. Sometimes, however, I suspected what I liked about dancing was the opposite: that when I was dancing I didn't need to control my body. On the dance floor I simply closed my eyes and gave myself up to the exciting, pulsating music.

It was only at the Latin American Ballroom, among strangers, that I allowed myself such sensual freedom. At the school dances I stumbled over my partner's feet, almost drowning out the music with a steady stream of apologies: *Sorry. My fault. Excuse me.* It was like leading a double life: in one, I was a bold, sensual woman, unafraid of my attraction to danger; in the other, an uncertain teenager, full of conflicts about the physical world of touch and feeling and intense longing.

Perhaps it was the memory of dancing at the Latin American Ballroom that made me suddenly decide I wanted to go dancing that night at Lincoln College.

I ran back to the porter's lodge hoping that Albert would still be there. When I arrived, breathless, he and the group were just setting out. I fell into step next to Ellen, who, I noticed, had changed from pants into a dress and high heels.

She greeted me with an amused look. "I see that maybe I am not the only one in need of some physical contact," she said, smiling.

When we reached Lincoln College, Albert led us into one of the buildings and through a maze of hallways and steps to a large, almost empty room where our dance instructor, Barry, awaited us.

There were folding chairs placed on the bare wood floors and in the corner an ancient record player was blaring out the Bee Gees version of "Stayin' Alive." A few couples and two or three young men were already there, practicing the complicated steps in a way that suggested they did this a lot. One of the young men, particularly—a stocky fellow dancing alone—was really into it. The concentration on his face was like that of a surgeon about to make the first incision in the brain of a patient.

I don't know what I expected, but somehow this stuffy bare room with its out-of-date sound system was not it.

Barry, however, was the greatest disappointment. Short, pot-bellied, and balding, Barry appeared to be in his early fifties. He wore a short-sleeved, wildly patterned Hawaiian shirt that stopped just beneath his pot belly. When he spoke, his accent was coarse and unpleasant. Despite all this, Barry exuded self-confidence. He seemed to see himself as Fred Astaire: dashing, debonair, and charming.

To my surprise Barry started us off with a lesson in the waltz. The married couples who'd come along had no trouble stumbling through their steps together; they after all had been partners for years and were used to one another's mistakes. For those of us who were single it was more difficult. I felt especially timid and retired to a corner chair to watch.

It was interesting to observe the two married couples who'd chosen dancing over Chopin. They were really enjoying themselves, enjoying the physical pleasure of dancing. From my window at Brasenose I'd watch both of these couples walk across the quad to breakfast. They were always holding hands. I watched them now, laughing and touching on the dance floor, and couldn't help but feel a surge of envy.

It was only then that I noticed Albert. Albert, who off the dance floor seemed quite reserved, was a sensational and exciting dancer. Tall and elegant, he turned into a different person when he was dancing.

By this time, everyone was having fun. Except me. I had accepted Albert's invitation to dance, but for some reason felt extremely uncomfortable dancing with him. Within minutes I found myself reverting to my awkward high school personality. *Excuse me. Was that your foot? Sorry. My fault.* My cheeks burned with embarrassment and humiliation.

After a brief turn around the floor, I thanked Albert and returned to sit on the sidelines. I didn't know why I felt so uptight; there were quite a few people making fools of themselves on the dance floor. So what was stopping me?

A man's voice interrupted my thoughts: "It's time you got up and danced," said the voice. It was Barry. Before I could say no, he pulled me out of the chair and onto the center of the floor.

"Now, with the aid of my partner," Barry announced to the class, "I'm going to show you how to do the quickstep."

Oh my God, I thought, he's going to use *me* to teach the quickstep to the rest of the group? The only thing I knew about the quickstep was that I'd seen it done a few weeks earlier in a movie called *Strictly Ballroom.* And that it was, well, quick.

"Barry," I said, "you'd better get another partner. I can't do this."

"Sure you can," he said. "Just follow me, lovey."

What can I say? It was like watching a caterpillar turn into a butterfly. Barry *was* Fred Astaire: incredibly light on his feet, graceful, gentle in his touch but firm in his lead. After a few minutes of tension I relaxed and gave myself up to the dancing. And to Barry.

Through the quickstep—*Quick-quick-slow; quick-quick-slow*—I let Barry lead me. And the cha-cha: *One, two, cha-cha-cha; one, two, cha-cha-cha.* Then the foxtrot and the samba. By this time when Barry told me to do something I did it.

Once again I was the sixteen-year-old girl at the Latin American Ballroom, uninhibited and in touch with my body. I arched my back. I pointed my toes. I turned my head, first to one side, then the other, dipping as I did so, just like the ballroom dancers I'd seen on television. It was almost laughable that I, who did not like to be given directions, who liked instead to do things my own way, was so willing to do exactly what Barry told me to do.

For hours we glided, dipped, swooped, and laughed our way across the hallowed floors of Lincoln College. I danced with almost everyone there, including the man who liked to dance by himself. He turned out to be quite good, I thought, when he had a partner.

By the end of the evening no one in the group had any defenses left. We were all quite willing to make fools of ourselves by performing, under Barry's instructions, some of the dances from *Saturday Night Fever.*

Standing next to one another in a straight line, we danced to the sound of the Bee Gees singing "Stayin' Alive . . ." I moved from side to side, first lifting one arm up toward the ceiling, index finger pointed; then swinging the same arm down across my body, I pointed to the floor. Just like John Travolta. Minus the white suit, of course.

We repeated this dance several times. The music grew louder and the room warmer. Perspiration dripped down my back and my hair stuck to my neck in a clump; I was sure my makeup had melted into an unflattering Phantom of the Opera look. But I didn't care.

And I didn't care that the music was corny and the dancing hopelessly unhip. This was not about being hip; it was about having fun. Pure, sheer, unabashed fun.

Why, I wondered, couldn't I feel this way more often? The answer, I decided, was that having fun isn't really what most of us do best. What most of us do best is work and worry. Often we combine the two into one consuming preoccupation: worrying about work. Are we doing a good job? Where do we stack up in terms of our colleagues? Do we work hard enough? Do we work too hard? And how can we do what it takes to have a successful career without sacrificing family life?

Worrying about children is high on the list, too. And it makes no difference, as I well knew, whether the children are three or thirty. A child is a child is a child. At least in the eyes of a parent.

Most of us are also quite skilled at worrying about money, about relationships, about our looks, about our health, and about weather. Worrying about weather seems to have become a national pastime. At least that's the impression given by the number of television hours given over to discussing rain, snow, heat, humidity, wind chill, barometric pressure, and jet streams of air arriving from somewhere or another.

I found myself trying to figure out how much of my life had been consumed by worrying. If totaled up in years, what would it amount to? One year? Five? Ten? Whatever the figure, it was too high.

I once read an article on the psychoanalysis of worry. In it a British psychoanalyst, a man named Adam Phillips, expressed his view that worrying is an attempt by the worrier to simplify his life. ". . . specific worries," he wrote, "can be reassuring because they preempt what is in actuality an unknowable future."

It made sense to me. Is there anything we dread more than an unknowable future? And is there anything more likely to obscure our fear of this unpredictable future than the act of worrying? If we worry about weather or a bad haircut, for instance, we are relieved of the need to worry that something terrible may be waiting around the corner, ready to ambush us.

But worrying, I found, was quite a difficult thing to do while dancing the quickstep with Barry. Having fun was not.

Later, walking home in the moist night air, the domes and spires of Oxford stabbing the dark-blue sky above, I felt completely relaxed and carefree. I glanced at my watch; it was nearly midnight. The lateness of the hour surprised me. Then I realized that while dancing with Barry and the others I'd not been measuring time. I'd been living it.

When I got back to my rooms at Brasenose, I took out my journal and began writing down my feelings about Barry and the way dancing made me happy and carefree. Then I started to think it wasn't *dancing* that made me feel that way; it was giving myself up to dancing. I wasn't used to doing that, throwing myself so completely into something that had no definable goal. Or at least I hadn't done it for a long time.

Still, it wasn't hard to remember how as a girl I walked miles in winter to skate on frozen ponds and, in summer, swam fast-moving rivers to lie dreaming on sun-warmed rocks. I had no goal when I did such things. Unless it was simply a not-yet-diluted instinct to enjoy the world I saw around me.

When that changed I wasn't sure. All I knew was that for the last couple of decades I had organized my life too much around the illusionary principle of success and failure. Naturally, it was the verdict of success I wanted the world to hand down to me. Maybe my reluctance to join the others in a night of ballroom dancing was simply my fear of not being very good at it. Of failing.

But somehow when dancing with Barry I never once thought about failing. Or, for that matter, succeeding. It was enough to be alive and having fun, surrounded by music and laughter and people who, though I barely knew them, seemed on this night as familiar to me as lifelong friends.

I suppose it will always puzzle me, the riddle of why an important lesson is sometimes taught by the unlikeliest of professors. By Barry, for instance. Perhaps I was just ready to learn. Maybe it's that simple. Although answers, once we've found them, always seem simple.

I wondered: was this then to be my Oxford learning experience? The lesson I would remember long after I'd forgotten rural England's economic history and patterns of settlement? Was Barry to be the Oxford instructor I would remember above all others?

As if to answer, the church bells in Radcliffe Square began sounding their midnight chimes, telling me: *Yes, yes, yes.*

Italy

MILANO

GOLDEN LINE

12

MOTHER OF THE BRIDE

Dear Alice,

Milan seems like home to me. It's one of the big surprises of my trip. Today, sitting in the sun in the Piazza della Scala, an elderly man asked if he could sit next to me. I nodded. The man, who looked down on his luck, opened a magazine of crossword puzzles, which he completed by copying the answers from the back of the book. Later when he saw me consulting a map, he asked in near-perfect English: "May I be of help to you?" It's a friendly—and surprising—town.

Love, Alice

When the plane landed at Malpensa airport outside Milan, the pilot's voice announced brightly that the ground temperature was a "mild" 78 degrees. No mention was made, however, of the rain that pelted the windows, or the wind that caught the rivulets of water in midstream, blowing them sideways across the glass. This omission did not surprise me. It is a truth universally acknowledged by those in the travel business that less is more when it comes to imparting bad-weather news to tourists. If this was not true, most travelers would ignore the guidebooks and, regardless of destination, simply pack three things: rainwear, a down parka, and clothing made of tropical see-through mesh fabric.

This was my first trip to Milan. It was also my first encounter with Malpensa airport. I whispered the name to myself: *Malpensa.* It was a forbidding name, I thought, one that summoned up Edgar Allan Poe. Or Bram Stoker, the man who created the strange, dark world of Count Dracula. My intuition was right. Malpensa turned out to be the Transylvania of airports: a place of such twists and turns that conceivably an innocent tourist might arrive only to disappear and never be heard from again.

All airports, of course, present the weary traveler with any number of obstacles; but the frustration mounts when a language barrier is added to the mix. Foolishly, I had counted on the Italian classes taken twenty-five years earlier to get me through the basics.

Too late I remembered that the sole purpose of all those classes was to foster a deeper appreciation for Italian opera. So unless I was prepared to stop a porter and say: *Such sweet warmth runs through my veins*, or, *I cannot tell if your cheerful mood is real or not*—words I seemed to recall as being from Donizetti's *L'Elisir d'Amore*—I was totally out of the conversational loop.

It was hot, humid, and crowded in the airport. It was also incredibly busy, with long lines waiting at every ticket counter and information desk. I needed some directions but couldn't bear the thought of standing in line. I was a tired, perspiring woman wearing a coat suited for upper Norway and I wanted out. It was time to turn to my secret weapon: a small glossary of useful phrases in Italian and English.

What I needed to know was where to catch a bus I'd been told about, one that would take me into Milan for one-third the cost of a taxi. I flipped through the section on travel. The closest thing I could find was *A che ora parte il treno?* "At what time does the train leave?" It wasn't perfect but I could work with it. I stopped a man who looked like an airport employee, figuring that I would change the word "train" to "bus" and then ask him to point out the direction. "*A che ore parte il bus-o?*" I asked, throwing in for good measure the extra Italian-sounding *o*.

The man in the cap stared at me. For some reason I repeated my question in English, saying "Where is the departing bus, *per favore?*" He stared again. Then he walked off. Similar inquiries produced similar results. Determined to find my way out of the airport, I moved into a stream of arriving travelers who seemed to know where they were going. I followed them straight to the bus. Their tour bus. Which was headed for Lake Como. I stood there in the rain and watched it pull away.

Buck up, I told myself. If Freya Stark can raft down the Euphrates River at the age of eighty-six, I ought to be able to find my way from the airport into Milan.

And sure enough, just thinking of Freya encouraged me to carry on. A minute later I spotted a taxi and, as though divinely inspired, I opened the door and jumped right in.

The taxi ride from Malpensa to my hotel in Milan took over an hour. Most of that time I'd practiced saying, sotto voce, the Italian words I would need to ask the fare at journey's end. "*Quanto costa, per favore?*" I said over and over again. It seemed simple enough. And it was. The driver understood perfectly what I meant and proceeded to answer me in Italian. Naturally I hadn't a clue as to what he was saying. A porter came to my rescue. "The fare, Signora, is 172,000 lire," he told me, picking up my bags.

A six-figure fare for a taxi ride! Trying to hide my alarm, I got out my currency converter. It was bad. But not as bad as I thought. Without tip the fare was $95. With tip it came to about twenty dollars less than I was paying for my hotel room. Worth every lire, I thought, just to get out of Malpensa.

I had chosen to stay in a big, modern, chain hotel that catered to foreign businesspeople. Recommended to me by one of the few people I know who'd actually spent a night in Milan—most of my friends cited Milan as a city that was "too industrial, too commercial," bypassing it for Florence or Venice—the hotel had offered a special promotional rate. I took it immediately, knowing how expensive a city Milan is.

It was busy inside, the lobby buzzing with the voices of men

wearing business suits and women in chic outfits speaking the language of business. No tourists here. Although it was not what the
French would call a *hôtel de charme,* I liked the looks of it. For one
thing, it seemed exactly like all the chain hotels I'd ever stayed in.
And given my language deficits and the fact that Milan was a complete cipher to me, it offered exactly what I needed: familiarity.

That's when I noticed something unusual taking place in the
hotel. Bridal gowns—racks and racks of bouffant white dresses and
tulle veils—were being rolled into a large area just inside the entrance. I watched as a small, excitable man speaking in rapid Italian
directed the operation. Each time a hotel guest passed by, he ges-
tured dramatically to the racks, saying loudly, first in Italian, then
English: *"Attenzione!* Look out!"

"What's going on?" I asked a porter standing nearby. He explained they were setting up a bridal trade show, one scheduled to
open the next day. I watched a few minutes more, then left for my
room. When I stepped off the elevator I walked into a blizzard of
white bridal gowns. The doors to almost every room along the cor-
ridor were open and inside I could see rows of silky beaded gowns
being arranged for display. A dummy wearing an ivory dress of
heavy embroidered silk with huge puffy sleeves stood in the hallway, an island of serenity amid a stream of workmen and seam-
stresses scurrying about. It led me to wonder if the excellent rate I
was paying had anything to do with my room being situated in the
middle of *Brideshead Revisited.*

Actually, I rather liked it, the activity and excitement generated
by all these people bustling around with their beautiful merchan-
dise. Instead of going straight to my room, a solitary guest in a large
hotel, I saw an opportunity to hang about and be a part of the fes-
tivities.

I wheeled my suitcase past more racks hung with creamy satin gowns, stopping in front of my room. I unlocked the door and stepped inside. It was dark and stuffy. After opening the curtains and raising a window, I sat down on the bed and looked around. It was a perfectly adequate room, the kind I often stayed in when I was on the road, reporting a story for the newspaper. It suits my mood, I thought, although I wasn't sure what my mood was. Then I suddenly caught sight of myself in the mirror opposite the bed. What I saw was a woman who looked a little lost; a woman who looked as though she were missing someone. Which I was. I was missing Naohiro.

I sat on the bed thinking about the three days we'd spent together in London. After an unexpected business trip to Paris, Naohiro had stopped in London to see me. He was on his way back to Tokyo. I had just finished my course at Oxford and, although I hadn't planned on returning to London, the prospect of seeing him sooner than we had planned was an unexpected gift. But the thought of meeting Naohiro again made me nervous. On the train from Oxford to London my head buzzed with questions. What if Paris had been a fluke? What if we met and one of us—or both, for that matter—felt nothing? Had I been wrong in feeling that Naohiro and I had connected in some deep way? The closer I got to London, the more nervous I became.

As if to summon up his presence, I pulled out from my travel case one of the letters he'd written me and began reading it. By the end of the first page—a very amusing description of his encounter in Paris with two French students who insisted on speaking to him in beginner's-level Chinese—I was laughing out loud. I had forgotten how sharp a sense of humor Naohiro had, and how despite our cultural differences we found many of the same things funny. By the time the train reached London I had read two more of his letters. They were the perfect antidote to my anxiety, I thought, hurrying off the train, eager to meet the man I'd unearthed again in his written thoughts.

Still, when I met Naohiro for lunch a few hours later, some of my nervousness had returned. He was already seated when I arrived at the restaurant. Immediately he rose and walked toward me. Watching him gracefully thread his way between the tables, I realized there was no need to wonder any longer if I would still find him attractive. My big worry now was: would *he* still find *me* attractive?

Suddenly Naohiro was standing in front of me. For a minute or two we stood face-to-face, not speaking. Naohiro broke the silence.

"It is good to see you again," he said, bowing his head slightly. Then he moved closer. "You are well, I hope."

"I am. And you? Did things go well for you in Paris?"

"Yes, I am happy to say. But not as well as they did the last time I was in Paris."

I looked at his face, trying to figure out if he meant what I hoped he meant. I decided to test the waters. "And when was that visit?" I asked.

"It was on the occasion of *Les cinq jours de l'Objet Extraordinaire.*" Naohiro paused. "I believe you were in Paris at the same time, were you not?"

"Yes, but I seem to remember many more days than five that were extraordinary."

He laughed. "So do I."

For the next three days Naohiro and I wandered through London like happy children: stopping to eat when we were hungry, popping into a shop or gallery that drew our interest, exploring the story-book houses in the tiny mews that dot London, and riding, with no particular destination in mind, the red double-decker buses.

One afternoon, after a trip to Harrods where Naohiro bought a watch for his daughter, we passed a movie house that was showing *Strictly Ballroom.* I had already told him about Barry and my night of dancing at Oxford. To my surprise, he seemed quite interested, asking questions about the difficulties of various dances. In Japan, he told me, ballroom dancing was considered rather exotic.

"Why don't we go in and see the movie?" I asked Naohiro suddenly. "I saw it before going up to Oxford and it's just wonderful. Funny and touching and . . . well, it's just wonderful."

Without hesitating, he agreed.

For the next two hours we sat together in the dark theater laughing and rooting for the "good guy" dancer to win the dance contest. When we stumbled out into the late afternoon light, I was exhilarated and happy. Naohiro's mood seemed to match mine exactly.

That night, Naohiro and I danced together for the first time. After seeing the movie, I had told him of my first evening in Paris; of watching a young couple dance under the paulownia trees in the place Furstemberg, oblivious to everything but each other. And I told him of how seeing them stirred up memories of my high school prom and the last slow dance with the boy I had a hopeless crush on.

"What does this mean, the last slow dance?" Naohiro asked. "It sounds sad."

I didn't quite know how to answer him. In a way, the last slow dance *was* sad. I tried to tell him about the custom at high school dances of ending the evening by announcing the last slow dance. "In some way," I said, "it's what everyone's been waiting for all evening. The chance to release all that pent-up teenage emotion by holding the other person in your arms."

"We have nothing like that in Japan," he said. "But perhaps we could turn on the radio and you could teach me this last slow dance."

We turned on the radio. The sound of Fred Astaire singing "The Way You Look Tonight" filled the room. Naohiro held out his arms. I entered them. We danced, our cheeks touching. He was an excellent dancer. I closed my eyes, lost in the music and the feel of Naohiro's arms around me. It was the high school prom all over again. Only much better.

When the music stopped, Naohiro said, "That was not sad at all. It was a very good last slow dance, was it not?"

"The best last slow dance of my life."

"Well, then, we should make a habit of doing the last slow dance each time we meet," he said.

An hour after arriving at the hotel in Milan I had unpacked and was ready to hit the streets. I needed a destination and had picked Milan's most famous attraction: the Duomo, a huge wedding cake of a cathedral, with 135 spires and over 3,100 statues. I marked on the map the location of my hotel; then the location of the Duomo. I drew a red arrow between the two. Maybe I'd get there and maybe I wouldn't; that was beside the point. What mattered was that when I stepped out of my hotel I knew which way to turn. Once I did that, the flow of the city would carry me along. Perhaps even to the Duomo.

Outside, the rain had stopped and the sun was struggling to

break through the clouds. The busy street that ran past the hotel was not very inviting; its gray buildings, mostly offices with a few banks and dreary coffee shops scattered between, depressed me. But I continued to walk, turning one corner and then another and then another. At the last turn I found the Milan that spoke my name.

Before me, at the center of four tree-lined streets, was a small green park, where two young women were walking, pushing babies in their strollers. An old man sat reading the newspaper. Children ran up and down the paths, their high-pitched voices shrieking in delight. A woman sold gelato from a stand, filling the cups with pale green pistachio ice. I bought some.

It was then I heard it; the sound of a tram rumbling around the corner, its *clang clang clang* as familiar to me as Grandmother's voice calling me to supper. It was the sound I grew up hearing in Baltimore, where trolleys plied the streets like pleasure boats, ready to take you wherever you wanted to go. They're gone, now—the streetcars of my youth—but here and there some of the metal tracks still gleam above the asphalt surface of a street.

I stood at the Piazza Quattro Novembre and watched the tram approach. It looked exactly like the Number 8 streetcar that Mother and I took downtown to see the newest MGM movies at the Century Theatre. So strong in my mind was this connection that when the tram stopped to let off passengers, I jumped on without a second thought. What did it matter where it was going? I thought. Getting lost was not a consideration. I was already lost— if lost means not having the slightest idea of where you are.

The interior of the tram was charming. I settled back into one of the polished wooden seats next to an Art Deco lamp and looked through the window. As the streets and shops and neighborhoods slid by—streets and shops and neighborhoods I'd never seen before but recognized anyway—the dislocation I felt dissolved. Odd, I thought, how the past makes its presence known no matter where we travel.

I spent most of the afternoon riding on trams, hopping off whenever I saw something interesting: a neighborhood, a church, a piazza, a street. By this time I was in love with Milan.

I was particularly drawn to a neighborhood called the Brera. Once the center of Milan's bohemian life, the Brera now combined an art student ambience with unique shops and galleries catering to the upscale shopper. Bookshops, bars, boutiques, and restaurants of every kind and price dotted its meandering cobblestone streets. After stopping to study the menus posted outside several of the restaurants, I decided to come back to the Brera for dinner that night.

Before returning to the hotel, I walked back through the Brera to La Scala. Although musical performances did not begin until December, guided tours through the beautiful opera house and its museum of operatic memorabilia were offered. I found the museum particularly fascinating. Verdi seemed to be the star here, with more than half the museum space devoted to his career. I studied his scores, in awe of the man who marked down these black notations that expressed so much in such small strokes.

A man's voice, that of an Italian speaking English, suddenly broke the silence. "He was a wonderful man, a great man, our Verdi." I looked up and saw an elderly man standing next to me, studying the scores. He was dressed in a dark suit, one that had turned shiny from too much cleaning and pressing, and a white shirt frayed at the collar.

We began to chat about Verdi. "When he died a great crowd turned out in the streets," the man said. He then went on to tell me of the Rest Home for Musicians that Verdi financed and built.

Composers were given preference at the Casa di Riposo per Musicisti, followed by singers, conductors, and orchestral musicians. As he spoke I wondered, but didn't ask, if he was a resident at the home.

Later, on my way back to the hotel, I thought of Verdi's Rest Home for Musicians and its similarity to Gertrude Jekyll's Home of Rest for Ladies of Small Means. Perhaps there are similar rest homes, I thought, scattered around the world like an aberrant chain of Hilton Hotels.

In my hotel, I stopped at the door of a room filled with voluminous bridal gowns. Inside, a short, heavyset woman stood ironing the hem of a dress. The deft manner in which she moved the iron across the tricky satin material was as delicate as a butterfly landing on a leaf.

As I stood watching, a pink-cheeked young woman who obviously had been out running—she was wearing a gray sweatsuit and Nike running shoes—paused at the door. "What's going on?" she asked in a voice that was unmistakably American. I told her about the trade show. "So if you're looking for a wedding dress," I said, "you've come to the right hotel."

Just then the woman ironing the dress gently removed it from the board and transferred it to a padded hanger. "Ah, look at that one," the young woman said. *"Bella,"* she said to the seamstress. *"Molto bella."* The seamstress smiled and replied with a nod. She began moving toward the door, carrying the bouffant gown high above her head. But a struggle ensued in the doorway: she was unable to get both herself and the dress through the opening.

"*Avanti dritto,*" the American said, taking hold of the front end of the dress and guiding it and the seamstress through the doorway.

"*Grazie,*" said the Italian woman.

"*Prego,*" replied the American.

We watched the woman and the dress march down the hallway together, a happy couple who, unfortunately, would soon be parted.

"You speak Italian?" I asked, turning to the American.

She laughed. "No. That's pretty much my entire repertoire. Except for *quanto costa.*"

She had an easygoing way about her, the kind of outgoing attitude that often is associated—rightly or wrongly—with Americans. Her appearance matched her manner: long, copper-colored hair casually pulled back into a ponytail and no makeup except a pale gloss of lipstick. I judged her to be in her early twenties. I asked if she'd been in Milan long.

"No. I arrived this morning. At least I arrived at the airport this morning. By the time I found my way out of there and got to the hotel it was afternoon."

"Ah, yes, the enchanting Malpensa," I said. "I had the same experience when I arrived there today."

After a few minutes spent in exchanging war stories about Malpensa, she asked if I knew of a good place for dinner. "A place where I would be comfortable eating alone."

"Not really," I said, explaining I didn't know Milan at all. "But I walked through an interesting neighborhood today. It's called the Brera and it's loaded with places to eat. I thought I'd head back there tonight for dinner." I hesitated, then decided to go ahead with what I was thinking "Would you like to come?"

"I'd like that very much," she said. "What time did you want to go?"

I suggested we meet in the lobby at 8:30. She agreed.

"By the way," she said, putting her hand out, "I'm Carolyn."

I laughed. "I can't believe I didn't introduce myself," I said, shaking her hand. "I'm Alice."

"The place we're looking for is somewhere near the end of a little street called Via Fiori Chiara," I told Carolyn, after consulting my map. The taxi driver had dropped us off in front of the Piazza della Scala, just opposite the opera house. From there we set out to find the Tuscan restaurant I'd spotted earlier that day.

The streets were pleasantly crowded with both locals and tourists out enjoying the evening. Carolyn and I fell into step, strolling along at a leisurely pace, stopping often to peek into a lobby or bar. We were in no hurry to reach our destination. In fact, we almost jettisoned the Tuscan restaurant plan for a piano bar that served pasta. But when we stepped inside, the noise level forced our retreat back to the street. After walking another block or two we arrived at Via Fiori Chiara. Ten minutes later we were seated in the Tuscan trattoria, raising our wineglasses in a toast.

"*Cin cin!*" Carolyn said.

"*Cin cin!*" I echoed, clinking my glass of Chianti against hers.

We decided to share several dishes offered on the menu. Each of us was surprised, pleasantly so, to learn the other ate little meat. After much discussion we narrowed down our choices to bean soup with pasta, baked omelet with artichoke hearts, and "Treviso salad," a combination of two varieties of radicchio. Dinner was a leisurely affair, with each course separated by as much as half an hour. By the time our warm zabaglione arrived, Carolyn and I were exchanging life stories the way old friends do.

Carolyn, I learned, was twenty-four and a graduate student in art history. She had interrupted her studies, however, to join her boyfriend, Rob, in Italy. They were engaged to be married.

"He's doing a year's graduate work in Florence, and it was too good an opportunity for me to pass up," she said. "Finally, after all the years of looking at pictures and reproductions of Renaissance art, I'll get to see the real thing." She planned to spend three days in Milan before taking the train to Florence. "There's some wonderful art in this city that I'd like to see. And who knows if I'll have the chance again?"

It was her first trip to Italy, but not to Europe. The daughter of a military man who moved from place to place, she had lived a few years in Germany during her early teens.

We finished our coffee and asked for a bill. The young waiter, who had been flirting with Carolyn all evening, made quite a show of saying in English, "It has made me the most happy to come to the table of so beautiful women." Later, I told Carolyn it was very smart of him to include me in his flattery; it had earned him a larger tip.

Although it was almost midnight when we arrived back at the hotel, a small band of people were still setting up bridal displays. Carolyn and I stopped again to peek in the door of a room on our floor. A smartly dressed woman was sitting inside, taking bites out of a sandwich and sipping wine. When she caught sight of us, she called out *"Buona sera."* Carolyn and I returned her greeting. "Good evening," we said, almost in unison. To my astonishment, the woman motioned us to come in. Then, in accented English, she said, "Are you here to buy from the show?"

I explained we were just guests at the hotel who couldn't resist the tempting display of silk and satin gowns.

"Oh, look at this one," Carolyn said, pointing to a champagne-colored satin dress that was elegant in its simple cut and lack of adornment.

"Yes, that is the right color for your hair and fair skin," the woman said, rising to pull the dress off the rack and spread it before Carolyn. She turned to me. "Your daughter has good taste."

Carolyn and I exchanged glances. "Yes," I said, "even as a little girl she showed a great deal of taste. Remember, Carolyn, how you would never wear frilly dresses?"

"Yes, Mom, I do remember." She paused. "I always wanted to be just like you."

Then Carolyn asked the woman a question that surprised me. "What does a dress like this cost?"

"Quite a lot," she answered. "I think in American dollars something like three thousand dollars. Are you getting married?"

"Yes, I am," Carolyn said. "In Florence. Next month."

"What a beautiful city to marry in. And what a beautiful bride you will make."

It was growing late. I could see the fatigue in Carolyn's face. I didn't need to look at mine to know I was dead tired. "You've been very kind, Signora, to take so much time with us," I said.

"No, it is my pleasure," she said. "Tomorrow will come only the buyers shopping for their stores. It is nice to see a real bride."

We left for our rooms. There were so many questions I wanted to ask Carolyn, but there would be time for that tomorrow. We already had agreed to spend the day together. But I had to know just one thing before we parted. I asked if it was really true that she was to be married in Florence the following month.

"Yes, it really is true," she said, turning to unlock her door.

Then, turning back to face me, she said: "Good night, Mom. See you in the morning."

Over the next few days Carolyn and I spent most of our time together. We visited museums, reconnoitered the lobbies of expensive hotels, ate in cafés, trattorias, and bars, explored hidden streets, sat peacefully in parks and churches, took a day trip to Lake Como, and, in a moment of heart-pounding madness, climbed the stairs to the roof of the Duomo for a breathtaking view of Milan.

I learned a lot about Carolyn in the days we spent traipsing around the city. First of all, that she was fun to be with. She was the kind of spontaneous traveler willing to ditch a preplanned schedule in favor of seizing the moment. We also shared a number of interests. Art, for one thing. And, for another, a view of the world that was equal parts affection and amused skepticism.

During one of our dinners together Carolyn talked with enthusiasm about her upcoming wedding. "We don't really have any plans about where or how we'll get married. The only thing we're sure of is that it will set the Guiness record for 'World's Cheapest Wedding.' " She said it matter-of-factly, with no trace of "poor me" in her voice.

I already knew Carolyn was on a tight budget; we factored that in each time we chose where to eat or what to visit. And she had talked a bit about taking a job in Florence to supplement her fiancé's foundation grant. "I'm thinking about teaching English, but I'll take any job I can find," she said. "After all, art history majors can't be choosers."

By the time our last day together in Milan arrived I knew I

wanted to give Carolyn some kind of wedding gift. What exactly, I didn't know. But since we had reserved the whole day for a tour of one of Europe's most fashionable shopping streets, Via Monte Napoleone, my plan was to surprise Carolyn with a small gift of her choosing.

By mutual agreement, Carolyn and I dressed more grandly than usual for the deluxe occasion. Which meant a black suit and white silk sweater for me; and for Carolyn, a nicely tailored khaki pantsuit worn with a white linen blouse. We called them our "power shopping clothes." Of course, once we hit Montenapo—as the locals affectionately call the street—we laughed at our attempts to look like the *gran' signora* and *signorina.*

The Italian women were gorgeous; the young ones as ripe and luscious as peaches, the not-so-young a glorious combination of elegance and mature sensuality. Draped in the latest fashion and wearing astonishing jewelry, they walked along the streets chatting and gesturing, carrying their shopping bags like badges of honor.

"And ye shall know them by their shopping bags," I said to Carolyn, as we ticked off the famous designer names imprinted on the chic bags: Versace, Pratesi, Fendi, Armani, Valentino, Bulgari, Missoni.

The shops themselves were imposing monuments to the power of achieving status through fashion. The saleswomen inside were no less imposing. As elegantly turned-out as their customers— some more so—each ruled her domain like a queen, favoring this one with a smile and that one with a look that said "tourist sightseer." It required a whole lot of Attitude just to enter such a shop. But Carolyn and I hit on an approach. Before pushing open a door, we took a minute or two to slip into the right Attitude. Like actors rehearsing for an audition, we practiced being haughty and dismissive. Sometimes it worked. And sometimes it didn't.

As the day progressed I grew worried about coming up with a wedding gift for Carolyn. She really hadn't expressed an acquisitive interest in anything and, more practically, nothing we saw was even remotely affordable.

After a late lunch at a café in the Galleria San Babila, we walked to the nearby Piazza San Babila. As we strolled along, we noticed that many of the women passing by had extraordinarily becoming haircuts. "Do you suppose they're models?" Carolyn whispered.

"I don't know," I said. "It's mysterious, seeing all these women with great hair walking around this small piazza. It's like seeing the Stepford Wives in Milan."

Another half-block, however, and the mystery was solved. From the door of a hair salon exited women with perfect haircuts of every style and length: short and spiky; curly and tousled; blunt-cut bobs; classic pageboys. Carolyn seemed transfixed. She moved to the door and peered inside. The interior was a model of good design; it looked very expensive.

Then, turning to me, she patted her ponytail and said, "Maybe I should get my hair cut. I've been thinking about it ever since I got to Milan. What do you think?"

What I thought—but didn't say—was that advising a friend about matters of the hair was fraught with peril. It was something I'd learned the hard way, more than once. The truth was, I thought Carolyn would look great with short hair. But suppose it didn't suit her or she hated it? She was, after all, getting married in a month. What if it shocked her fiancé? I brought up this last point.

"How do you think Rob would feel if you looked like a totally different person at your wedding?" I asked. "I've always thought it was nice if the bride looked natural on her wedding day, not like some stranger walking down the aisle."

Carolyn laughed. "Oh, he's been after me for a long time to cut my hair. Besides, he'll have a month to get used to it." Having said that, she opened the door and walked into the salon. I followed.

Carolyn began to speak in halting Italian, but the receptionist cut her short. "I speak English," she said, speaking English. "How may I help?"

After explaining to her that she had no appointment, Carolyn asked if it would be possible for someone to cut her hair that afternoon. The receptionist's exquisitely arched eyebrows shot up in alarm. "Without an appointment! I think it is not possible." She consulted her book. "But we could take you one month from today."

"I think it is not possible," Carolyn said, "as I will be getting married in Florence in one month." She said it with her usual sly humor but her face showed her disappointment.

A young man standing nearby interrupted, telling the receptionist in good but not perfect English, "Yes, but I have been canceled. Now I can take her."

The receptionist looked at Carolyn who, for some reason, was hesitating. "Vincenzo is very good," she said reassuringly to Carolyn.

By this time Carolyn's face was quite flushed. "I'm sure he is. But I need to ask . . . I should have asked first . . . but what I wanted to know is . . . what do you charge for a haircut?"

"For Vincenzo that would be 210,000 lire." Carolyn's flushed face turned pale. By this time we both were able to convert lire into an approximate dollar figure without consulting a currency converter. The haircut would cost close to $150. I knew Carolyn couldn't afford this. Suddenly I knew what my wedding gift would be.

"She'll take the appointment," I told the receptionist. Then turning to Carolyn, I said, "Please allow me to do this. It will be my gift to you. After all, I am the mother of the bride."

I waited in the reception area, relishing the chance to watch some of the most stylish women in Milan enter and exit. It was like being at the theater, only here the drama lay in the expectations, hopes, and disappointments surrounding a new hairstyle. I worried that Carolyn might be among those who emerged disappointed. Or worse, that Vincenzo, like many hairstylists, might get carried away and do something drastic. I looked at my watch. An hour had passed. What could be taking so long? I grew apprehensive, as though this were a hospital waiting room and Carolyn a patient.

Five minutes later, Carolyn reappeared. She was smiling. And with good reason. She looked wonderful. Her hair was parted on the side and cut to a length that just brushed the top of her shoulders. "Well, Mom, what do you think?" Carolyn asked.

"I think you're going to make a beautiful bride," I said.

The next morning Carolyn went off to Florence to get married and start a new life. We had said our good-byes the night before, but I walked down to the lobby with her for a final farewell.

"Be a good daughter now and write," I said.

"I will, Mom. Promise you'll write back."

I stood outside and watched her walk toward the train station, her newly cut red hair bouncing up and down with each step. I envied her, off to start a new life. But even more than that, I envied the fact that if her new life didn't work out, she had plenty of time to start another one. Carolyn had made a commitment, a big one, but there were many more important choices to be made in her future.

I thought about my own life and wondered: would there ever be another large commitment in my life? Or would my life now become just a series of small ones? It occurred to me that perhaps, in the long run, small was better.

Right now I had two excellent commitments to carry out: to spend my last day visiting, if I could find it, the Casa di Riposo per Musicisti; and to get ready to leave for Venice, where I planned to hook up with a group traveling south to Tuscany, Umbria, and the Amalfi Coast.

True enough, neither of these plans amounted to a major life commitment. Still, I found myself thinking that such small steps may be all a person needs to set out on a new path. The thought cheered me, although until that moment I wasn't aware I needed cheering.

Along with the cheer came a surge of optimism. It was a totally unearned optimism; mysterious in its source but real nonetheless. Then, in what I guessed was a sly trick of association, I thought of E. B. White's observation that "once in everyone's life there is apt to be a period when he is fully awake, instead of half-asleep."

I started walking. When I approached the corner, I wondered: should I turn right? Or left? Then I realized it really didn't matter. Either way, something new—perhaps a tiny adventure—awaited my arrival.

I hurried down the street. Whatever was around the corner, I didn't want to miss a minute of it.

13

WE OPEN IN VENICE

Dear Alice,

    When it comes to travel I'm more convinced than ever that less is more. Yesterday I left Perugia at 7:45 A.M. (up at 6:30); took the train to Rome; lunched in Rome; took the train (under a threat of strike) to Naples; then a bus to Pompeii (where I took a two-hour tour); and arrived at Sorrento at 7:30 P.M. Whew!

                    Love, Alice

At caffè Florian the morning music had just begun. Tired-looking tourists sitting over their cappuccinos seemed to perk up as the band launched into a medley from *Cabaret*. I could see feet tapping under the tables, keeping time with the beat.

Late morning was a nice time to sit in the Piazza San Marco. The crowds had yet to arrive and the large square, half in sun and half in shadow, could be appreciated for what it was: one of the most beautiful and romantic spots in the world. Sitting at a table facing a domed, pink-and-gold church that glowed jewellike against a cloud-puffed sky of azure blue, I thought: it's unreal. It's like a stage set painted by children for a school play.

Of course, my being here was just as unreal. October was around the corner, but there were still mornings when I woke up, surprised to find myself in Italy and not in Baltimore. At home, the Japanese maple in my garden would be turning gold; at work, the newsroom would be back in full swing after the doldrums of late summer. Sometimes I thought I should be there, writing columns and rushing from place to place, not here, leisurely drinking espresso while contemplating the shimmering mirage of Venice.

But it was easier now than it had been six months earlier to let go of such thoughts. Usually I had only to ask myself one question: how stupid would it be to get stuck in the past or the future when I could sink into a morning like this?

So much was going on. I watched the waiters glide from table to table, swooping down at the last minute to present with a flourish a cappuccino or an iced Coca-Cola. An important-looking couple swept in, accompanied by an entourage of Prada-clad young

men carrying cellular phones. Across the square at the Quadri, a
rival café to Florian's, a second band of musicians could be heard
tuning up. Then just as Florian's quintet segued into "Smoke Gets
in Your Eyes," the Quadri's group burst into a medley from *Okla-
homa.* Dueling cafés, I thought.

I ordered another espresso. The waiter bowed and went off, ex-
pertly threading his way between the tables that now were quite
crowded. I sat alone, looking around and eavesdropping.

Behind me a man said to a woman, "The canals are pretty, but I
hate not being able to rent a car and go where I want to go when I
want to go." At another table where four women sat, one said,
"Does anyone have any idea of how to get back to the hotel?" Two
tables away I noticed an attractive man sitting alone reading *Le
Monde.* Was he French? I wondered. To my chagrin, he caught me
staring at him. He nodded, then smiled. I smiled back, then turned
away, embarrassed. But I was also pleased. This small attention from
a handsome stranger was like a bone thrown to my vanity. I resisted
the temptation to march ahead into full-dress fantasy.

Still, I did allow myself to recall *Summertime,* an old movie filmed
in Venice. In it, Katharine Hepburn played an aging, unaccompanied
spinster visiting Europe for the first time. Wandering one late afternoon into the Piazza San Marco, she sits alone and sad at a café table,
watching the couples around her. Then, just when she's all teary-
eyed—in the way only Katharine Hepburn can be teary-eyed—*poof,*
the handsome Rossano Brazzi appears. They fall in love. She falls
into a canal. They part, knowing their relationship has no future.

A sense of discomfort followed my reprisal of the movie's
romance-fantasy plot. The sad truth, no, the *pathetic* truth, was that
it struck too close to home. It was not a scenario I wanted to examine in detail. Not now, anyway.

Three days had passed since I'd left Milan with a group of travelers.
After Venice, our first stop, we were headed for Tuscany, Umbria,
and the Amalfi Coast. Of the sixteen people traveling together, all
but three—myself and two other women—were traveling with a
partner of one sort or another. Our guide was a smart, formidable
Australian woman who had lived in Italy for many years. She was
also tall, an attribute that proved to be almost as valuable as her flu-
ent Italian. When separated from the group by crowds or a ten-
dency to malinger at a shop window, her long neck and elegant
head bobbing above the thronging tourists proved a reliable com-
pass.

We had traveled by train from Milan to Venice, stopping over in
Verona for lunch. In Verona, by pure chance, I sat at a table with the
three people who would become my closest pals on the trip: Marta
and Bernie, a middle-aged married couple from Connecticut; and
Vivian, a writer from New York whose husband had died two years
earlier. Vivian was, as the French like to say, a woman of a certain
age. Although I became close to Marta, Bernie, and Vivian, it did
not follow that we were a foursome. My friendship with Marta and
Bernie existed separately from my relationship with Vivian and, as
the trip progressed, each had its own dynamic.

Marta, a short dark-haired woman with a quick, intelligent face
and an acerbic wit, was amazingly well-read. She also was overweight; so much so that it sometimes physically slowed her down.
Her husband, Bernie, was also quick-witted and well-read. I liked
being around them. They obviously enjoyed one another's company and were respectful of their differences. I was impressed that

Bernie, energetic and always ready to go, showed no impatience when Marta was unable to keep up. When such a situation arose, Bernie, in subtle ways, saw to it that his wife did not feel left out or self-conscious. Relaxed in both attitude and attire, Marta and Bernie seemed living examples of the what-you-see-is-what-you-get approach to life.

Vivian, on the other hand, was always perfectly turned out. Even racing to catch a train in the morning, Vivian was an exemplar of exquisite grooming and detailed accessorizing. In appearance and philosophy, Vivian was a true romantic. She believed in and was motivated by the idea of keeping romance alive in a marriage or re-lationship. To her this meant never allowing your significant other to see you if you were not coiffed and looking your best.

"Men want to see the finished product," she told me, "not the work in progress."

I could only imagine the enormous effort required by this ap-proach but, according to Vivian, it kept alive the romance in her marriage until the very end. Professionally, Vivian put the same phi-losophy to use. She wrote romantic novels—a genre not to be con-fused with romance novels of the bodice-ripping kind.

But for all her attention to matters of appearance, in the end it was not color-coordinated outfits or attentive grooming that de-fined Vivian. She was a novelist, after all, and what interested her most—after the feats of self-adornment had been gotten out of the way—were other people's stories. In conversation, she was surpris-ingly adept at asking the kind of unexpected question capable of teasing out a person's intimate feelings.

"Are you in love?" Vivian asked me on our second night to-gether in Venice. We were having dinner, the group that is, on a beautiful candlelit terrace overlooking the Grand Canal when Vi-vian, sitting next to me, brought up the subject of love. Ordinarily,

I would find such a question out of line if asked by someone I'd known for only two days. But traveling friendships are different from normal friendships, and I found Vivian's question perfectly reasonable. Still, it was not one I could answer with any clarity.

"Oh, there are moments when I think of someone and find myself missing him," I said. "But I don't know if it's love I'm feeling. In a way, it seems more like feeling the absence of love."

"That's interesting, although I'm not sure what it means," Vivian said.

I laughed. "I'm not so sure I know what it means either."

Earlier that day Vivian and I had spent part of the afternoon visiting the Peggy Guggenheim collection of twentieth-century art. We had taken the vaporetto across the Grand Canal to Dorsoduro; from there we walked along the narrow *calli* to the Palazzo Venier dei Leoni, where Guggenheim had lived until her death in 1979. Now her modern art collection is there, existing side by side, like a debutant among dowagers, with the High Renaissance art at the stately Accademia Gallery.

Although Vivian and her husband had visited Venice several times, she'd never seen the Guggenheim collection. "Hal and I were not much drawn to modern art," she told me as we entered the quiet, shady courtyard at the rear of the palazzo. Vivian often linked her observations to those of her late husband, Hal; occasionally she would accidentally slip into the present tense. I had the impression that part of Vivian lived in the past; that often what she enjoyed or did not enjoy was linked to memories of traveling with Hal.

I understood this. Although Mother had been dead for almost ten years, more than once on this trip I'd had the urge to phone her: "Hello, Mother," I could hear myself saying, "you won't believe it, but today in a private garden I saw the most beautiful three-hundred-year-old yellow rose growing against a pink brick wall."

But Vivian, I found, was also capable of enjoying new experiences. When we emerged from the Peggy Guggenheim museum, she was genuinely enthusiastic about the collection. I told her I admired her for being open enough to let go of her prejudice against modern art.

Her answer was not what I expected. "I just wish I weren't so prejudiced against the future," she said. "At my age it's a constant struggle to look ahead and be optimistic."

If appearance and energy were any indication, Vivian could be in her fifties. However, certain biographical facts mentioned by her suggested she was closer to seventy. Marta, who liked Vivian, leaned toward the higher figure. "I think she's had a facelift," Marta said. "It's subtle, but there's something about the mouth." Bernie, who said he didn't know from facelifts, said, "What does it matter? I'd be happy to have that kind of energy at any age."

It was true. Vivian seemed tireless.

"Let's walk back to the hotel," she said after leaving the Guggenheim collection. She was suggesting a walk of at last two miles; more, if we got lost in the narrow, winding *calli* that snaked through Venice with no obvious beginning or end. Walking in Venice, I had found, was like white-water rafting: once you entered the eddies and swirls of these small streets the only thing to do was go with the flow. To me, being swept along to some mysterious destination was part of the city's magical allure.

After forty minutes of walking, we emerged from one of the

narrow *calli* onto the vast open space of the Piazza San Marco. Vivian didn't seem or look tired. In fact she suggested we stroll around the arcade and do some window-shopping. A few shops down from Florian's, Vivian stopped in front of a window display of expensive jewelry. She told me of her husband's habit of buying her a gift, usually jewelry, on each of their trips. In Venice, he had surprised her with a turquoise bracelet.

"The one I'm wearing," she said, raising her arm to show me a lovely blue-green rope of turquoise. "He bought it here, in this shop." Vivian paused. "I've thought about getting earrings to match it." She paused again. "Would you like to go in with me?"

I agreed and we entered the shop. Immediately, a well-dressed man with coiffed silver hair approached us. "May I help you?" he asked.

Vivian showed him the bracelet and explained she was interested in turquoise earrings. "My husband bought the bracelet here and I thought you might be able to match the color." Vivian and I were then seated in chairs before a glass case on top of which were flat black velvet pads. The man left, returning with a small case of turquoise earrings. I could see at once they were not at all the same color as Vivian's bracelet. Vivian could, too, but was polite enough to try on one of the earrings before pointing out the difference. When she did, the man became annoyed.

"But that is as close as you can get, signora. If you know turquoise you know this is a good match."

"But I have seen turquoise in just the shade of my bracelet," Vivian said.

"Well, perhaps, signora, you should buy *that* turquoise," the salesman said curtly, removing the turquoise earrings from the black velvet pad. He was dismissing Vivian. And she knew it.

"That would never have happened if I'd been with Hal," she

said, walking back to the hotel. "Or if I were a younger woman." She sighed. "That's the worst thing about growing older. People dismiss you. As though you were a child."

"Oh, Vivian, you're much too much of a force to be dismissed," I said. My reassurance, however, did not cheer her. For the first time on the trip, she looked tired.

As I lay in bed that night I thought of Vivian's remark about optimism. Or, more to the point, her observation about the difficulty of maintaining optimism as you grow older. I thought about the bittersweet feelings I had in Milan as I watched Carolyn go off to begin a new life. Everything was ahead of her, I had thought then. Including the idea of time as an infinite presence. Unlike me, she had not yet heard the faint sound of a clock ticking.

But as I lay in bed in Venice, thinking about the people I'd met on this trip and the challenges and excitement that each day brought, I heard no ticking. Instead I thought about how I had surprised myself this year by jumping in to reshape my life before life stepped in to reshape it for me.

And, I reasoned, if I could reinvent myself once, I could do it more than once.

The next morning brought a surprise. When I arrived at Florian's for my cappuccino, the Piazza San Marco was almost entirely under water—in some places by as much as a foot. To allow pedestrians to cross the square, catwalks had been set up on metal trestles that rose a few feet above the water. Fascinated, I watched as people struggled to navigate the narrow wooden planks. Since pedestrian traffic flowed in both directions like a two-lane highway, crossing required not only balance but nerve. Particularly disadvantaged were the new arrivals to Venice, those just deposited by vaporetto and searching for their hotels. They had the added burden of dragging their luggage with them across the makeshift platforms.

"It's the *acque alte,*" said the waiter, standing next to me in the arcade outside Florian's. "The high waters from the lagoon."

I had read about the *acque alte.* I knew that each year, usually between October and April, exceptionally high tides poured through the three gates and into the city. The Piazza San Marco was particularly vulnerable, the waiter told me, because it is the lowest point in Venice.

After watching for several more minutes, I mounted a plank that would deposit me near the less-crowded Castello neighborhood. The group was leaving for Florence after lunch, and before we left I wanted to check out an inexpensive *pensione* recommended by a friend. I already knew I wanted to spend more time in Venice, and this place sounded quite nice.

Sadly, I never got there.

Halfway across the catwalk a major pile-up occurred when some school kids, out for a joy walk, decided to play a version of "chicken" on the narrow planks. After placing themselves on a collision course with oncoming tourists, they would wait to see who would give way first. Naturally it was always the adults who chickened out, jumping into the foot-deep water. When my turn came I decided it was better to jump than fall. Several tourists behind followed me, like lemmings, into the water. A big splash ensued. I got soaked.

Later, sitting in my room, my clothes hung on a chair to dry, I consoled myself with thoughts of what a good story it would make when I got home. Although it wasn't exactly like Katharine Hepburn falling into a canal—I did jump, after all, not fall—there were some similarities. It involved Venice, for one thing, and water, for another.

In the next few weeks, as the group worked its way south, the days and the towns passed by quickly. We were like a touring company of actors: always on the move, packing and unpacking, checking in and checking out of hotels, catching trains and buses on a schedule that allowed us to wake up in Perugia, have lunch in Rome, and go to bed in Sorrento.

And like any group thrown together in a strange situation, we developed the sort of we're-in-this-together, for-better-or-for-worse camaraderie that I found appealingly familial. It was something I missed, the sense of sharing those small, daily experiences that, as far as I can tell, are really what life boils down to.

I particularly enjoyed being around Marta and Bernie. Often we shared meals together, using the time to agree on or argue about books, politics, personalities, and what we liked or didn't like about the trip. If I had to pinpoint what drew me to Marta and Bernie, beside their humor and interest in the world, it was this: the three of us just liked one another. And we all knew it.

It was in the hill towns of Tuscany and Umbria, however, that the depth of Marta's character began to reveal itself to me.

Because Marta's weight limited the amount of walking she could do on the steep streets of towns like Amalfi and San

Gimignano, she sometimes spent the afternoon sitting in a café or on a hotel veranda with a view. There, with the town's activity going on around her and the olive groves stretching out beneath, Marta sat, taking in the essence of that particular place. Sometimes, when I grew weary of long lectures inside museums and churches, I would abandon the lecturer—as Whitman had abandoned his "learned astronomer"—to join Marta outside in her quiet vigil of the Italian countryside.

On one such occasion in Assisi—a town with streets so steep it was like walking up the face of a cliff—Marta said, "I know some of the others think I shouldn't have come on a trip that involved so much walking and climbing. But I don't feel I've missed a thing. Just look out there."

It was late afternoon and we were sitting in the warm sun of the Hotel Subasio overlooking the Umbrian countryside. Beneath us, stretched out as far as we could see, was a patchwork quilt of hills, olive groves, and terraced vineyards.

"You're right, Marta," I said. "I can't imagine anyplace I'd rather be."

The hotel just outside the city walls of Siena looked fabulous. An historic sixteenth-century villa surrounded by olive groves and gardens, it was the epitome of Tuscan charm. It was a little after six in the evening and we were lined up at the receptionist's desk, waiting to check in. We were all tired and hungry and not looking forward to the predictable delay that accompanied the processing of a late-arriving group.

"I hear the rooms here are lovely," Vivian said, as we stood in the lobby waiting to be shown to them. I could tell she was anxious. It was becoming clear to her that single travelers, despite paying a surcharge, did not get the best rooms in the house. Although I thought the practice of penalizing someone for traveling alone was unfair, I'd grown used to it. Vivian, on the other hand, had not. It distressed her to be assigned to what usually amounted to a small room with little or no view.

When our turn came to follow the bellhop to our rooms, he ushered us, along with the third single woman in the group, through a door leading away from the main hotel. After climbing a flight of steps and crossing a hallway, we found ourselves in a modern annex. There was no sign of any other guests in this part of the hotel. The bellhop stopped to open one door, and then another and another. I stepped into mine. It was a dreary room with a musty smell. Since it was dark outside I couldn't tell if it had a view.

Oh well, I thought, it's only for two nights. I started to unpack; in an hour we were to drive into Siena for dinner. I heard a tap on my door. It was Vivian. "Is your room as bad as mine?" she asked. I could tell she was upset.

"Maybe worse," I said, waving her in. She looked around but said nothing. "So, what do you think?" I asked.

"It's just like my room. Dreary and depressing. I'd call down and ask them to move me but I'm just too tired."

I put my arm around her. "Vivian, what you need is a great dinner and some good wine. So go change your clothes, put on some fresh lipstick, and we'll hit the road."

After Vivian left I looked around the room. She's right, I thought. It *is* a depressing room.

To my surprise, Vivian was in fine form by the time we sat down to dinner. We had been joined by four others at our table: Marta and Bernie, and a couple from Chicago, Betty and Herb. The restaurant, located near the breathtaking Piazza del Campo, was casual and charming, with delightful food and local wine. It turned out to be the perfect antidote for travelers' fatigue, a malady that, to a greater or lesser degree, we all felt. For three hours we sat, eating and drinking and talking and laughing. With each course we raised our glasses and toasted each other: *Cin cin!* Then others in the small restaurant began joining in, calling across the room, *Buon appetito. Cin cin!*

Although Vivian clearly was enjoying herself, sometimes I caught her glancing at a table nearby. There, a young couple sat, whispering and holding hands across the table, oblivious to anything but each other.

"Tell me the truth," Vivian said as we were leaving. "Wouldn't you give anything to be like them? To be in love and part of a couple?"

The truth was, it had never occurred to me. I was having a wonderful time.

But later that night, alone in bed, I thought of Naohiro and a certain dinner in Paris, one during which nothing existed for me but the man across the table.

In Perugia I had a room with a view. Situated at the top of a winding road that leads up to the old city, the hotel commanded a panoramic view of the Umbrian countryside. From my room I looked down into the tops of the trees lining the road and beyond that to the Tiber valley.

It was early morning, the start of a long day, and I was tired. I'd spent a restless night, dozing mostly between long stretches of wakefulness. At one point I'd gotten up to get a drink of water, only to find I couldn't remember where the bathroom was. Was I in Siena? Was the bathroom to the left? Or was I in Florence and the bathroom to the right? For a minute or two I stood there, totally disoriented. It frightened me, this black hole in my thinking; I wondered if this was how elderly people felt when unable to retrieve a memory.

Through the window I saw the light of dawn rising, a curtain lifting to reveal the day. I opened the shutters and stood looking out for a few minutes before gazing down into the treetops below my room. There, nesting in the upper branches, were dozens of birds. It was an odd perspective, looking down into the nests of birds instead of up. I felt like a voyeur. Then, as if some secret signal compelled them, they suddenly rose into the air, a graceful white-and-gray squadron. As they lifted off, the branches beneath them swayed slightly and the leaves shivered. The small sound reverberated in the air like a tuning fork as it nears the end of its vibrations.

From Perugia, we were to travel by train to Rome and then to Sorrento. On the bus to the station we were told that a train strike, already affecting travel north of Perugia, might force a change of plan. Of course, anyone who's ever taken a train in Italy knows the threat of strike is always lurking about and ignores it. But this strike was genuine. And it was traveling, as we were, from north to south. In Perugia we were able to board the train to Rome. But what would happen in Rome, where we changed trains? All day long we felt as though we were moving just ahead of a giant wave, one that was about to break and drag us under.

Still, nothing—neither anxiety nor fatigue—could dull the sharp pleasure of the landscape between Perugia and Rome. Through the train window I gazed out at the hills set in bold relief against the horizon. Along the top ridges, rows of tall trees marched in single file like an army on the move.

In Rome, the train station, as usual, was noisy and crowded; this time, however, an element of chaos was added to the mix. After a long lunch in the city we returned to find that our train to Naples was still scheduled and on time. The train was sleek and fast and like most of the others I slept sprawled across the seat until we arrived. In Naples we boarded a bus headed for Sorrento. But first we stopped at Pompeii.

Because it was late in the afternoon, Pompeii was almost empty. We wandered leisurely through the ruined city where men and women and children lived in their time as we live now in ours, believing then, as we do now, that death was far off in the distance. We saw where once they slept and baked bread and made love and raised families. Now, only stray dogs, sleeping in Pompeii's cool shadowy tombs, offered any signs of life.

But the drive from Pompeii to Sorrento banished the eerie spell cast by the ghostly city. The fertile beauty of the Campania region is a reaffirmation of life itself. We drove as the sun set in a ribbon of light across the shimmering Bay of Naples. Through the windows of the bus I could see olive groves slanting down to the water, covered with gauzy harvesting nets that looked like communion veils. And finally, into view came Sorrento, glorious Sorrento, with its colorful tiled roofs and scent of orange blossoms, perched on sheer cliffs high above the deep blue Bay of Naples.

I felt we had entered a different country. Here, there was little of the commerce of Milan or the brooding mystery of Venice or the art-filled museums and churches of Tuscany. We had arrived in a country ruled by the Mediterranean climate; by the intense heat and sun that even in October left most of the city streets empty between late morning and late afternoon. Here, everything flowed from that heat: the pace of life, the daily routines, the lush foliage of the palms, crepe myrtle, and orange and lemon trees.

For a brief time, we stayed in Sorrento. Settled into our glorious hotel high above the Bay of Naples, we ate fine food and swam in the pool and visited Capri and sat on the gorgeous terraces sipping cold drinks, thoroughly enjoying the chance to do nothing.

From Sorrento we rounded the tip of the peninsula and began the drive up the Amalfi Coast, along the Gulf of Salerno. The Amalfi Drive, a narrow winding road that cuts in half the whitewashed villages tumbling down the slopes of the Lattari Mountains, was breathtaking. So were the towns that we visited. Sun, flowers, coves to swim in, turquoise skies, and unparalleled natural beauty surrounded us: it was heaven on earth.

The problem for me was: I seemed to prefer earth on earth. The Amalfi Coast was almost too much of a good thing. The gorgeous countryside and picture-book villages approached the level of a fairy tale. I yearned for the dark alleys of Venice or the busy streets of Milan.

Enough is enough, I thought one day upon arriving in yet another sun-drenched whitewalled village dripping with red and white oleander, smart shops, and ten thousand steps to climb. But then I remembered what some philosopher or other had pointed out: you cannot know what is enough until you know what is too much.

But just when I thought I'd arrived at the point of knowing "too much" apropos the Amalfi Coast, we pulled into our last stop of the trip: a little village called Ravello.

The road to the medieval village of Ravello rises from the sea and zigzags up a long steep incline terraced with vineyards and lemon groves that, from a distance, look like yellow confetti scattered across the hills.

Because of its isolated location, Ravello is not as much on the tourist circuit as other towns in the area. The day we arrived, the streets were pleasantly uncrowded; an air of normalcy prevailed as the local villagers went about their daily errands.

To reach the center of town required a long walk up many steps. I lagged behind with Marta, ducking in and out of tiny shops and peering through gated doorways. In the courtyard of one house we spied a family of cats. A few were full-grown, but most—at least a dozen—were kittens of various sizes. Marta, also a cat fancier, stopped with me to watch the feline circus going on inside the gates. While the adult cats engaged in a hilarious round of territorial strutting, the kittens proceeded to stalk blades of grass, pounce on sticks, bite each other on the neck, tip over pots, and fall into small ditches before dozing off, one on top of another.

"Makes you homesick for your cat, doesn't it?" Marta said, laughing at their antics.

"More than you know," I said.

Actually, a small breeze of homesickness had been blowing over me for the last few days. I suspected, however, that I wasn't homesick for anything I would find at home when I returned. The longing was for what I wouldn't find: the past and all the people and places and cats that were lost to me. I'd been thinking a lot about that lately—the inevitability of separation, in one form or another, from all those we love and, in a different way, from ourselves as we were in the past.

But there would be time enough to face down those feelings in the weeks ahead; this was my last day with the group and I intended to enjoy it.

Although I do not believe in love at first sight—not with a man, anyway—I do believe it's possible to fall instantly in love with a place. As soon as Marta and I emerged from the narrow lane and entered Ravello's pristine town square, I felt the *zing* of Cupid's arrow hitting my heart. I was smitten instantly. But why Ravello? I wondered. Why didn't I fall for sparkling Amalfi or dazzling Positano? For some reason I found myself comparing the three towns to men. If Amalfi were a man, I thought, he'd be dressed by Calvin Klein and reading Tom Clancy. Positano would wear Armani and carry a book by John Le Carré. But if Ravello were a man—ah, Ravello!— he would be in chinos and a fresh white oxford shirt with no tie, buried in a book by Graham Greene.

After spending the morning touring one of Ravello's spectacular cliffside villas, the entire group gathered for lunch. We met at Salvatore's, a family-run trattoria overlooking the Gulf of Salerno. For me it was a good-bye luncheon; after returning to Rome that night I would be leaving the group.

We ate outside on a vine-covered terrace that jutted out over the cliff's edge, above the blue basin of the sea; it was like being suspended in midair. Since Salvatore and members of his family cooked each dish from scratch, there was time between courses to enjoy a brief stroll through the nearby cypress trees, or change tables to catch up with the others, or, best of all, to simply sit breathing in the lemon-scented mountain air as it moved through the lemon groves and down the hillside to us.

I looked around at the faces that over the past weeks had become familiar to me. *La famiglia,* I thought. Family. I knew, of course, that most of the faces, and the names that went with them, would fade quickly once normal life took over again. But in a way we had briefly, *very* briefly, been a family. And who's to say that just because something lasts only a short time, it has little value?

By the end of the afternoon, as we trudged back to the bus waiting to take us to Rome, it came to me, the reason I'd fallen for this village. Unlike the spun-sugar appeal of other Amalfi towns, Ravello personified simple elegance. It had the kind of austere beauty found in Shaker furniture. A classic example of this was the pristine white church in the town square, its only ornamentation a pair of bronze doors and four ancient columns. As the others walked ahead, I ducked into the church.

It was cool inside. The walls were a blinding white, embedded with delicate traces of frescoes. I stood for a while, then moved to the altar and bowed my head. There, alone in the silent church, I whispered the names of those gone from me: *Father. Mother. Grandmother. Jean. Marion. Ducky. Max. David.*

In my life, I loved them all.

14

SPANISH STEPS

Dear Alice,

    I have remained a stranger in Rome. Which is why I send you this happy reminder of a city I love: Venice. Rome and I are not lovers. We are not even friends. I can only hope that Camus was right when he wrote that "what gives value to travel is fear." I suppose it's possible that a little dash of fear gives *value to more than just travel. For one thing, it can teach us to be brave.*

Love, Alice

Three days after arriving in Rome I had my first real brush with danger. Until then I'd encountered only the routine mini-scares faced by most tourists. Yes, there was the evening in Paris when I was window-shopping along a quiet street near St. Sulpice and a burly man approached me, demanding I give him money. He took off, however, when several people emerged from the door of a nearby café. And there was that Sunday in London when two menacing young men circled me while I waited to change trains in an out-of-the-way Underground station. But then the train came and I jumped on, leaving them behind.

The incident in Rome was different. For one thing, I already had negative feelings about the city. Although I knew it to be a premature and unfair judgment, Rome struck me as frenetic and indifferent, a place where everyone seemed unfriendly, hassled, and in a hurry. Where was that warm, laid-back attitude that prevailed in the other Italian cities I'd visited? Not here.

Here, I seldom walked along a street without someone bumping into me or rudely pushing their way ahead of me. Here, I walked in a tense, alert state, always on the lookout for the noisy, polluting motorbikes whose drivers seemed to extract pleasure from terrorizing pedestrians.

Noisy, polluted, indifferent, crowded: this was my impression of Rome.

I knew it was a superficial one; I knew that if I dived deeper into the real city beneath the tourist attractions, my view of Rome would change. But I had no desire to ingratiate myself with the city, as I had done in the past with Paris or Milan or Venice. I had made a feeble attempt the day before, crossing over the Tiber River to visit the old Trastevere district where, despite rampant gentrification, the authentic Rome was said to reside still. And it was true.

In Trastevere I wandered through a maze of narrow streets and alleys, walking occasionally beneath a canopy of wash hung out between buildings to dry. Although I'd been told to look out for purse-snatchers in Trastevere, I was quite at ease walking by myself through the area. This was a real neighborhood, one where mothers walked with children to and from the market and shopkeepers stood at their doors calling out to passers-by. At times I had an eerie feeling that somehow I'd wandered onto the set of a Sophia Loren movie.

Of course, it had its beauty spots, too. I was particularly drawn to the lovely Piazza di Santa Maria in Trastevere, which I wandered into quite by chance. With its elegant raised fountain and charming sidewalk cafés, the square was an oasis of pleasant neighborhood bustle—minus the motor scooters. I had an iced coffee, and then headed across the piazza to the twelfth-century church of Santa Maria in Trastevere. I was unprepared for the majesty of the church's interior: its enormous, glowing nave and gigantic columns were as beautiful as any I'd seen.

Still, as pleasant as my visit to Trastevere was, it was not enough to change my mind about Rome. I remained a stranger, wandering through a city as indifferent to me as I was to it.

It didn't matter that deep down I recognized my disenchantment with Rome for what it was: an attempt to deny that I was homesick. It was much easier to blame Rome than to deal with my longing for the comfort of routine. I yearned to have lunch with my friends at the paper; to dig in my garden and feel the damp earth between my fingers; to hear the sound of neighbors calling in their dogs late at night; to shop at the neighborhood market, where everybody knows my name; and to lie in bed, waiting for the soft thud that signals the arrival of my cat.

To counteract such feelings, I devised a plan. During my short stay in Rome—a week's stopover, really, before working my way north to Tuscany and the Veneto—I would seek out all things familiar. Meaning: I ate at English tearooms, visited John Keats's house at the bottom of the Spanish Steps, went to lectures given in English at a nearby school, and saw the original English-speaking version of *Roman Holiday* with Audrey Hepburn and Gregory Peck. One day I even had a Big Mac and french fries at McDonald's, something I never did at home.

As silly as it was, *le plan d'Angleterre*—as I came to call it—actually worked. My homesickness or anxiety or whatever it was began to dissipate and my curiosity returned. At last Rome beckoned. And I responded. So I set out to do what I always do in a strange city: walk and walk and walk. I even responded to the Romans, chatting with the clerks in bookshops and with espresso-drinkers in the stand-up coffee bars.

My flirtation with Rome, however, proved to be a brief one. It ended abruptly two days later on a busy, fashionable street near my hotel on the Via Sistina.

After spending the morning and early afternoon visiting art galleries on the Via Margutta, I decided to walk over to a coffee bar I liked: the Antico Caffè Greco. Something of an institution in

Rome, the 200-year-old café was a hangout for writers and artists, as well as a rest stop for wealthy shoppers on the Via Condotti. I'd discovered the café on my first day in Rome and liked it instantly. It was a great place to sit and observe the Italian scene. Soon I was going there almost every day; sometimes for a quick espresso at the stand-up bar, sometimes to linger over a cappuccino.

Standing next to me at the bar on this particular day was a man I recognized as a café regular. He had the look of an artist about him, I thought, studying his scruffy corduroy jacket, uncombed hair, and gaunt face. But then again, for all I knew, he could be an eccentric billionaire, the Howard Hughes of Italy.

I drank my espresso and left, planning to walk directly back to my hotel. To my surprise the streets outside were pleasantly un-crowded. I looked at my watch. It was a little before three. The shops, closed down for the traditional long lunch break, would not reopen for another hour. The perfect time, I decided, to explore this fashionable district; to window-shop and read the menus posted outside restaurants and duck into the occasional bookstore or gallery still open.

It was on the Via Borgognona, near the bottom of the Spanish Steps, that I first sensed someone was following me. I began paying attention to a tall man dressed in a corduroy jacket and pants who, I noticed, stopped whenever I stopped and started walking again when I did.

Was he following me? I wondered. Or was it just my imagina-tion? But after two blocks of being trailed in this way I was sure his presence was no accident. When he began closing the distance be-tween us I saw it was the man I'd noticed in the café. Suddenly I was afraid. Then another man, a stocky fellow in dark pants and a checkered shirt, approached me from the opposite direction.

I knew then I had not imagined myself to be in danger; I *was* in danger. I'm going to be mugged, I thought, my heart pounding; or worse. I tightened my grip on my handbag, braced myself, and looked around for help—a person or an open door or even a motor scooter that I could stop. I saw nothing and no one. I cursed myself for not being more vigilant. At that moment the tall man brushed up against me, grabbing my arm. Without hesitating I broke into a run and started screaming for help.

The two men ran after me. I continued making as much noise as I could, overturning some trash cans along the way, hoping the noise of the rolling metal, plus my screaming, would alert someone. It did. By the time I reached the corner of the main street, doors had opened and several people appeared on the street, yelling at the two men to stop. It worked. The men chasing me immediately took off in the opposite direction.

After watching them disappear I sank to the curb. I sat shaking, the adrenaline still pumping through me, my head and ears pounding. I hadn't yet allowed myself to fully acknowledge the fear I felt. That would come later. Mainly I was embarrassed. What must the small crowd gathered round me think of this crazy woman who'd run screaming up the street?

But that seemed not to be what they were thinking about at all. What was on their minds was my well-being. I was touched by their concern and kindness as they helped me compose myself, asking over and over again if I was all right.

Si, si, grazie, I am all right, I said. I kept repeating it—*Si, si, grazie. I am all right*—until the crowd dispersed.

But I wasn't all right. Something had happened to me, something that left me feeling vulnerable in a way I'd not experienced for a long time. It was as though a tiny hairline crack had suddenly appeared in the self-sufficient image I had constructed over the years.

Not since my mother's death ten years earlier had I felt so painfully aware of how little control I had when it came to the grand scheme of my life.

Things happen, I thought, and we respond. That's what it all comes down to. To believe anything else, as far as I could tell, was simply an illusion.

Over the next few days I found myself unable to stop thinking about the incident on the Via Borgognona. First came the self-recriminations, and the attempt to deal with feelings of guilt that somehow I was responsible for what happened. My thoughts raced: *I should have taken another street. I shouldn't have been wandering around alone. I should have been more alert. I should have carried pepper spray or Mace. I shouldn't have looked at the man in the café.* Intellectually, I knew none of these things applied, knew that I hadn't done anything wrong or anything I hadn't done safely a hundred times in the past. Still, a voice kept saying: *My fault. My fault. My fault.*

Worse, however, was the loss of confidence that settled over me. I was overcome with a heavy inert feeling, one that prevented me from entering into life with any sense of trust. I tried putting into action the theorem I'd attributed to Albert back in Oxford—M=EA (Mishap equals Excellent Adventure)—but to no avail. I simply hadn't the energy or desire necessary to make such a plan work.

Now when I was out on the streets, I was so busy looking for danger that I barely saw the city. At night I slept with the bathroom light on, comforted by its dull glow through the half-closed door.

Sleep, however, did not refresh me. I awoke fatigued. It was trauma fatigue, I decided one morning after waking to a memory of the chronic tiredness I'd felt years earlier after serious back surgery.

It was time, I decided, to get out of Rome.

Intellectually I knew Rome wasn't the problem; that I was the problem. Still, when I changed my train tickets to Florence for an earlier departure, I breathed a sigh of relief. From Florence I planned to take the bus to Siena, a town I remembered as quiet and serene, one bereft of motor scooters and dangerous situations.

In the two days left before my departure, I spent my time taking bus tours organized for tourist groups. That way I was never alone. In the evening I followed the routine of eating dinner at a fancy hotel near mine and then returning to my room to sit outside on an adjoining veranda.

The veranda had come as a pleasant surprise in an otherwise disappointing choice of hotel. I'd discovered the outdoor balcony only a few days earlier, after opening a door hidden behind a curtain in my room. Like my room, it was in need of sprucing up—dead leaves lay scattered on the stone floor and the metal chairs were rusted—but I liked it anyway. It had a nice view of the Via Sistina and I found if I leaned over the stone balustrade and looked to the right, I could catch a glimpse of the Spanish Steps. Given my mood, the veranda was exactly what I needed: a retreat where I could sit and think. Or, more often, sit and *not* think.

In the evenings I'd sit there drinking wine and smoking an occasional cigarette, a habit I'd retrieved after the attempted mugging. I'd wait until the light faded and the lamps came on over the Spanish Steps before walking up the hill to have dinner at the usual place. Afterward I would return and, wrapped in a blanket, sit outside looking at the stars.

On my last night in Rome the rains came, turning my veranda

into a shallow swimming pool. Reluctantly, I abandoned my usual routine. Instead I propped myself up in bed and turned to my old friend Freya, hoping to find comfort and, perhaps, advice in her books, her observations. As usual, she did not disappoint.

"The unexpectedness of life, waiting round every corner, catches even wise women unawares," she wrote. "To avoid corners altogether is, after all, to refuse to live."

Reading this, I let out a small shriek of recognition. It was as though someone in charge had said to me: not guilty. Permission granted to continue on with your life as usual.

It would take some time, I knew, to regain my confidence about approaching life's corners. But, as Freya pointed out, avoiding them would be the same as saying "no" to life. And I wasn't about to do that.

I had been asleep for only an hour or two when a loud, booming sound awakened me. For one wild moment I thought a bomb had exploded. I sat upright, still groggy. Then I heard it again. *Boom!* It was even louder than the first one. Suddenly a great burst of light lit up my room. I ran to the veranda door and looked outside. Rain was pelting the empty streets below and forks of lightning illuminated the dark sky like arteries exposed on an X-ray. Thunder rolled across the city in great waves.

I looked at the clock. It was 3:00 A.M. I was already packed and ready to leave for Florence later that morning. If I went back to bed right away, I thought, I could catch maybe another three hours of sleep.

But I already knew I wasn't going to do that. Instead I put on my Reeboks, threw a raincoat over my pajamas, and left the hotel. It was as impulsive an act as anything I'd ever done. But something in me said: never again will you have the opportunity to stand at the top of the Spanish Steps with Rome lit up and spread out beneath you.

Put that way, I had no choice.

Outside, the streets were empty. The lightning and thunder were now off in the distance, but the rain had not let up. Leisurely, almost playfully, I walked the short distance—a hundred feet or so—from my hotel to the top of the Spanish Steps. There, like a sentinel I stood watch over the sleeping city of Rome.

With the city stretched out beneath me I looked off into the distance, across the Tiber. I watched as silent flashes of lightning, like strobes going on and off, revealed briefly domes and towers and church spires set against the sky. For the first time I felt the ancient majesty of Rome. Caught up in the strange beauty of the storm, I imagined all the Romes buried beneath this one. It was like being back in Pompeii. Watching, my thoughts excavated the city back through the centuries, back to a time when all roads led to Rome.

As I stood at the top of the Spanish Steps—a temporary traveler passing through Rome, and through life, in *anno Domini* 1993— an intense feeling of awe and respect came over me. Rome had endured. And when I was gone from Rome, and from life, she would still endure. It was then that I bowed with respect, like a younger member of the tribe, to the wisdom and tradition possessed by this honorable elder.

When I returned to the hotel I was no longer sleepy. The rain had stopped so I stepped out onto the veranda. Again, I wondered why I'd acted so impulsively. Was it because I needed to feel in control again? Perhaps. Perhaps not. For some reason the question no longer interested me.

I stood looking down over the streets near the hotel. Directly below on the Via Sistina a few people were venturing out: early risers, dog-walkers, people coming home from jobs that ended as day began. The street lamps were still on, but dawn was moving up quickly into the sky, turning it into a pale pink dome.

I ran back into the room and got my camera. Then, leaning out as far as I could over the veranda wall, I faced the Spanish Steps and gently squeezed the shutter release. It was my first photograph of Rome. And my last.

Whatever I wanted to remember of the city, I decided, would be there, in that single picture of Rome after the storm.

15

JANE EYRE IN SIENA

Dear Alice,

    The city of Siena is famous for the Palio, a horse race dating back to 1656. It is a brutal race, the horses often crashing into stone walls as they race around the main square of the city. Mattresses are placed on the walls, but they offer very little protection. I was told that it is the only race in the world in which the horse

can win <u>without</u> a jockey! Last year only two of the ten riders fin-
ished. How sad that the spectators think so little of the cruelly in-
volved.

Love, Alice

The minute I stepped off the bus in Siena I heard the music: strange noises created by drums and what sounded like high-pitched wind instruments—recorders perhaps. Whatever it was, the sound was captivating. It set my imagination spinning off into the Middle Ages, evoking powerful images I'd stored up; dark, fairy-tale scenes of fierce battles and axes and terrible deaths from the plague. For me it was part of Siena's appeal, this ability to tap into the primitive, mythic remnants of childhood fantasy that lurk beneath the adult sensibility.

Immediately, I checked my suitcase with a porter and ran toward the odd-sounding music. There, on a street lined with thirteenth-century stone buildings, men dressed in medieval costumes paraded by the shadowy arches and tall wooden gates that opened into private courtyards. In solemn rows, filling the width and length of the Via della Galluzza, they marched to the music; men both young and old, some carrying flags that floated in the air above their heads. A few marchers wore armored breastplates, calling to mind Siena's history as a powerful fortress once capable of defeating the Florentines in battle.

As I stood watching, a wide shaft of sunlight angled its way down into the narrow street, highlighting the buildings opposite me. Suddenly I saw two parades: the real one and a parade composed of shadows marching across the sunlit stone walls. The ghostly figures reminded me of the Halloween night parade in Baltimore; of how as a child I loved the excitement of moving through the stream of goblins and witches wandering the streets on that one night. Safe behind my own mask, an anonymous observer, I was free to watch without being seen.

In the narrow streets of Siena I felt all the same things: excitement, pleasure, and the safety of anonymity. It was as though the girl who loved Halloween and the woman who had just arrived in Siena were standing together, enjoying this medieval parade.

How odd, I thought, that within minutes of arriving in this remote Tuscan hill town I—or perhaps it would be accurate to say *we*—should feel so utterly at home.

The next day I set out to find a bookstore I recalled from my visit to Siena with the tour group. Marta and I had discovered the shop about a half hour before we were to leave for Perugia. To our surprise, it had a phenomenal collection of hard-to-find books, many available in English. Marta and I were able to spend only a few minutes there, but I'd written down the address, along with a note to seek it out when I returned. Unfortunately the note and address were lost somewhere along the line. However, Siena was a small town and I knew that in the course of wandering around I'd stumble across the bookshop.

I didn't have to stumble very long. About five minutes after leaving the old converted palazzo where I'd taken a room, I found the shop. It was near the Via di Città, a central street where many of the best antiques and pottery shops were clustered. When I pushed open the heavy door to the shop, the familiar dusty smell of old paper and leather greeted me like a welcoming friend.

My intention was to look for books on Siena's history. I was particularly interested in learning more about the famous Palio, a savage horse race dating back to the 1600s that still takes place twice a year in Siena's main square, Piazza del Campo. But I never made it to the history section; I was waylaid by Jane Eyre.

Miss Eyre lay primly on a table along with two other women I knew and loved: Elizabeth Bennet and Dorothea Brooke. I considered the three of them old friends. To me they were the grown-up versions of the three girls who'd helped me through my childhood and adolescence: Jo March and Nancy Drew and the orphaned Mary Lennox, whose secret garden still exists in my head as a real place.

I saw all of them as curious, independent girls and women who through necessity went out in search of their destinies. I also was not unaware that all—with the exception of Elizabeth Bennet— were bereft of one or both of their parents; through death, through absence, through sickness. Growing up—and well past that—they were my companions and sometimes my grief counselors. So even though I was on holiday in Italy I could not pass by Jane Eyre without stopping to say hello.

I stood at the table skimming the book's pages, stopping to reread this passage and that, as though I had no hidden agenda. But a part of me, I knew, was searching for a specific passage; the one describing the rainy night when the orphaned, ten-year-old Jane is delivered by carriage, alone and frightened, to the austere Lowood School. It still sent chills through me, the thought of Jane's abrupt introduction into yet another cruel reality of the unprotected, motherless child.

I found what I was looking for on page seventy-five. As I read the words, I relived young Jane's first encounter with Lowood and the stern woman who approached the carriage:

" 'Is there a little girl called Jane Eyre here?' she asked. I answered 'Yes,' and was then lifted out; my trunk was handed down, and the coach instantly drove away."

By this time I was sniffling and fighting back the tears. I got out a Kleenex and was dabbing at my eyes when a male voice, a very proper-sounding British voice, said, "See here, if you get the pages wet, you'll have to buy the book."

Startled, I looked up. The owner of the voice was a big man, tall and muscular, with thick reddish hair and a strong face dominated by a hawklike nose and a quizzical expression. In his arms he carried several heavy books that kept getting tangled with the horn-rimmed eyeglasses hanging from a cord around his neck.

"I was planning to buy the book anyway," I said sheepishly, thinking he was the shop owner.

"Well then, you're in the clear, aren't you?"

Was he serious? Or making fun of me? I couldn't tell. Either way I found him annoying and was about to tell him so when he interrupted.

"Alas, I wasn't so lucky. A week or two past, I dropped a book I was looking through, broke the spine—the owner made me pay for it. Worse luck, it was a book I can't abide."

"What book was it?" I asked, unable to beat back my curiosity.

"The *Decameron.* Paid a pretty penny for it, too. But that's water over the dam, isn't it? What have you there?" he asked, looking at the open book I held.

I hesitated, slightly embarrassed. The *Decameron* vs. *Jane Eyre?* No contest, I thought. But then my deep affection for the Brontë book took over, chasing away the snob in me. "*Jane Eyre,*" I said, catching myself just as I was about to add the word "sir"—as Jane might have done when addressing Mr. Rochester.

"Ah, yes. Quite a good book, that. It's held up rather well, don't you think?"

I was about to answer when an avalanche of books—the ones he held in his arms—began crashing to the floor. The noise attracted the attention of everyone in the shop, including a salesclerk who ran over and breathlessly asked, "Is everything all right, signore?"

"Yes, yes, quite all right, thanks," said the red-haired man who, stooping to gather up the books, seemed unfazed by the commotion he'd created.

I knelt down to help him. "I guess you'll have to buy all these books now," I said, smiling, hoping he'd get the joke.

He did. "I was planning to buy them anyway," he said, returning my smile.

"Well, then. You're in the clear, aren't you?"

We both laughed at the sudden reversal of roles. Then, as I helped him carry his books to the cashier's desk, he stopped and asked, "Aren't you forgetting something?" He nodded in the direction of the English table where *Jane Eyre* resided.

"Thank you, sir," I said, the word "sir" slipping out before I could edit it.

"You're welcome," he said, looking either puzzled or amused, I couldn't decide which.

At the cashier's desk I noted the authors of the books he had selected: Samuel Beckett, James Joyce, W. B. Yeats, Brendan Behan, Sean O'Casey; all Irish writers. I started to say something, but by this time he was halfway out the door.

It wasn't until we were on the street that he introduced himself. His name was Harold Ladley and he asked if I would like to join him for tea. "I know a nice spot nearby," he said, leading the way back to the narrow, winding Via di Città. Within minutes we were seated at a table in the Victoria Tea Room. It was a small place with tiny tables and chairs barely able to accommodate someone of his size.

But Hal Ladley, as I would learn over time, had a way of fitting comfortably into whatever situation presented itself to him. Whether it was a chair too small or an ill-fitting social gathering, he found a way to adapt and enjoy himself. I found it a very appealing quality.

Over tea and sandwiches I learned that Hal Ladley was not a tourist. He lived in Italy, in the nearby Chianti area.

"We Brits call it Chiantishire," he said, "because so many of us have moved here." At the moment his house was being occupied for two weeks by his honeymooning niece; it was his wedding gift to her. "So for the next fortnight I'm a nomad," he said. For the time being he was staying at a friend's house in Greve, a small village about a half-hour's drive from Siena.

A former professor of mathematics, Hal had left his university position in London after receiving a small inheritance from an aunt. "She was always a great one for saying that it was your time, not your money, that you should spend wisely."

"So, how do you spend your time wisely here in Chiantishire?" I asked.

"I travel. I cook. I have visitors. And I read a fair amount. But not anything to do with mathematics. Right now I'm working my way through the Irish writers."

"Yes, I noticed that back in the bookshop."

"So, ye read my book titles, did ye?" he said, smiling and leaning forward across the table. "And have ye an opinion of them?"

"No," I said. "No opinion about the books. But I have one about the reader. I think anyone who reads Joyce and Beckett—and is a mathematician to boot—must be very smart."

"And now I've gone and disabused you of that notion, have I?"

"Time will tell," I said. We both began laughing, but not because anything witty had been said. What had happened, I think, was we each recognized how much at ease we were with the other and that put us—at least it put me—in a good mood.

Later that evening, while walking alone through the town square, I found myself thinking of *Casablanca;* particularly of the final scene when Bogart's Rick says to Claude Raines's Inspector Renault, "I think this is the beginning of a beautiful friendship."

It was how I felt about Hal Ladley. And, I hoped, how he felt about me. But real friendships, I knew, are as rare as happy childhoods.

Over the next several days, Hal and I saw a lot of each other. Often we would spend the day driving through the beautiful Chianti countryside, taking the narrow, meandering Strada Chiantigiana instead of the modern highway. We'd drive through the valley, its sloping hillsides planted with silvery green olive trees and rows of vineyards, stopping to take a walk or have lunch or sample the local wine along the way. Hal, who knew the area and its history, was a perfect guide.

To my surprise, he also turned out to be a perfect traveling companion. Deep down, though, I recognized it was not so much Hal's aptitude for the give-and-take of such an arrangement that surprised me; it was my own. Although our inner clocks were totally mismatched—Hal liked to start the day late and dine at nine or nine-thirty; I was at my best early in the morning and disliked eating after 7:30 in the evening—I adapted as easily to his schedule as he did, in turn, to mine. It wasn't that we had discussions and made decisions about such things; whatever Hal and I did together just happened spontaneously and, despite our differences, was more often than not agreeable to the both of us.

Sometimes, driving home at the end of the day, we wouldn't talk at all. We'd just sit in the car, perfectly comfortable with the silence, enjoying the view or listening to music. Other times we never stopped talking. We talked about everything, from how to make the best bread soup to the reasons why Communism failed. And sometimes, usually after a glass or two of wine, we talked about our personal lives.

Hal told me about growing up in Oxfordshire and going off to study mathematics. His father, a mathematician who'd proved some well-known theorem or other, had been influential in Hal's choice of vocation. "I think I always knew it was not a true passion of mine," Hal said one day. "That it was a case of the son following the father."

We exchanged, too—but did not dwell on—our personal histories. Married young, divorced young, no children; that was Hal's summation, more or less, of his family life. My description to him was almost as brief. Married young, divorced in my early forties, two sons, now grown. With anyone else I would have thought it strange, these shorthand versions of our lives. But it seemed right for us.

When we traveled together, Hal and I seemed to have an unspoken agreement that we could go our own separate ways once we'd got to our destination. Sometimes we'd arrive in a town and while Hal went off to tour some church or sit in a café, I strolled through the streets or sought out a pottery shop. But we always met for lunch. And we were always eager to tell each other, over pasta and wine, what we did that morning.

Seeing a place through Hal's eyes added a new dimension to the trip. He was a person who seemed pleasantly surprised by everything. The appearance of a dog on the street. The sight of a little girl combing her doll's hair. Once when a sudden rainstorm swept through Siena, catching us off guard at an outdoor café, Hal seemed surprised but delighted.

"Unusual, this rain. But there's nothing more refreshing than Italian rain, is there?" he asked, after we'd taken shelter under one of the café's awnings.

Hal and I also enjoyed taking part in the *passeggiata*, the traditional before-dinner stroll observed in many Tuscan towns. It's a neighborly time, when young and old take to the narrow streets, window-shopping and stopping to gossip. Young lovers, too, came out to enjoy the *passeggiata*. But they walked in their own world, each in thrall to the other. The older townspeople smiled at the sight of the young lovers as they passed by. Hal and I, walking arm in arm, smiled too.

"Romeo and Juliet, eh?" Hal said, nodding in the direction of one young couple. "Caught up in the *folie à deux* known as young love."

"Ah yes, I remember it well," I said. "Too well, I fear."

"I suspect we all do. Romantic love is likely responsible for most of us marrying the wrong person." Hal laughed. "It was in my case, anyway."

I was caught off guard by his remark. Despite his love of writers like Yeats and Joyce, I never thought of Hal as having a romantic nature. It was hard for me to imagine him driven by overwhelming passion into a marriage, or even a relationship. Certainly ours was a platonic relationship. But I'd suspected from the beginning that Hal and I would never be a romantic couple, that we were destined instead for friendship.

The truth is, my relationship with Hal turned out to be one of the least romanticized I'd ever had with a man. I didn't imagine him or invent him, as I often did with men who attracted me. I liked him for the person he actually was. And when I noticed something about him I didn't like, it was no big deal. As far as his feelings about me, well, I liked not having any of the bloated self-awareness that comes with romantic chemistry or the need to see myself reflected favorably in a man's eyes. What I saw in Hal's eyes was: Hal.

Sometimes I thought Harold Ladley was just the kind of man with whom I could share a life. But other times I suspected that I would miss the leap of the blood, as a friend of mine calls the physical chemistry between a man and a woman. It is the tension, as every woman knows, that gives a relationship its extra spring.

I felt it, the leap of the blood, one morning in Siena when a letter arrived from Paris. It was from Naohiro, suggesting we meet in Venice. Immediately I wrote back, agreeing. On my return from posting it, I stopped to look at some pottery in a shop window. In the glass I saw my reflection. Looking at my flushed face, I decided that the leap of the blood, among other things, was very good for one's complexion.

On the day before I was to leave Siena for the Veneto, Hal suggested we visit the nearby town of San Gimignano. "It's among the most remarkable of all the Tuscan towns," he said. "Very well-preserved and quite haunting, I think."

I agreed and we left within the hour, driving the short distance from Siena to San Gimignano through rolling farmland and air fresh with the scent of cypress trees.

As we drove, Hal explained that San Gimignano, once known as San Gimignano of the Fine Towers, had a savage past, one that included fighting and plunder by barbarians, and terrible plagues. At the end of the eleventh century, seventy-six towers were built, from which San Gimignano's great families could wage war. As usual when Hal went into the history of a place, he made it quite entertaining.

Listening to him, I often was reminded of my father's stories about the exotic places he'd visited. I'd been thinking about my father a lot lately. Sometimes when I came across a place that seemed unusually exciting and foreign to me—the kind of place I imagined he would like—it was as though I was seeing it through my father's eyes as well as my own. More than once I found myself wondering if I was trying to, as an analyst might put it, "incorporate" my father. I knew it was a necessary emotional task I'd never been able to complete. It even occurred to me, on the way to San Gimignano with Hal, that of all the roles assigned to me in my lifetime, the one I'd never played to a mature conclusion was that of daughter. Daughter to a father, anyway.

I was about to ask Hal how close we were to San Gimignano when a skyline of tall buildings appeared on a distant hillside. The shapes, silhouetted against the sky, struck me as mysterious, almost ominous. If I squinted, they resembled giant warriors standing guard over the town.

"Those are the thirteen remaining towers of San Gimignano," Hal said. "The most that are left, I think, in any of the hill towns."

As we approached the walls surrounding the town, my excitement grew. I was attracted to the dark history that lay inside these ramparts, just as I had been drawn to the medieval pageantry of the parade in Siena. Why this was so, I wasn't sure. But the minute I entered the walled city, where no cars are permitted, a little thrill of pleasure passed through me.

Hal had decided to search for a church fresco he wanted to see, so I walked alone up the steep Via San Giovanni. Halfway to the top I stopped and leaned against a doorway. I stood there imagining how, long ago, whole families living on this street were wiped out by the cruel and terrible Black Death. Now there were shops and cafés filled with tourists drinking Vernaccia, the delicious local white wine. Looking past the town ramparts I could imagine fierce battles being waged, filling the air with smoke and the pitiful cries of the doomed. Now I smelled the fragrance of almond biscuits baking and heard the high, sweet sounds of music.

Since Hal and I had agreed to meet at the square—the Piazza del Duomo—I headed in that direction. The fresco Hal was looking for was inside the large cathedral on the west side of the piazza.

I was about to climb the steps leading to the cathedral's entrance when I saw Hal. He was standing at the opposite side of the piazza, leafing through a book. The sight of him in his familiar brown tweed jacket, his red hair shooting off sparks in the sun, made me smile. I waved. He didn't seem to see me.

As I started to walk back down the steps to cross the square I heard the music. It was the same sound of recorders I'd heard earlier. Hauntingly beautiful, the music reminded me of Andean folk music, sad and delicate, filled with longing. I spotted four men standing at the entrance to a street; they were playing different-sized wooden pipes. The limpid sounds floated through the piazza, each note hanging in the air like a memory of home.

As I listened, a strange, mixed-up feeling came over me. Part of it had to do with standing in a small Tuscan hill town waving—waving good-bye, really—to a man I liked and admired. But another part was about the past, about wanting to wave good-bye to my father. Not the kind of good-bye that was forever, but the kind I waved to Mother when I left on the bus for Girl Scout camp or to Ducky Harris when we parted after walking home from school.

I thought of all the years I'd spent trying to piece together a picture of my father's face. Now, for the first time, I wished he could see me, see what I looked like, see who I was.

I wanted to say: *This is me, Dad. This is your little girl grown into a woman. And I'm standing here far from home, alive and excited and thinking of you.*

Instead, I said to the red-haired man running up the steps of the Duomo toward me, "I was wondering if you saw me. I've been waiting for you."

16

PAST PERFECT

Dear Alice,

   I think it was Jung who pointed out there is a big difference between falling and diving. At the beginning of this trip I was falling, I think; a figure at the mercy of gravity and whatever passing object I could grab on the way down. Like maps or friendly cafés or people who spoke English. Now, even though my *form is far from perfect, I am better able to dive into new waters, leaving behind barely a splash as I enter.*

Love, Alice

It was to Asolo, a Renaissance town perched high in the green foothills of the Italian Dolomites, that Freya Stark came to live out the end of her life. And it was to Asolo that I had come to pay my respects to Dame Freya and to end my trip.

It seemed the right thing to do, to spend the last days of my journey with a woman who had become my travel companion. Over the months I often had relied on her spirit to guide me when I hesitated, uncertain of the way. Usually it was her idealism and desire to understand that inspired me. But Freya also made me laugh. Sometimes out loud. Who else could offer up, after writing with elegance and insight about the culture and people of Baghdad, an observation such as this:

"I suppose that, after the passion of love, water rights have caused more trouble than anything else to the human species."

The irony was that had I come to Asolo just seven months earlier I might have run into her. Indeed I might have seen Freya at the very villa where I was staying; she was said to occasionally take dinner there. But just as I was beginning my trip in Paris, Freya was ending her lifelong journey. She died in her beloved Asolo at the age of 100 and was buried in the local graveyard. In Arabian robes, so the story goes.

No wonder she loved this village, I thought, as I sat drinking espresso in Piazza Garibaldi, the central square of Asolo. With its honey-colored buildings and winding, colonnaded streets too nar-

row to allow two-way traffic, Asolo's quiet beauty for centuries attracted composers, painters, and poets, Robert Browning among
them. "The most beautiful spot I ever was privileged to see," he
wrote of Asolo. After his death the street he lived on was renamed
Via Browning.

Asolo's beauty was astonishing. But it was the quiet serenity of
the place that appealed to me most. Sometimes at night I would get
up and walk through the terraced gardens just outside the door to
my room, listening to the silence. Rising in the morning, I would
open the heavy wooden shutters and hear only the sound of birdsong or the soft thud of raindrops dripping from the roof above to
the grass below. Beyond the gardens was the view I looked out on
each morning: pale blue hills, and beyond them, the snowy
Dolomites, their peaks ringed like Saturn with bands of swirling
mist.

In Asolo I purposely fell into a routine; I wanted to make one
day indistinguishable from the next. Breakfast was taken on the terrace outside my room or in the main villa: espresso, fresh fruit, and
a slice or two of panforte, a bread made with raisins and nuts. Then
I walked into town, stopping to peer in every window and study
each building along the way. One day a British tourist staying at the
villa accompanied me on my walk, pointing out the house where
Eleonora Duse, a great actress born in Italy in 1858, had lived. She,
too, was buried in Asolo.

Occasionally, I would stop to pick up a paper before heading
for Caffè Centrale in the main piazza. There, in front of the imposing fifteenth-century water fountain, under the fierce gaze of the
stone lion of San Marco, I would try to decipher the news by
matching the Italian words with the accompanying pictures. More
often, I simply sat drinking espresso while observing the townspeople as they went about their daily routines.

In Asolo there were no cell phones ringing or motorbikes whizzing by; no harried commuters on their way to jobs that occupied most of the space in their lives; no weary-looking tourists with timetables to meet and must-see churches to visit. The tourists in Asolo at this time of the year, mostly English travelers and well-to-do Italians from Milan, seemed to have no agenda—except to relax and enjoy themselves.

In Asolo, life went on in a quiet fashion. Children played around the fountain, splashing one another with water that still flows through a Roman aqueduct. Mothers pushed babies in strollers. Men sat reading the papers, halos of pipe smoke rising above their heads. Women walked home from the market, carrying bags of fresh fruit and vegetables. Once I saw a wedding party walking to the church, the bride's white veil blowing up from her head like gauzy wings.

The piazza was home base for me. Often I ate lunch there; soup, usually. The *pasta e fagioli*, a thick pasta-and-bean soup, was my favorite. Then in the afternoon I'd explore the small, fascinating shops in the arcaded walkways, stopping in at the embroidery school and pottery shop to watch the artisans at work.

At night, after dinner, I would stroll up to the square and have a glass of Ferrari, a sparkling white wine from the Alto Adige. Often on such evenings I thought of my sons.

Sometimes I found my mind roaming over the past, briefly returning to me the two boys who used to live in my house. I saw them sitting at the table, one building airplane models, the other arranging his baseball cards in stacks. I saw them playing with the cats—Pussums, Graysie, Pussums, Jr., Mittens, Pumpkin, Tasha—who still, in their minds and mine, formed a feline map of our past together. I saw the boys waving good-bye from the bus that took them to summer camp and saying hello when they came home from college for Christmas. It never occurred to me then to mark such seemingly ordinary moments before they slid into obscurity. After all, how was I to know that somewhere a clock was quietly ticking away, moving the three of us into the future?

More often, though, I tried to imagine what the future held for my sons. Although I used to think I had a pretty good handle on who they were and where life would take them, now I was less sure. To my surprise, I liked my new attitude better. It seemed to signal a letting-go of the notion they were set on some immutable course that could not be changed. That left me to face the problem of how to give up my desire to keep them close to me in a way I still needed but they didn't.

What a long, painful process it is, letting go of those you love, I thought, walking back to the villa one night. Still I knew that slowly it *was* happening. The odd thing is, letting go of the two young boys I loved didn't make me feel as lonely as I had feared. It seemed to be freeing up more space for the men they had become.

One morning, while loitering near the entrance to the villa, I watched the arrival of two new guests in a chauffeur-driven car. Along with several pieces of expensive luggage, the couple—a tall, regal-looking woman with silver hair and an impeccably dressed younger man—moved toward the receptionist's desk. I, naturally, moved along with them, curious to learn what I could about this rather intriguing couple. Were they mother and son? I wondered, although the gap between their ages seemed too wide for that. Was he a paid companion, perhaps, for a wealthy woman? A nephew? Maybe a grandson?

Pretending to study a brochure about sightseeing in Treviso, I took up a position near the reception desk. The check-in procedure yielded several pieces of information. One, they were British; their accents definitely patrician. Two, the woman—in her seventies perhaps, but quite striking—did most of the talking. Three, the young man—in his early thirties perhaps—had quite a pleasant demeanor. Four, they were staying in separate rooms.

What I planned to do with this information I hadn't a clue. But they were by far the most interesting people I'd seen at the villa. And they spoke English. Who knows? I thought, perhaps our paths will cross. Perhaps we'll meet one morning at breakfast. Or in the village. Or in the garden.

A day later I did meet the British couple. But not in any of the likely places. We met at Asolo's graveyard, the cemetery attached to the small church of Sant'Anna. It was the place, I had been told, where Freya Stark was buried.

The walk to the graveyard, situated on a high spot outside the town's center, took about thirty minutes. When I reached the tidy little cemetery, I was out of breath and slightly dizzy from the altitude. I seemed to be the only visitor. Looking around at the rows and rows of tombs crowded together, I realized I had no idea as to the actual location of Freya's grave. But what the heck, I thought, that wouldn't have stopped Freya and it won't stop me.

At the end of an hour I still hadn't located what I'd come to find. Tired, I sat on a tombstone to rest. It was then that I saw them approaching, the British couple from the hotel. Embarrassed to be caught sitting on top of someone's gravesite, I jumped up and blurted out, "Hello. I'm an American and I'm staying at your villa."

The silver-haired woman smiled. "Well, I wish it *were* my villa," she said. "But, alas, it's not." Up close, she appeared even older than I'd imagined, but still quite lovely.

"Are you looking for someone special?" asked the young man.

"Yes, I am. Freya Stark."

The mention of her name drew an instant response from the silver-haired woman. "Oh, my, what a dear old gal she was. Wonderful woman, Freya Stark. Is she buried here?"

I told her yes, I thought so, but that I hadn't been able to find her.

"Did you know that just last month a memorial service was held for her in London?" the woman asked. "At St. James's Church. In Piccadilly. I heard it was really beautiful."

I knew that church; I had visited it three months earlier. Quite by accident I'd popped into the modest-looking building to take a rest after a long walk through Piccadilly and Mayfair. From a plaque posted at the entrance I learned that Sir Christopher Wren designed the church in 1674 and, after its destruction by bombs in 1940, it was completely rebuilt.

When I walked inside the church I saw a choir about to rehearse a hymn. I sat listening as they began to sing:

Morning glory, starlit sky
soaring music, scholars' truth,
flight of swallows, autumn leaves,
memory's treasure, grace of youth:
open are the gifts of God.

If I closed my eyes now, in Asolo, I could still see St. James's interior: a vast, simple space surrounded by two-tiered windows beneath a barrel-vaulted ceiling. It struck me that St. James's, an edifice plain on the outside but soaring and beautiful within, was the perfect place to honor Dame Freya.

The British couple, unlike me, had found the site they'd come looking for: the grave of Eleonora Duse. It was set apart from the rest of the cemetery, they told me, in a small patch of woods.

I had planned to stay for another hour or so, searching, but the light was fading and so was my energy. I walked back to the main road with the woman and her friend to their parked car. A chauffeur stood beside it, smoking a cigarette. Seeing them, he quickly stamped it out.

"Could we give you a lift back to town?" the young man asked.

"That would be very nice," I said. He held open the door and I climbed in.

"By the way, I'm Jack Upton," he said, holding out his hand. "And this is Mrs. Margaret Spenser."

"I'm delighted to meet you," I said, introducing myself and wondering, even as I did, what to say next. For some reason I felt the burden of conversation lay with me. As I rummaged through my head looking for something interesting to say, Mrs. Spenser broke the silence.

"Have you been enjoying your stay in Asolo?" she asked.

I told her I was enjoying it immensely, especially the quiet, pastoral setting.

"Yes, it's quite restful, isn't it? Particularly after the crowds we found in Venice. I must say, though, I find Venice simply charming. Have you been?"

"Yes, I have. And it is beautiful. No wonder painters could never get enough of Venice. I've read somewhere that the light in Venice actually changed the course of painting."

My remark seemed to interest the two of them, particularly Jack. "It has been said you can classify Venetian painters by the light they preferred," he said. "Bellini liked morning light, Veronese the midday, and Guardi the evening."

"Are you a painter?" I asked.

"No, but I am interested in art."

"Jack is too modest," Mrs. Spenser said. "He's quite an expert on Renaissance drawings."

I was about to ask more when the car pulled up in front of the villa. Jack spoke to the driver in Italian, then helped Mrs. Spenser and me from the car.

"I told him to pick us up tomorrow afternoon at two," he told Mrs. Spenser. "Maser is only four miles from here and Villa Barbaro is only open in the afternoon." He turned to me. "One of the reasons for our visit here is to see the Palladian villas in the region. Particularly Villa Barbaro. Some think it's Palladio's masterpiece."

"Yes. I've read about the Villa Barbaro. It's on my list, too."

We walked into the small lobby together. They were staying in the villa; my room was in a smaller, more modest building nearby. We said our good-byes and parted, going off in different directions.

That night I broke my usual routine. Instead of going to the square after dinner for a glass of wine, I sat in the garden thinking about Venice. About Venice and about Naohiro.

Just before leaving for Asolo I had spent my last weekend in Venice with Naohiro. When he arrived by plane from Paris on a Friday afternoon I was there at the small, crowded airport waiting for him. As usual, I was excited by the thought of being with him.

I spotted him first. He wore a black leather jacket and was moving quickly, but with his usual elegance, through the crowd. Watching him, I felt it: the leap of the blood. I wondered—no, I *hoped*—that he would feel it, too.

Naohiro, I could tell, had seen me. He walked to where I stood and put his suitcase down. Then in traditional Japanese fashion, he greeted me by bowing his head. In similar fashion I returned the greeting. By now I was used to the formality that surrounded our meetings in public places.

"I trust you are well," he said, stepping close to me. He smelled of fresh pine needles.

"I am. And you?"

"I am very well. And very happy to see you."

We took a water taxi from the airport to Venice. In the small speedboat we sat side by side, our bodies touching. When finally the city of Venice began to take shape on the horizon, Naohiro put his arm around my shoulder. He had never done this before. It was such an American gesture and so foreign to Naohiro's usual public demeanor that it caught me off guard. I found it endearing. And exciting, too.

It confirmed my belief that restraint is often more exciting than unbridled emotion. Up to a point, anyway.

The small boat entered the Grand Canal, moving past the glorious white-domed church of Santa Maria della Salute to Ponte dell'Accademia, the bridge connecting the San Marco section of the city to Dorsoduro. After getting off on the Dorsoduro side, we walked to the *pensione* where I was staying. This was my favorite part of Venice.

To get to the *pensione* we had to cross a small wooden bridge over a narrow canal. The water beneath the bridge shimmered in the sunlight. Halfway over we stopped to admire the dappled patterns moving across the water.

"This reminds me of the bridge over the water gardens at Giverny," I said. "Only there, we watched water lilies floating by. Do you remember?"

Naohiro took my hand. "I remember."

"And what else do you remember?" I asked.

"That you wore a black dress to dinner that night." He stopped and smiled. "And that I learned Laredo is not concrete but a city in Texas."

Why this moment should make me as happy as it did was a mystery to me. But I accepted it as one accepts the arrival of an unexpected windfall: with complete pleasure and no questions as to its origins.

Over the next two days, Naohiro and I rose early and retired late. After all, there weren't that many hours in a weekend; we didn't want to waste too many of them sleeping.

Our favorite time was early morning, when Venice was just waking. On the first morning, with no map or destination, we walked holding hands through the quiet streets, changing direction if a certain square or canal path attracted us. Gradually, as we walked, the city came to life. Men and women appeared on their way to work. Smells of breakfast cooking, of bacon and coffee, floated from windows into the narrow streets. Dogs pranced along the sides of narrow small canals, their noses to the ground, sniffing. Sleepy-eyed children, carrying books, entered the church school on the Campo San Agnese. Shopkeepers could be seen moving around inside their still-closed establishments.

We stopped at a caffè bar to have espresso. We sat there for an hour, exchanging news of our children and detailed information about what we'd been doing since our meeting in London. Once again, I was struck by the immediacy of our relationship, by how much it was set in the present. I felt no need to retrace in detail Naohiro's life before he met me, and Naohiro, it seemed, shared this feeling. It was as though we recognized that the past—and the roles we had played with others in that past—had no dominion over who we were to each other.

By the time we crossed the bridge to have a proper breakfast near the Piazza San Marco, we were both quite hungry. It was while walking through one of the narrow, mazelike streets leading into the piazza that Naohiro and I were met by Death. He approached us slowly, a tall, gaunt figure dressed in a voluminous black cape and three-cornered hat, his face covered by a skeletal white mask. In one gloved hand he carried a scythe; in the other a cardboard tombstone.

He drew close, close enough for us to read what was written on the tombstone: *Fugit hora, memento mori.*

"What does it mean, I wonder, the words on the tombstone?" Naohiro said.

"You've come to the right person," I said, thinking about all the days I had spent studying tombstones with my grandmother. "It's a Latin phrase often inscribed on tombstones. It means, 'Time flies, remember you must die.' "

We watched as the spectral figure continued on, in the direction of two women studying a window display of expensive leather bags.

"I suppose he's a walking advertisement for some mask shop," I said. There were many such shops in Venice, where mask-making is an art form, one whose origins go far back in the city's history.

Naohiro said nothing. But a look passed across his face, one I couldn't identify. Was he offended by the tombstone admonition? I realized how little I knew about death and burial traditions in Japan. It was something I would ask him about, I decided, over breakfast.

It was a little after nine when we arrived at the terrace café in the Hotel Monaco. In a perfect setting overlooking the Grand Canal we ordered cereal and fresh fruit, a basket of sweet rolls, and strong coffee. Just as I started to ask Naohiro about the ceremonies and customs associated with death in Japan, he asked me a question.

"I have been thinking," he said. "Why do they say on their tombstones that 'Time flies, remember you must die'? Would it not be more useful to say that 'Time flies, remember you must live'?"

It was such a simple observation. But profound, I thought. It reminded me of the way children think; of how they try to understand the world by asking the obvious or naive question. It was a great gift, I thought, to retain such directness as an adult.

I looked at Naohiro and felt a tenderness usually reserved for my sons. "You are right," I said. "It is more useful to remember that we must live."

On Sunday afternoon we boarded the Number 1 vaporetto for a leisurely ride along the length of the Grand Canal. It was a quiet time along this watery thoroughfare. Quiet enough for Naohiro and me to hear the soft lapping sounds of water meeting land and the echoes of children playing in the narrow *calli* near the canal.

On Sunday afternoons there was none of the early-morning commerce of boats delivering fresh produce or the sight of rubbish barges picking up refuse. Nor any of the midday rush of tourists, many of whom had already left after spending a weekend in Venice. The vaporetto that Naohiro and I boarded was almost empty.

For the next hour we sat mesmerized by the changing light, by the white palazzo steps that disappeared into the canal, and the tethered gondolas riding up and down on the water like restless black steeds.

Naohiro was the first to spot the silver-haired gentleman standing on the balcony of his grand palazzo, an elegant greyhound by his side. Later it was I who called to Naohiro's attention the gauzy fabric covering the palazzi being renovated; it was as though the artist Christo had come to Venice and wrapped the buildings in thin white nets.

Later that night we walked back to our *pensione* under a moon that glowed silver through the fog, like a light shining through ice. Giddy with happiness we crossed bridge after bridge, turned down one narrow street after another, walked along the quays of small canals. And then it dawned on us: we were lost.

We ducked into a piano bar on the Zattere to ask for directions. After listening to directions given in a combination of Italian and English by a very kind patron, Naohiro and I still had no idea of how to get back to the *pensione*.

"Maybe we should have left a trail of bread crumbs, so we'd be sure to find our way back," I said, forgetting that Naohiro probably was not familiar with the fairy tale about Hansel and Gretel.

"Or perhaps we should not try to find a way back," he said. "Perhaps the answer lies in finding a way to go ahead."

As I sat on the terrace in Asolo remembering all this, the phone in my room rang. I ran inside and picked it up.

"This is Jack Upton," the voice said. "I do hope it's not too late to call. But Mrs. Spenser and I were wondering if you'd like to drive with us tomorrow to the Villa Barbaro."

The call startled me somewhat. I was still back in Venice. But after a few seconds of readjustment I accepted his offer. It was just what I needed, I decided, turning out the light and climbing into bed.

The drive to Villa Barbaro took less than fifteen minutes. On the way there, Jack Upton explained that only a portion of the sixteenth-century villa was open to the public.

"The present owners—the Volpe-Buschetti family, I believe—reside there and do not open up their private quarters to visitors. But what is open is magnificent." This was his second visit to the villa, he said.

"Have you been to the villa before?" I asked Mrs. Spenser.

"Not inside. But we have driven by and, I must say, the façade is quite breathtaking. But it's the Veronese frescoes I'm longing to see."

Suddenly, the Villa Barbaro appeared through the car window. None of the photographs of the villa had prepared me for the real thing. Set on a slope, the graceful building stood at the end of a long gravel pathway surrounded by manicured lawns. The perfect symmetry of its long arcaded façade and pillared entrances, so pure and simple, made the villa one of the most beautiful structures I had ever seen.

Across the road was another glorious sight: a rounded building with three cupolas protruding from its dome. I asked Jack about it.

"That is the round temple," Jack said, "also designed by Palladio."

We drove off the main road and into a parking lot adjacent to the villa. From there we walked across gravel pathways to the front of the building, where we purchased tickets and put felt scuffs on over our shoes to protect the highly polished floors.

Inside the villa we climbed to the top of a staircase and were met by a young woman leaning through an open door. She was dressed in a green silk gown, her blond hair pulled back from her fresh-scrubbed, cherubic face. It took me a second to realize I was seeing not a real woman but one of Veronese's witty trompe l'oeil frescoes. We were in fact surrounded by such painted women: courtiers dressed in taffeta peered down from a balcony; women flirted from behind fans; naughty winged Cupids teased a love-struck woman.

Across the room I saw Jack and Mrs. Spenser standing before a large painting, engaged in animated conversation. They seemed to have forgotten me. Which was fine. I liked wandering about on my own.

I was about to take a stroll outside when I came across an out-of-the-way alcove. Looking in, I saw it was empty except for a trompe l'oeil of an elegant room as seen through a glass door. I stepped in and walked over to the painted door, which this time turned out to be the real thing: a real door leading into a real room.

Reverting to my reporter's habits, I tried to open the door. It was locked.

I peered through the glass. Inside was an elegant, comfortable room, furnished with large, soft chairs and antique rugs. Glass vases filled with flowers and silver-framed photographs sat on top of gleaming wooden tables. A soft light fell from tall floor lamps, revealing an upturned book left behind on the arm of a chair. Beyond the room was a hallway; I could see umbrellas protruding from a stand carved in the shape of an exotic bird.

I decided I liked the people who lived here. The Bolpe-Vuschetti or Volpe-Buschetti—or whoever they were—seemed to have made a home out of what easily could have become a museum. Signs of real life were everywhere: in the books and flowers and pictures and umbrellas and lamps that someone forgot to turn off.

As I was thinking this, a woman appeared in the hallway beyond the glass door. She seemed to see me. Embarrassed, I turned and quickly retreated to one of the public rooms. Then, after checking to see that Jack and Mrs. Spenser hadn't left, I turned in my felt scuffs and went outside to take a walk.

I stood on the front veranda and looked down the long formal walkway and across the Veneto plains that ran off into the distance. *How beautiful this is,* I thought. *This view, this house, the ravishing frescoes inside.*

But a part of me already knew that my most vivid memory of Villa Barbaro would not be the vanishing perspective of the Veneto plains or the trompe l'oeil or any other "trick of the eye." No, what I would remember most would be the sight of that one private room so redolent with real life.

The rain started to fall just as we began the drive back to Asolo. Jack and Mrs. Spenser were eager to exchange views of the villa.

"Well, I've not seen its likes before," Mrs. Spenser said. "It certainly was a treat, wasn't it?"

"You really have to return again and again to a place like this to fully appreciate it," Jack said. "What did you think of the Veronese?"

"Splendid, simply splendid," Mrs. Spenser said.

It seemed to be my turn, so I said, "I was surprised to see how witty Veronese was. His work seemed more contemporary than I expected."

"Well, yes, in a way, I suppose you could say that," Jack said. I could see that Jack didn't agree but was too gallant to say so.

I changed the subject, asking them where they were off to next.

"To Montreux. To a spa near there to rest and relax," Mrs. Spenser said. "And you? Are you off to someplace interesting?"

"Yes. I'm going home."

When I arrived at the Venice airport the next day I learned my flight was delayed by two hours. It annoyed me, this glitch in the schedule. But it annoyed me more that such a minor event had the ability to annoy me. Where was all that laid-back mellow outlook I thought I'd cultivated during my travels?

I bought a newspaper, thinking it would take my mind off the delayed plane. Instead I found myself wondering what was going to happen when I returned to my job at the newspaper. Did I still have the skills to report a story or write a column? Or had I lost my edge, maybe even my drive, when it came to newspaper work?

Don't do this to yourself, I thought. *Don't spend your last minutes in Italy worrying about the future.*

So I did what I'd done so many times while traveling: I spent a few minutes with Freya. I leafed to a passage that had to do with reaching one's destination. She wrote it from Persia:

"This is a great moment, when you see, however distant, the goal of your wandering. The thing which has been living in your imagination suddenly becomes a part of the tangible world. It matters not how many ranges, rivers or parching dusty ways may lie between you; it is yours now for ever."

It occurred to me that nowadays there was no such place as Persia; it had become a country named Iran. But whatever its name, Freya at least had a moment in which she reached a tangible destination and made it hers. Forever.

I had no such tangible destination. There was no goal to my wandering and nothing that I could claim as mine forever. But Freya's words still spoke to me.

There was an hour left before departure. I stepped outside, onto the pier where travelers to and from Venice catch water taxis to the city. I walked to the spot where Naohiro and I had last stood together. As I watched the boats arrive and depart with their cargo of passengers and luggage, rain began to fall. The raindrops bounced lightly off the water between the boats.

In the distance a mist was gathering. Slowly the white vapor moved like a ghostly presence toward the pier, enveloping everything but the tethered boats bobbing up and down. I stood at the pier and watched a departing vaporetto penetrate the misty curtain and then disappear.

This is mine, I thought suddenly. *This is what I will have forever. The memory of this moment, of rain falling on Venice.*

I began to imagine other rains that would be mine forever. I saw the rain streaming down the Spanish Steps. Blowing beneath the awning of a café in Paris. Sweeping through the piazza in Siena. Splashing against the shop windows along Sloane Street.

I glanced at my watch. It was time to go. I took one last look in the direction of fog-shrouded Venice and then hurried inside to catch my plane.

ILLUSTRATION CREDITS

The photographs in the book are reproduced courtesy of those listed below.

page 3 *Le petit déjeuner devant Nôtre Dame de Paris*
    R. Deschayes, Éditions du Pontcarré, France

page 19 *Colette et son chat*
    Roger-Viollet

page 33 *Propriétaire*
    Magnolia, Délphine de Largentaye

page 49 *Les Escaliers de Montmartre*
    H. Veiller (Explorer)

page 65 *Île Saint-Louis, Paris, 1975*
    Edouard Boubat/Agence TOP

page 85 Patrick Branwell Brontë: *The Brontë Sisters*
    The National Portrait Gallery, London

page 109 *Your Britain—Fight for It Now*

page 129 William Hogarth: *Marriage à la Mode: IV. The Countess's Morning Levée*
    The National Gallery, London

page 149 *View from All Souls College, with Spire of St. Mary's Church and Dome of Radcliffe Camera*
    James Allen Shuffrey, BWS

ABOUT THE AUTHOR

ALICE STEINBACH, whose work at the *Baltimore Sun* was awarded the Pulitzer Prize for Feature Writing in 1985, has been a freelance writer since 1999. She was appointed the 1998–99 McGraw Professor of Writing at Princeton University and is currently a Woodrow Wilson Visiting Fellow. She lives in Baltimore, Maryland.

ABOUT THE TYPE

This book was set in Weiss, a typeface designed by a German artist, Emil Rudolf Weiss (1875–1942). The designs of the roman and italic were completed in 1928 and 1931 respectively. The Weiss types are rich, well-balanced, and even in color, and they reflect the subtle skill of a fine calligrapher.